PIONEERS OF
OLD HOPEWELL

Ralph Ege

PIONEERS of OLD HOPEWELL

With Sketches of Her Revolutionary Heroes

By

RALPH EGE

Reprinted with the addition of index and introduction

Southern Historical Press, Inc.
Greenville, South Carolina

This volume was reproduced
from a personal copy located in
the Publishers private library

Please direct all correspondence and book orders to:
SOUTHERN HISTORICAL PRESS, Inc.
PO Box 1267
Greenville, SC   29602-1267

Originally published 1908
by: Race & Savidge, New York, NY
ISBN #978-1-63914-234-7
Printed in the United States of America

PREFACE.

The genealogical articles contained in this book were begun in May, 1901, for publication in the Hopewell Herald, and at the time of the author's death, August 7, 1905, thirty-three of them had appeared in the columns of that paper. These, together with fifteen unpublished manuscripts, have been collected and are now put into permanent form. Although many changes have taken place in families mentioned, as well as in the ownership of property in the few years that have elapsed since these were written, it has seemed best to published them as they came from the author's pen.

Ralph Ege, the author of "Pioneers of Old Hopewell," was born November 23, 1837, in a house erected about 1715, by Dr. Roger Parke, "on the north side of Stony Brook at Wissamenson." A part of the 400 acre tract was purchased by Samuel Ege, mentioned in article 1, the great grandfather of Ralph Ege, and remained in possession of the family for nearly one hundred years. This farm is described in article 32, and the whole Parke tract in article 33.

Adam Ege, mentioned in articles 25 and 26, the great great grandfather of Ralph Ege, was born about 1725 and came to this country from Germany when about thirteen years of age. He was accompanied by two brothers, George and Martin. George settled in Cumberland Co., Pa , where a large number of his descendants still reside, and are eminent in church and state. The name of Martin appears as one of the witnesses to a deed given to Adam in 1759, and is supposed to have settled in Philadelphia. That the family was of prominence in Germany, is evident from the fact that the Ege coat of arms is to be found on the tombstone of one of the family, who many years ago was Burgomaster of the town of Esslingen, Wurtemburg, Germany.

A genealogical family tree was drawn by Ralph Ege some years ago. It is seven feet in height and carrying the descendants of Adam Ege to the present day, contains about eleven hundred names.

Adam Ege was left in the care of Mr. and Mrs. John Hobbs who had no children of their own, and brought him up as their son, giving him a liberal education for the times. In a deed dated April 14, 1759, for the sum of one hundred pounds, they conveyed him their farm one half mile southeast of Woodsville, and it remained in the family for one hundred and thirty years. Mr. and Mrs Hobbs were prominent in the history of the Baptist church of Hopewell and much interested in Isaac Eaton's school (article 10 and footnote article 24). At Mrs. Hobbs' death she left a legacy to the school, for the "education of young men for the ministry." Mr. and Mrs. Hobbs are buried in Hopewell near the corner of the church, their graves being marked by tall brown stones.

Adam Ege married about 1748, Margaret, daughter of Thomas Hunt and they had eight children, viz: Samuel, Jacob, Elizabeth, Sarah, Nathaniel, Hannah, George and Andrew.

Samuel Ege, the eldest son of Adam, born June 24, 1750, married May 28, 1774, Anna, born June 7, 1755, daughter of John Titus, Jr., and Anna Smith who was the daughter of Andrew Smith and Sarah Stout (articles 14 and 21). They settled on the homestead near Woodsville, and in 1776 Adam moved to Harbourton where he spent the remaining years of his life. He is buried in the Harbourton church yard. Through the Titus family the line is traced to Rev. John Moore and the Howell family (article 29). Samuel Ege and Anna Titus had ten children, viz: John, William, Sarah, Andrew, George, Mary, Anna, Titus, Mahala, Nathaniel. Samuel Ege died August 22, 1829. John Ege, the eldest son of Samuel, born May 6, 1775, married first, Jan. 15, 1801, Mary, born December 12, 1779, daughter of Ralph Schenck of Amwell. She died Jan. 15, 1834. John Ege married second, Zilpha Decker, widow of Jonathan Hunt (article 7).

The Schenck genealogy is one of the most complete ever published. The family is said to have derived its name from Edgar De Schencken, chief butler to Charlemange, who about the year 798 granted to Edgar a title of nobility, and assigned him a coat of arms, the shield being in the form of a goblet, and the name De Schencken signifying the "cup-bearer." The line of descent is traced from Edgar, through the Barons of Fautchberg, to Christianus of 1225, then to Wilhemus and Ludovicus to 1346, when it is taken up in direct line. (1) Hendric Schenck Van Nydeck; (2) Hendrick ; (3) Derick ; (4) Derick; (5) Derick; (6) Derick ; (7) Gen. Peter; (8) Martin; (9) Rocliff, emigrated from Holland in 1650, settled at Flatlands, L. I. ; (10) Garret; (11) Roeliff; (12) Garret; (13) Roeliff (Ralph); (14) Mary, married John Ege. John Ege and Mary Schenck had three children, viz ; Ralph Schenck, Anna and Andrew. John Ege settled on the farm purchased by his father for him in 1801, and lived in the house now occupied by Amos Sked until his death, November 24, 1860.

Andrew Ege, youngest son of John Ege, born February 16, 1813, married November 16, 1836, Sarah Ann, born November 24, 1818, daughter of Abraham J. Voorhees, the sixth generation in the line of Steven Coerte Van Voorhees, whose history is given in a foot note to article 12. Abraham J. Voorhees married Maria, daughter of Uriah DeHart of Ten Mile Run, (article 22, foot note) who was the sixth generation in the line of Simon DeHart a French Huguenot who emigrated to this country in 1664 and settled at Gowanus, L. I. Uriah DeHart married Margaret, daughter of Henry Van Arsdalen, great, great grandson of Isaac Van Arsdalen, (foot note, article 12). The mother of Abraham J. Voorhees was Sarah, daughter of Simon Wyckoff and Alche Van Doren, who was the eighth child of the famous Christian Van Doren family of seventeen children.

Andrew Ege and Sarah Ann Voorhees settled in the house built by Roger Parke, where their only son Ralph Ege was born. They had one daughter Mariana who married Martin Nevius, son of James Van Zandt of Blawenburg. They reside in Des Moines, Iowa, and have three children, Claudius Maxwell, Dora Vroom and Herbert Voorhees. Their second son, Ralph Ege, died in 1905 aged twenty-one years.

Ralph Ege, married October 18, 1864, Mary Emma, daughter of Abraham Skillman, and grand daughter of Esquire David Stout, and had five children, viz : (1) Albert Augustus, married August 24, 1896, Florence Adelaide Murtha of Michigan, and resides in Trenton. (2) Sarah. (3) Andrew Howard, died at Pasadena, Cal., October 26, 1891, aged 21 years. (4) Ida Skillman, married May 18, 1904, Marion Moore Voorhees. (5) Mary Henrietta.

Ralph Ege was a man of wide interests. In his native town his memory will be cherished as a public-spirited citizen, ever giving time and money freely for the advancement of its industries, the preservation of its historic landmarks and the uplifting of the people. In early manhood he became superintendent of the Sabbath School, which office he held for forty years. His cheerful disposition, his kindly welcome, his hearty singing and his organizing ability won for him a large place in the hearts and lives of over a thousand children who came under his influence during that period. For many years he was an elder in the First Presbyterian church of Pennington, and was instrumental in organizing a Presbyterian church in Hopewell in 1877, of which church he was an influential member as clerk of the session, trustee, member of the choir, and superintendent of the Sabbath School, until his death in 1905.

Although he avoided the strife and contention of political life, his voice was often raised and his influence given for the betterment of mankind. He was prominent in Masonic circles, and as a progressive and up-to-date farmer he was well known by reason of his connection with the State Horticultural Society and the State Agricultural College.

From his boyhood days he loved the traditions of the Hopewell valley, and was fond of relating them to ready listeners as he drove over the hills in after years. That no tradition, record or relic should be lost through his negligence seemed to be an ever present thought, as shown by his valuable scrap books and diaries covering nearly fifty years.

In 1901, he was induced to write for publication, and his extensive reading and tireless research have made the information which he possessed invaluable to all who are interested in local history. It is a matter of much regret that he was claimed by death before the completion of his genealogical work, and before he had written all that he knew concerning "The Pioneers of Old Hopewell."

July 1, 1908.   M. E. E.

NUMBER I.

Although scarcely two centuries have elapsed since the first white settler built his log cabin in the Hopewell Valley, and although there are persons now living who have conversed with the children of the pioneers, it is a matter of universal regret that so little is known of their history.

There will always exist in the minds of their decendants a feeling of profound respect and admiration for the noble men and women who had the hardihood and courage to brave the perils of a wilderness, which was still the hunting grounds of the once powerful and warlike Lenni Lenape.

The pioneers have long since passed away and are sleeping their last long sleep in obscure corners of the fields they cleared and cultivated, their graves overgrown with a tangled mass of weeds and briars, so that we are filled with an unutterable feeling of sadness when we attempt to find the stones which mark the spot of their last resting places, and to deciper the moss grown inscriptions which have been almost obliterated by the ruthless hand of "Father Time." The same may be said of the noble sons of the pioneers—the old Revolutionary Heroes—who were our country's brave defenders in the hour of her gravest peril.

As we pass the monument (in our beautiful cemetery) erected to the memory of that grand old hero, Hon. John Hart, and read the inscription, "Honor the patriot's grave," it is a matter of profound regret that there are so many whose memory we delight to honor because of their heroism, but whose graves are unknown and neglected.

Where many of the old revolutionary soldiers are buried cannot now be definitely ascertained, but it is still possible to locate the places of their residence at the time of the revolution—most of them at least—and it is a matter of local interest to know this, and more especially to those who now occupy the farms where they lived.

It is a fact not generally known, that standing on the farm

owned at that time by Hon. John Hart and looking westward over Stony Brook as far as the road, then known as the "great road," leading from Marshall's Corner to Woodsville and including a strip of country three miles in length and about one and a half miles in width, there lived over a score of patriots who served either in the state troops, militia, or Continental army.

We will mention them in their order on adjoining farms, and will give something of their history in a subsequent article.

Hon. John Hart on the farm now owned by Mr. W. I. Phillips.

Col. Joab Houghton lived in early life on the farm now owned by Mr. A. L. Holcombe, and at the time of the revolution on the farm now owned by Mr. R. J. Birch.

Mathew Hixson on the farm now owned by R. S. Kise, between John Hart and Col. Houghton.

Abraham Golden on the farm now owned by Mr. A. L. Holcombe.

Wm. Golden where his great grandson, Mr. Wm F. Golden, now resides.

Jacob Golden on Mr. Holcombe's lower farm along the Trenton road.

Ensign Moses Stout on the farm now known as the Baptist parsonage farm. After the war he removed to Amwell.

Wm. Jewell on the farm lately owned by Mr. A. G. Reed.

Corporal David Hunt on the Railroad quarry farm.

Sergeant Jonas Wood on a lot adjoining David Hunt on the corner of Stony Brook road, near the old mines.

Captain Timothy Brush, Jr., on the farm adjoining the Golden's on the west, now owned by Mr. E. S. Titus.

Sergeant Roger Larison on the farm now owned by Mr. Amos Sked and Mr. E. S. Wells.

The father of Lieutenant William Parks also resided on that farm before the Larison's.

Elias Golden on the farm adjoining the above, now owned by Mr. Joshua J. Hunt.

Sergeant William Larison on the farm adjoining Mr. Hunt on the south, now owned by Mr. E. S. Wells.

Charles Sexton on the farm adjoining Timothy Brush, now owned by Mr. Wm. C. Velit.

Judge Jared Sexton, member of assembly 1777-1778, also resided on the above farm.

Abraham Stout and Absalom Stout, father and son, on farm adjoining the Sexton's on the northwest, now owned by Mr. William S. Stout, a great grandson of Abraham.

Captain Phillip Snook on the farm north of Mr. Stout's, now owned by Mr. Abraham S. Golden.

Samuel and Jacob Ege where Mr. Peter Titus now resides, the farm now owned by Mr. Titus and ex-Sheriff A. T. Ege, who is a grandson of Samuel.

John Humphrey on the farm adjoining, also owned by Mr. Titus.

John Larison where Mr. John L. Burroughs now resides.

In extending the same narrow strip of country west to the Delaware river we find the old homes of the Hunt's, Hart's, Smith's, Van Cleve's, Field's, Phillips', Muirheid's, Wilson's, and many others, and it has been said that every house was the home of a patriot. In the vicinity of Woodsville and Linvale were Capt. John Reed, Richard Reed, Lieutenant Richard Corwine, Samuel Corwine, John Corwine, John and Joseph Hixson, John Stillwell, Sergeant Jacob Decker, Philip Young and perhaps others.

Hopewell township extends but one mile east of the borough, and nearly all the valley was owned by the Stout family, who were nobly represented in the patriot army, as we hope to be able to show as we proceed.

There is great difficulty experienced in obtaining accurate and reliable data concerning the families of some of the revolutionary soldiers named above, from the fact that almost immediately after the close of the Revolution many of the old soldiers emigrated with their families to the "Lake Country" of New York State, to western Pennsylvania, Virginia and Kentucky and their descendants are scattered over every state and territory of the West.

Among these adventurous and enterprising spirits were the five sons of Hon. John Hart and the four sons of Col. Houghton, and in about twenty years after the war not one of them remained in New Jersey.

They all went to western Pennsylvania, West Virginia and Kentucky, except William Houghton, who was the last of the nine to go, and he went to Cortland Co., New York, with his wife, Margaret Sexton, and they are buried at Homer, about five miles from the City of Cortland, N. Y.

Excepting also John Hart, son of the signer, who, when only 22 years of age, went to Port Coupee, La., and from there to Cuba, returning to New Jersey before the close of the Revolution.

His remarkable business career, in making and losing three fortunes, in about ten or twelve years, is comprehensively stated in a paragraph of about one hundred words in Dr. Cooley's " genealogy of the early settlers of Trenton and Ewing."

In the rooms of the Historical Society of Pennsylvania at Philadelphia is to be found a manuscript containing the family record of Hon. John Hart, with a brief sketch of his life and public services, which has never been published. It was written for the society by Hon. John S. Darragh, of Beaver, Pa., who is a son of Deborah, and grandson of Jesse Hart, the oldest son of the signer, who resided on the homestead at Hopewell during and for some years after the Revolution.

The writer copied the family record and portions of the history of the family from the manuscript, but as it does not differ materially from the published biography of Mr. Hart, and as his life and distinguished services have been so eloquently portrayed from the platform and in these columns in recent years, the writer has thought best to refrain from any attempt to give a history of his family, as it would be impossible to do so without a repetition of much that has been already published, and is as familiar as household words to most of your readers.

With this explanation and apology for passing by such a distinguished man and such an illustrious family we will step across the Hart farm to the Houghton's, whose home for many years was on the farm now occupied by Mr. A. L. Holcombe.

May 1, 1901.

NUMBER II.

In a very valuable work entitled "National Biography," published in London, England, in 1898, we find the first reference to the family of "Houghton."

The very eventful history of Adam de Houghton, who was Bishop of St. David's and chancellor of England would fill a volume.

Of his birth and nationality the historian says, "that he was born at Caerforig, in the parish of White Church, near St. David's, but his name clearly shows his Norman or English origin." His death occurred in 1389.

The next reference in the same work is of John Houghton, who was born in 1488, and died in 1535. His biographer says of him that he was "born of honorable parentage, educated at Cambridge, became a very noted minister, and had a great career." He is described as slight of stature, elegant in appearance, shy in look, modest in manner, sweet in speech, chaste in body, humble of heart, amiable and beloved by all.

We have quoted the above from the biography simply to prove the English origin of this branch of the Houghton family, and that Col. Joab Houghton, the Hopewell hero of Revolutionary fame, was a worthy scion of an illustrious family, which was very distinguished and prominent at an early period.

The first record we have of the family in America is found in "The Genealogy of New England Families," and is of Ralph Houghton, who with his wife, Jane, emigrated from Lancaster, England, to Massachusetts, about 1654.

Their children were Mary, born January 4, 1654; John, born April 28, 1655; Joseph, born July 6, 1657; Experience, born October 1, 1659; Sarah, born February 17, 1662; Abigail, born July 15, 1664.

It cannot be stated positively, but there seems to be good reason for the belief that the John Houghton of the above family is identical with the one of the same name who on January 11, 1696, purchased 200 acres of land of Thomas Warne, at the bend of Stony Brook, near the present site of Port Mercer, about two miles southwest of Princeton, and bounded by the Province line on the west. Warne's tract comprised 1400 acres, 1200 of which were sold to Benjamin Clarke on October 28, 1696.

The deeds for the above tracts are on record in the office of the secretary of State, at Trenton, and the fact that Richard Stockton, William Olden, John Houghton, Benjamin Clarke, Joseph Worth, and several other prominent English families, settled at Stony Brook the same year, would seem to indicate that they all came together, although it is possible that the John Houghton who, on June 16, 1688, purchased 250 acres of land at Lower Hooke in Gloucester County, and who is described in the deed as a "Chirurgeon" or surgeon.

It is a fact very familiar to those who have had experience in tracing the genealogies of the families of the early settlers of this State, that there was a great migration of English families from the New England States to Long Island during the period from 1665 to 1675, and that many of these same families came to New Jersey a few years later, and settled in Monmonth, Middlesex, Burlington and Hunterdon counties, and this Houghton family was doubtless of the number.

With very rare exceptions the pioneers of Hopewell township were the children of the pioneers of New England, Long Island, and of Monmouth, Burlington, and other older settled counties of our own State.

Just over the Province line, only one mile east of our borough, the pioneers were almost exclusively the children of the Holland Dutch Emigrants, who, fifty years previous, had settled on Long Island, and in the vicinity of New Amsterdam.

The pioneers on either side of the line represented the best elements of the sturdy yeomanry of their respective nationalities, and had been reared amid the hardships and privations incident to pioneer life.

The will of John Houghton is dated January 24, 1709, and is filed in the office of the secretary of State at Trenton.

He gives his residence as "Stony Brook* in ye county of Middlesex,† and State of New Jersey," and it was written before all his children had attained their majority.

He mentions his children as follows : John, the eldest; Joseph, Richard, and Thomas the youngest.   He also names one daughter, Alice, and leaves property to two other daughters whose names are not given.

He gives to his two sons, John and Joseph, 320 acres of land on "Stony Brook at Hopewell in the county of Burlington,"‡ and is described as between "Joshua Ward and Samuel Allen, divided by a line running from Stony Brook to Thomas Smith's land."

His dwelling house and plantation he left to his wife and his son Thomas, "when he comes of age." (This Thomas was the father of Col. Joab).

One of the daughters, not named in the will, was doubtless the "Jane Houghton," who was one of the subscribing witnesses to the will of Richard Stockton, April 25, 1709.

The next account we have of Thomas Houghton is on April 23, 1726, when he purchased of Robert Tindall, "of Nottinghham, in ye county of Burlington, within the western division of Nova Ceserea, Yeoman," 300 acres of land, "lying in Hopewell." This is the tract now owned by Mr. A. L. Holcombe, Mr. Wm. F. Golden, Mr. Charles A. Holcombe, Mrs. Laura Rankin, and the portion of Mr. D. P. Voorhees' farm which lies on the east side of the public road.

At the time of the Houghton purchase, John Hixson owned the farm now owned by Mr. Wm. I. Phillips. Richard Ketcham and James Mattison owned the lands on the south, on the Trenton road.

The lands lying west of the Houghton purchase will be described later.

This Houghton tract was surveyed by Thomas Revell, agent for the West Jersey Society, for Thomas Tindall, on February 27,

---

*The Indian name for Stony Brook was "Wapowog," and the little hamlet known as "Stony Brook" was located on the east side of the brook opposite the present site of Joseph H. Bruere's mill, and at the crossing of the old Indian path. This village, which was the nucleus of the little Quaker settlement, had an existence and a name, about thirty years before the first house was built on the present site of the Borough of Princeton and from 1690 to 1725 all correspondence and public documents were dated "Stony Brook."

†Middlesex county extended west to the Province line at that time, and for many years the main street in Princeton was the boundary between Middlesex and Somerset counties.

‡Burlington county at that time extended to New York state line, and included Mercer, Hunterdon, Warren, Morris and Sussex counties.

1696, and was without doubt the first farm located in the Hopewell Valley.

On November 10, 1699, a deed was given by Thomas Revell, agent for "Ye Hon,ble The West Jersey Society in England" of the one part, and Thomas Tindall of the other part, for the above tract, the consideration being "ten pounds per hundred acres," or fifty cents per acre in our currency, which was the regulation price for all the societies lands of the thirty thousand acre tract. The above deed describes the 300 acres as a part of the thirty thousand acre tract "lying above ye ffalls of ye Delaware."

On this tract John Pullen, a son-in-law of Thomas Tindall, built his cabin soon after the above purchase and was one of the first, if not the first, pioneer white settler in this immediate vicinity.

May 29, 1901.

NUMBER III.

In the year 1691, Dr. Daniel Coxe transferred the right of government of West Jersey to a company of proprietaries called "The West Jersey Society of England," for a valuable consideration.

This society appointed Thomas Revell their agent, and he claimed the right to sell lands and give deeds for the same in the name of the society.

Great inducements were held out to the New England and Long Island settlers as well as to those of the older portions of this state, to avail themselves of the cheap and fertile lands of the thirty thousand acre tract, and scores of them were induced to come and settle, only to find that after they had subdued the wilderness and established their homes, that their titles were utterly worthless.

Fifty of these settlers (among whom is found the name of Thomas Houghton) entered into a solemn compact to stand by each other in a law suit with Dr. Coxe.

After a long and tedious trial at Burlington, the case was decided against them, and this verdict caused the most distressing state of affairs in this township that was ever experienced in any community.

Writs of ejectment had been served on them as "tenants" of Dr. Coxe to pay for their lands the second time or "quit."

Their lands had cost them only fifty cents per acre to purchase, it is true; but they had purchased them in good faith and spent the best years of their lives in clearing them. Many had mortgaged them to pay the expense of improvements, consequently not being able to incur the additional expense, they were compelled to leave their homes and seek new homes elsewhere, risking for the second, and some of them for the third time, the perils of the wilderness.

Many of them went to the northern part of the county which at that time extended to the New York state line, the county of Hunterdon, including Warren, Morris and Sussex counties, and an examination of the records of those counties between 1735 and 1750, will reveal many names that are very familiar to the people of old Hopewell.

The writer has a copy of this original writ of ejectment, together with the names of those on whom it was served, dated "May term of Supreme Court of New Jersey 1733," and a number of interesting documents in connection with it, which will appear later.

Thomas Tindall, who in 1696 purchased the 300 acre tract referred to died in 1713, and in his will dated July 18, 1713, leaves to son John, the tract in Hopewell "where John Pullen now dwells."

This tract passed from John Tindall to his brother Thomas, Jr., and from him, by will dated April 6, 1715, to his brother Robert.

These wills of Thomas, Sr., and Thomas, Jr., were witnessed by their neighbors in Nottingham, viz: Isaac Atkinson, Mary Embly, John Rodgers and Joshua Wright to the first, and Jacob Baillerjeau, Edmond Beakes and Wm. Embly to the second.

Thomas Houghton, the purchaser of this tract, had at least nine children, viz.: John, Absalom, Thomas, Joab, Elizabeth, the first wife of Abraham Stout; Sarah, wife of John Merrill; Annie, wife of John Smith; Mary, wife of William Drake, and Alice, second wife of Abraham Stout.

Only one of the four sons of Thomas Houghton left a will, viz: Thomas, Jr   His will is dated December 21, 1784, proved April 4, 1795. So far as we have been able to ascertain he never married, and resided in the vicinity of Harbourton, possibly with Josiah Hart or his son Nathaniel, who, with his neighbor, John Muirheid, was made executor of the will, which is a lengthy and very interesting document, proving him to have been a man of more than average ability, and blessed with a fair share of this world's goods.

His white beaver hat, silk coat and jacket, silver knee and shoe buckles, (which he divides between his nephew, Joab Stout,* and his friend, Nathaniel Hart) show him to have been a man who dressed in the style of the period, and becoming a gentleman of the old school.

The first bequest in his will is to his nephew, Joab Stout, to whom he leaves silverware, saddle and bridle, large bible, and a

---

*This Joab Stout was the nephew and namesake of Col. Joab Houghton, and also a nephew of "Esq. Nathan" Stout, who wrote the Stout history. [See "History of the Stout Family," page 18.] Joab Stout lived on the farm now occupied by his grandson, Wm. S· Stout, two miles west of the borough.

number of other articles, and also all the money on the note of
Peter and John Phillips, and a piece of woodland which he purchased of Wm. Drake.   He leaves to his nephews and nieces, Eli,
John, Mary and Rachel Stout, "all the money due in bank," and
household goods to be divided between them, and a considerable
sum of money to Eli and John in addition.†

He gives the nephews, William Houghton and Joab Houghton,
Jr., (sons of Col. Joab) household furniture and a considerable sum
of money, and to Catherine, wife of Col. Joab, mentioned as Joab
Senior, and his neices, Elizabeth Houghton, Mary Drake and
Sarah Merrill, bedding, etc.

He gives all his remainder of his wearing apparel to his two
brothers, Joab and Absalom.

The following is the closing clause of the will : "I give and bequeath to the Presbyterian congregation of Hopewell‡ eight pounds,
to be paid within one year after my decease, and all the balance of
my estate to the children of my brothers, John and Joab Houghton."

This will is witnessed by the neighbors of Thomas Houghton,
viz.: Daniel Howell, Jonathan Muirheid and George Muirheid.

July 10, 1901.

---

†The above named children had a brother, Solomon, who deserves special mention as
a hero of the revolution.   He was killed in the battle of White Plains, New York, October
28, 1776, in the unequal contest of 1600 Americans against 13000 well drilled troops under General Howe.   Abraham Stout, the father of Solomon, was in the same battle, and will be giv-
en special notice in a subsequent article.

‡The Pennington Presbyterian Church was organized probably as early as 1710, and
was designated on the records as "The Presbyterian Church of Hopewell," which name it
bore for about one hundred and seventy years, and until the Presbyterian Church of Hopewell was organized in the village of Hopewell in 1877, when the Pennington church dropped
the name of Hopewell and the name Pennington was substituted.   Thomas Houghton, Jr.,
was a liberal contributor to the salary of Rev. John Guild in 1769.

NUMBER IV.

On December 30th, 1734, Thomas Houghton, senior, sold to Joseph Golden 200 acres of the tract which he purchased of Robert Tindall April 23, 1726, the tract being described in the deed as "200 acres of the eastermost part thereof," the consideration being three hundred pounds.

This is the tract now owned by Mr. A. L. Holcombe and Mr. Charles A. Holcombe.

On July 19, 1750, Thomas Houghton sold to Thomas Mershon of Princeton the balance of the original 300-acre tract.

Thomas Mershon sold it to James Larison of Hopewell, and on the same date James Larison sold it to Joseph Golden.

By this purchase Mr. Golden secured the whole of the Houghton tract, a part of which is still in possession of the family.

Wm. F. Golden, the present owner, being a great, great grandson of Joseph and his children being the sixth generation who have resided on that farm.

In Barber and Howe's "Historical collections of New Jersey," published in 1846, it is stated that at the time of the Revolution Col. Joab Houghton lived in the house occupied by Mr. Wm. Suydam.

This historic old relic is still standing one mile north of the borough, in a good state of preservation and is owned by Mr. Rensaler J. Birch.

It is one of the very few homes of the old heroes of '76 that is left in this locality. One by one they have been ruthlessly torn away to make room for more modern structures, and the few which remain should be preserved, that they may be pointed out to the rising generation as the homes of our country's brave defenders in the darkest hours of the nation's history, and serve to keep alive the spirit of '76 as they are thus reminded of the noble patriots whose memory a grateful nation delights to honor.

It is said of the old colonel that he was of a very jovial disposition, and loved a good story, and after the close of the war this old house was a favorite place for the old veterans to gather, and seated around the wide fire place, which still remains unchanged, they loved to talk over the exciting experiences of the camp, the march and the battle field, and the "burning memories of that glorious drama of freedom," in which they bore such a noble part. At times the old hero's feelings would be so wrought upon by reminiscences of the war, or the utterance of some patriotic sentiment, that he would be moved to tears.

His grandson, Rev. Spencer Cone, says of him that he was a fine singer and a great lover of music, and that only a short time before his death his grandchildren sang "Hail Columbia" for him, and he was completely overcome and wept like a child.

Mr. Cone was the son of Conant Cone and Alice Houghton, and was one of the most distinguished Baptist clergymen of his day, and the following sketch of Col. Houghton is from his pen :

"Joab Houghton was one of those who first began to take measures against the Royal government, which resulted during 1776 in the organization of the Provincial Congress of New Jersey, and the arrest by Col. Heard of the Royal governor (Franklin) who was afterward handed over by order of the Continental Congress, sitting in Philadelphia, to the custody of Governor Trumbull of Connecticut. [Life of Lord Sterling.]

"Joab Houghton was also among the first appointments of field officers made by New Jersey for the Contingent Army, raised for the army of the United Colonies, and when a state government was erected by the choice of representatives to the two houses of council and assembly, and the election of Livingston as governor, he was one of the first members of the assembly returned from the county of Hunterdon.

"It was in the old Baptist meeting house at Hopewell that Joab Houghton received the first news of the battle of Lexington, and the defeat of the Earl of Northumberland, the haughty descendant of the hero of Chevy Chase, by the half-armed yeomanry of New England.

"Stilling the breathless messenger Mr. Houghton sat quietly through the services, and when they were concluded passed out, and mounting the great stone block* in front of the meeting house, beckoned the people to stop.

"Men and women paused to hear, curious to know what so un-usual a sequel to the service of the day could mean.

"At the first words a silence stern as death fell over all ; the Sabbath quiet of the hour and the place was deepening into a terri-ble solemnity.

"He told them all the story of the cowardly murder at Lexing-ton by the royal troops, the heroic vengeance following hard upon it, the retreat of Percy, the gathering of the children of the pilgrims around the beleaguered hills of Boston.   Then pausing and looking over the silent crowd, he said slowly, 'Men of New Jersey, the red coats are murdering our brethren of New England !   Who follows me to Boston ?' and every man of that audience stepped out into line and answered, 'I'.

"There was not a coward or traitor in old Hopewell meeting house on that day."

Col. Houghton first received his commission as captain in the First New Jersey Regiment October 19, 1776.   (Col. Isaac Smith).

Lieut. Col. Abraham Hunt resigned on March 15, 1777, and Capt. Houghton was promoted to the position and was transferred to Col. Taylor's State Troops October 9, 1779.

He was a brave officer, greatly beloved by his men, and served with distinction all through the war, and in 1784 to 1787 served in the State Legislature and filled other positions of trust and re-sponsibility until the close of his life.

In a short sketch of Col. Houghton published in Barber and Howe's "Historical Collections " page 262, the incident is related that he and a few of his neighbors succeeded in capturing a ser-geant and a detachment of Hessians, who were plundering a house near Moore's Mill, about two miles from Col. Houghton's home, but the historian omitted to state that he marched his prisoners to Coryell's Ferry (now Lambertville) and placed them in charge of a detachment of American troops then stationed there.

---

*This great stone, which was used by the ladies in mounting their horses and dis-mounting, is about eight feet in length by four in width, and on July 4, 1896, it was placed as the cap stone of a memorial tablet erected by the people of Hopewell to the memory of Col. Houghton, and the memorial exercises were attended by a great throng of people anxious to honor his memory. A very interesting sketch of this memorial celebration was written by Prof. Nomer Gray, and published in pamphet form by Mr. C. E. Voorhees, editor of The Hopewell Herald.

The name of Col. Houghton was a terror to the Hessians, when they were on their raids in this region, and they made frequent attempts to capture him and his illustrious neighbor and co-patriot, John Hart, but without success.

There is a tradition that on one occasion when the colonel was visiting his home for a short time he was so closely pressed that he had no chance of escape from the house, and hastily climbing the wide chimney, sat securely perched on the "lug pole" while the house was being searched.

Shakespeare has said that "the better part of valor is discretion," and we admire the old colonel's discretion in this instance with such heavy odds against him.

August 7, 1901.

NUMBER V.

The tract of land on which Col. Joab resided during the revolutionary period, was a part of the thirty thousand acre tract owned by Dr. Daniel Coxe, of London, and was purchased about 1750 of his heirs by Philip Rogers of Huntington, Long Island, who sold 125 acres to his brother-in-law, John Stout,* who soon after sold it to their brother-in-law, George Sexton. About 1765 George Sexton sold it to Joab Houghton for 430 pounds, and on May 17, 1796, he sold 100 acres of the tract to his son, William Houghton, who, in 1805 sold it to William Suydam, who resided there until his death in 1845.

The tract is now owned by R. J. Birch, Esq., who kindly presented the old deed to the writer.

Joab Houghton married about 1748, Catharine, daughter of his neighbor, Aaron Runyan,† and had children as follows: Aaron Houghton married Elizabeth Sexton, February 23, 1780; Elijah, Joab, Jr; William, Sarah and Alice.

Four of the above children, viz: Aaron, Joab, Elijah, and Sarah, wife of Amos Corwine, moved to Mason Co., Kentucky, about 1790.

---

*Philip Rogers married at Huntington, L. I., June 24, 1735, Esther, daughter of Charles Sexton, Jr., and with his father-in-law came to Hopewell soon after and were among the pioneers of this region. This John Stout was the son of Zebulon, and grandson of Jonathan, one of the very first of old Hopewell's settlers and married Mabel, youngest daughter of Charles Sexton.

†This Runyan family were among the earliest pioneers of Hopewell Township, and were descended from a distinguished and eminently pious French Huguenot family, who resided in the Province of Poitou, on the west coast of France, and were driven by fierce religious persecutions to seek refuge, first in the isle of Jersey, and from thence emigrated to America. The first records we have of any of the family in New Jersey, is of Vincent Rougion of Portiers, France, Mariner, who in 1668 was granted a license by Philip Carteret, the young governor of East Jersey, to wed "Ann Boutcher, daughter of John Boutcher of Hartford, in England." [See genealogy of the Runyan family published by Henry Runyan, Esq., of Princeton, N. J.] Thomas Runyan, doubtless a son of Vincent, of Piscataway Township, Middlesex Co., N. J., purchased in 1708, the farm on which Enoch A. Titus now resides, on the west side of Stony Brook, two miles south of our borough, where he lived many years and reared a family among whom were Vincent, Aaron, Ephraim and others.

After the death of Col. Joab, his widow also left New Jersey and resided with her children in Kentucky until her death, which occurred about 1820, at a very advanced age.

There had been such a large migration of the old families of Hopewell to Kentucky during the period from 1790 to 1810, that Mrs. Alice Cone wrote in 1817, "That whilst old Hopewell and Princeton recalled the memories of her youth, most that remained of the old familiar faces were to be seen about the newer settlements of the West, and chiefly in the neighborhood of Maysville, Kentucky."

Elijah, son of Col. Joab, married Charlotte, daughter of Nathaniel Hart, and granddaughter of Hon. John Hart, and resided at Maysville, Ky., where she died at the age of 33 years, and he married for a second wife a Miss Jackson.

William, son of Col. Joab, born September 25, 1757, married Margaret Sexton, who was born October 29, 1775.

She was the daughter of Judge Jared Sexton of Hopewell, who represented Hunterdon county in the legislature 1777-1779, and filled many public offices until the time of his death, which occurred May 10, 1785, at the age of 48.

William Houghton and Margaret Sexton had children as follows, viz: Sarah, born August 7, 1794, died 1873 unmarried; Nancy, born January 28, 1796, married Palmer Price; Caroline, born March 31, 1798, married Joseph Hart; William Sexton, born 1803, died 1805; John Sexton, born September 9, 1805, married Lucy A. Alvord, and died at Marengo, Ill., August 28, 1865; Aaron, born January 22, 1807, died March 1, 1837; Joab, born February 25, 1810, and died at Las Vegas, New Mexico, January 31, 1876, leaving a wife and six children; Elizabeth, born November 28, 1812, married Jeremiah Devoe; William, born December 26, 1816, died in Chase Co., Kansas, January 25, 1890, leaving a wife and six children, all now deceased.

William Houghton, Sr., owned a beautiful farm of about 400 acres, at "Houghton's Hill," near Homer, Cortland county, New York.

When he removed to New York State he selected a tract of land located much the same as the old home of his grandfather at Hopewell, which were the farms now occupied by A. L. Holcombe, Wm. F. Golden and Charles A. Holcombe.

William Houghton, Sr., died June 29, 1835, aged 78, and his

widow died March 6, 1864, aged 88. They are buried in the At-
water Cemetery, near Homer, New York.

Sarah Houghton, daughter of Col. Joab, born about 1760,
married Amos Corwine‡, who was born near New Market, N. J.
(now Linvale) in 1756. They emigrated to Mason County, Kentucky, at the time of the great migration about 1790, and had children as follows, viz: Joab Houghton, Richard, William, John,
Clarissa, Aaron Houghton.

Of the above children, Joab, born 1788, married Elizabeth,
daughter of General Samuel Lucas, and became an editor and publisher of considerable note in the West.

He published the Maysville Eagle, the first newspaper in
Maysville, Ky., and afterward the "Dove," the first paper in Washington, Ky. In 1833, he removed to Cincinnatti, Ohio, and published the "Cincinnatti" Courier, but soon removed to Louisville,
Ky., where he died May 20, 1837.

All of his sons became widely known as editors, publishers and
politicians in the southwest, and held several appointments of
great trust and responsibility under different administrations.

Aaron, son of Amos Corwine and Sarah Houghton, became an
artist of considerable repute, and resided in Cincinnatti, Ohio,
where he took rank among the first of his profession.

His portraits were singularly true to the originals, and to the
present day are highly prized by those who are so fortunate as to
possess them.

In 1829 he started for Italy for the purpose of perfecting his
art by foreign study, but in conseqence of failing health abandoned
the idea after reaching London, and returned to this country and
died in 1830.

October 9, 1901.

---

‡George Corwine, the father of Amos, born July 12, 1718, married Abigail, daughter of
John Hixson, another of Hopewell's pioneers, who lived on the farm, afterward owned by
Hon. John Hart, and now owned by William I. Phillips, Esq. Bartholomew Corwine, the
father of George, born June 21, 1693, married Esther Burt, daughter of John Burt, of England.
He, Bartholomew Corwine, was a man of education and business ability, and was one of
Hopewell's most prominent citizens from the time of his settlement here in 1717, to the time
of his death, which occurred May 9, 1747, at the age of 54. His father, Sheriff George, was so
unfortunate as to be the Sherriff of Essex County, Mass., at the time of the Salem Witch-
craft trials and executions in 1692, and was very severely persecuted by the friends of the
sufferers. This was doubtless the cause of his only son, Bartholomew, seeking a home in
the New Jersey wilderness He and several of his family are buried in the old cemetery on
the farm of John S. Hunt, deceased, about three miles west of our borough. The old and
distinguished Corwine family are traced back several hundred years, in "The Corwin
Genealogy," published in 1872 by Rev. Edward T. Corwin, of Millstone, N. J.

NUMBER VI.

The writer has in his possession copies of two old letters—one written in colonial time, dated January ye 16, 1755, written by the Corwines in Amwell, Hunterdon Co., N. J., to their cousins in Boston, Mass., and the other of more recent date written by Amos and Sarah Houghton Corwine of Maysville, Kentucky, to John and Rebecca Stillwell Corwine* of Snydertown, N. J.

The last is in the Houghton line and will be read with interest, manifesting, as it does, a spirit of such fervent piety and deep religious feeling.

Dear Brother and Sister:

After the compliments common to letters, we inform you that we are in a reasonable state of health at present. Blessed be God for it, and all other mercies from time to time bestowed on us. We hope these few lines will find you and your family in the same state. It is a long time since we heard from you

Alice Cone wrote us last fall and she tells us that she saw and conversed with you not long before, and it gives us unspeakable satisfaction to hear that you partake of the sweet seasons of the out pourings of God's grace upon the church at Hopewell. She likewise informs us that some of our old acquaintances have been turned from the ways of darkness to the light of the knowledge of the glory of God in Christ Jesus our Lord, for which we trust we join in unfeigned thanks to God.

As a church we once enjoyed that fullness of harmony you now enjoy but alas! we are overshadowed by a cloud of thick darkness which we trust the Lord will remove in his appointed time.

Mother continues same as she was when I wrote to you the last time, but in as good health as is common for her age. She wishes to be remembered to you and children and all relatives and friends.

---

*This John and Rebecca Corwine were the parents of Gideon Reed Corwine of Pennington, N. J., and the grandparents of our esteemed fellow townsman, Cornelius T. Corwine, who is the last male representative in this region, bearing the name of this once numerous and influential family in old Hunterdon County.

Dear brother, our ardent desire is that you could make it convenient to come and partake of the goodness of the soil of our fertile country. We by experience do know that with one-half the expense you are at where you are would maintain you better, and we should be happy in the enjoyment of you.

Please remember us to John Reed† and family, let him know that we have not forgot him, and all enquiring friends.

Send us information of your welfare by the first opportunity.

No more at present. We conclude, remaining your affectionate brother and sister until death.

AMOS AND SARAH CORWINE,
MARGARET CORWINE,‡
RUTH CORWINE.

Mason Co., Ky., April 20, 1800.

To John and Rebecca Corwine.

Alice, youngest daughter of Col. Joab Houghton, married Conant Cone, of Princeton, N. J., who was a co-patriot and companion in arms of Col. Joab.

They had children as follows: Spencer Houghton, born at Princeton, April 30, 1785, became one of the most noted preachers in the Baptist church and was pastor of the First Baptist Church of New York City; Catharine, who married John Norvell, a partner of Spencer H. Cone of the Baltimore Whig and removed to Lexington, Ky., and afterward to Michigan, and was United States Senator from that state; Eliza, who became the wife of James Leslie, Esq., of Philadelphia; Martha and Amelia, single; Joseph who was an artist and engraver in Baltimore and married Mary Ann Diffendaffer.

The history of the life and most remarkable career of Rev. Spencer Houghton Cone was published in a volume of 500 pages, by his sons, Edward W. and Spencer W. Cone in 1856.

He was a student in Princeton College at twelve years of age, a full grown man in size and a teacher at fourteen—a celebrated actor, playing in the best theatres in New York, Philadelphia and Baltimore at twenty, and a soldier and captain of artilery in the war of 1812.

He was also an editor and publisher and during the last forty years of his life one of the most talented and popular preachers of

---

†John Reed resided at New Market (now Linvale) and was the great grandfather of Levi H. Reed, Esq., of our borough.

‡Margaret and Ruth Corwine were maiden sisters of Amos residing with him.

his generation, possessing as a public speaker extraordinary endowments.

Such was his command of language that he never hesitated for a word, or recalled one that he had uttered.

He was married May 10, 1813, to Miss Sally Wallace Morrell, daughter of Robert Morrell of Philadelphia. She died in August, 1854, and he August 28, 1855.

His mother, Alice Houghton Cone, united with the Baptist Church of Hopewell in 1785, when her eldest child, Spencer, was but a few months old, and was a woman of extraordinary piety and consecration, which, coupled with a mind of rare culture and refinement, stamped itself upon all of her children, who, like their mother, became earnest devoted members of the Baptist church in early life.

In closing the articles on the family of Col. Houghton we will quote in part from references found in the life of his grandson, alluded to above, which will be of interest, emphasizing as it does the fact that "great hearts are tender hearts" and "the loving are the daring."

He says: "The last we remember of grandfather Houghton was once when mother took all of us children up to his house. He would have us sing for him, and we sung 'Hail Columbia' as best we could.

"He was completely overcome and cried like a child.

"Our father Cone was just like him and easily moved to tears.

"They both sung finely. Uncle Houghton said that they could hear grandfather sing three-quarters of a mile.

"Both of them used to set the tunes in church, I remember hearing them.

"My dear brother's voice was hereditary. It ran in the Houghton and Cone families.

"Our father had naturally all the qualities of a public speaker. His language flowed easily and naturally.

"He was a philanthropist and greatly injured himself and family by his too great generousity.

"He spoke at grandfather Houghton's grave.§ What a strange transmission of qualities! His son inherited the same strange compelling sense of duty.

---

§The grave of Col. Houghton is in the old cemetery, only a few feet north of the meeting house, while the memorial tablet, erected by the citizens of Hopewell in 1896, stands within a few feet of the Hart monument, and near the street.

"It is evident that there was no one there when the old soldier was laid to rest, who could do him justice but Conant Cone. He felt it. He had been his fellow soldier, and fought with him in the the same holy cause. He felt it to be his duty.

"That simple idea, heroic in its simplicity, bore down everything else ; put back the tears, conquered all but the high sense of duty to the dead, and he stood up and spoke for him to the living.

"It is not a little singular, too, that three generations of the same stock should not only be controlled by the same all powerful sentiment of duty, but also that in each of them it should take the same development in love of country, lofty patriotism, perpetually looking to the people as the source of all power, and the object of all effort politically ; and in religious affairs to the propagation of Baptist sentiments.

"Three generations thought, spoke and acted as one ; all looking from remote and various periods of time to one object, and working for one glorious faith of civil and religious independence.

"Grandfather, father and mother were all at one time members together of the old Hopewell Baptist church.

"The meeting house is a square, old-fashioned stone building of some size and is pleasantly situated in the lower part of Hunterdon county.

"There are hundreds like it scattered through the land, and few can fail to picture from their own memory such a place with its plain, high backed pews, made neither for ornament nor ease ; its square pulpit, perched high up in one end ; its whitewashed walls and general air of rude and simple solemnity.‖ One feature is peculiar—before the meeting house still flourish trees, now almost centenarians, and beneath whose shade many generations have met in the pleasant hush of the Sabbath to exchange weekly their kind greetings before entering together the house of prayer."

November 20, 1901.

‖So far as known the above is the only description in existence of the old meeting house erected in 1748.

During the 23d, 24th and 25th of June, 1778, when the hill north of the borough was covered with the tents of the Continental Army, it rained constantly, and hundreds of the soldiers were on the sick list, and this venerable old structure described above was used as a hospital, and here many brave men, who had faced the cannon's mouth, were forced to abandon the struggle and are buried in the old cemetery. Their last resting place is marked by a plain marble slab, which was erected through the exertions of one of Hopewell's most patriotic and public spirited citizens, Joseph M. Phillips, Esq., now deceased.

NUMBER VII.

There was no period during the long struggle for American Independence, when the horrors of war were so severely felt in the Hopewell Valley, as during the month of December, 1776, when the state of New Jersey was completely under the control of the victorious legions of Lord Cornwallis, who occupied the towns of New Brunswick, Princeton and Trenton, with strong detachments of Hessian troops.

The patriot army under General Washington had been defeated in every engagement with the enemy at White Plains, Brooklyn Heights, New York, Fort Lee and Fort Washington, and with the discouraged and disheartened remnant of his army, now reduced to less than three thousand men, he was compelled to make a hasty retreat across the state into Pennsylvania, closely pursued by the victorious army of Cornwallis.

So close was the pursuit that he entered Princeton just one hour after Washington had left it, and pressed on with all possible speed, confident of capturing the whole American Army before it could cross the Delaware and thus end the war in the colonies in less than six months after they had declared their independence.

The advance column of the Hessians reached Trenton about midnight of December the eighth—just as the last boat of Washington's rear guard had safely crossed the Delaware, and not being able to obtain boats the pursuit had to be abandoned, and leaving a strong detachment of Hessian troops at Trenton and Princeton, Cornwallis returned with the main body of his army to New Brunswick.

Several prominent Princeton and Trenton families made their escape with the American army into Pennsylvania, and the exciting scenes at the ferries above Trenton were described by an eye witness as follows :

"To my youthful imagination they called up the day of judgment. So many panic stricken and frightened people, together

with sick and wounded soldiers, assembled at the ferries, all flying
for their lives, and with scarcely any means of crossing the river.''

During this dark and gloomy period between the retreat into
Pennsylvania, and the battle of Trenton on December 26th, a large
proportion of the people of this state became so discouraged that they
despaired of a successful issue of the struggle for liberty, and accepted the terms of Lord Howe's proclamation, offering pardon and
protection to all who would lay down their arms and take the oath
of allegiance to the British crown within sixty days.

It is a matter of history that for over two weeks the daily average of those who took ''protection papers'' was about 200, and the
whole number 2,703.* The great majority of them being along the
route of the conquering army, including Newark, Elizabethtown,
New Brunswick, Princeton and Trenton. So widespread was this
disaffection that even Samuel Tucker of Hunterdon county, chairman of the committee of safety, treasurer and judge of the Supreme
Court, took protection of the British and vacated his offices.

It may be said to the honor of Old Hopewell that the great majority of the people were staunch old patriots, who spurned with
disdain the offer of pardon and protection, and stood gallantly by
their noble leaders, Hart and Houghton, who never faltered for a
moment, or lost confidence in the cause of freedom, even in this the
darkest hour in our nation's history.

Those timid and faint hearted people who had so promptly tak-
en the oath of allegiance to the crown, and received protection soon
found to their great consternation and dismay, that they had been
terribly deceived, for during the brief period that the British held
undisputed sway the country was ravaged by the Hessian soldiers,
who could not read a word of the English language, and when these

---

*The following is a copy of one of these ''protection'' papers, given by Col. Mawhood,
who a little more than two weeks later was defeated by General Washington at Princeton.

"I do hereby certify that the bearer, ———— of ————, came and subscribed the declaration specified in a certain proclamation published in New York on the 18th day of November last, by the Right Honorable Lord Howe, and his excellency General Howe.

"Whereby he is entitled to the protection of all officers and soldiers serving in his
Majestie's Army in America, both for himself, his family and property, and to pass and re-
pass on his lawful business without molestation.

"Given under my hand this 18th day of December, 1776.

"C. MAWHOOD, Leut. Col."

"protection" papers were exhibited, regarded them no more than if they had been passes from General Washington, and showed them no more mercy than to the patriots who remained true to the cause of liberty.

Property was destroyed without distinction of persons. Stock was driven off, furniture that could not be carried away was wantonly destroyed and houses were completely striped of bedding, leaving women and children and the aged and decrepit without a blanket to cover them.

These crimes and others too horrible to relate were committed in this valley, and no portion of the state within a few miles of the British lines was exempt. These atrocities had the effect of uniting the people as one man to resist the invaders, and revenge personal injuries, so that when Washington recrossed the Delaware and won his great victory at Trenton, they flocked to him by hundreds, anxious to show their sincerity by burning their so called "protection papers," and renewing their allegiance to the United States.

If all the exciting and thrilling events and incidents which occured in this valley during the short period intervening between the hasty retreat of Washington toward the Delaware the first week of December, 1776, and the still more hasty retreat of Cornwallis' demoralized troops toward the Raritan only one month later, could be gathered and published, they would be of intense interest to those who now occupy the old homesteads of the patriots who figured conspicuously in those events.

At the time alluded to, the enemy was making daily raids through this region and the minds of the people were in a state of constant fear and alarm.

Hon. John Hart was absent from his home, recruiting for the army and his farm, and those of his neighbors were plundered and their families driven from their homes to seek refuge in the Sourland Mountain, at that time an almost impenetrable wilderness which the Hessians never had the courage to explore.

John Hart's nearest neighbor was Abraham Golden, who resided on the farm now owned by A. L. Holcombe and who was a member of Capt. John Stryker's Light Horse Troop of Somerset County Militia, which at this time performed almost constant service in skirmishing with the enemy's outposts near New Brunswick and Princeton, and in keeping the country near the British camps as

free as possible from the plundering bands of Hessians.† Mr. Golden had returned home one night from one of these scouting expeditions, and being very much exhausted threw himself across his
bed without taking off his uniform and fell into a very sound sleep,
from which he was rudely aroused toward morning by a squad of
Hessians, who hustled him in line with a number of his neighbors,
who like himself had been "caught napping."

It was nearly daylight when they started on their march toward Princeton, and we can but faintly imagine the emotions of that
little band of patriots as in the gray dawn of that cold December
morning, they marched in grim silence before their insolent and
brutal captors, thinking of the helpless and defenseless families
they had left behind.

The march was not an altogether silent and uneventful one,
however, as they had one very refractory and irrepressible prisoner
who was bent on making things lively.

This prisoner was Jacob Lane Golden, a nephew of Abraham,
who on account of his diminutive size was known in the community as "Little Jake."

He was about sixteen years old at that time, but not larger
than the average boy of twelve and would have remained at home
unnoticed had it not been for his characteristic failing of endeavor-
ing to make up in noise and bravado what he lacked in size.

This unfortunate trait in his character was very conspicuous on
this occasion, and while the Hessians were getting their prisoners
together, and helping themselves to all the provisions in sight and
whatever else of value they could conveniently carry away, he made
use of all the profanity he was master of in expressing his contempt
for the whole British nation and this squad of Hessian robbers in
particular.

---

†Capt. John Stryker was the son of Peter Stryker and Antje Deremer, and was
born March 2, 1740, and died March 25, 1786. His father had bequeathed to him his "silver
hilted sword," which he used very effectively during the war for independence. He was
commissioned captain of a troop of Light Horse of Somerset Militia, and afterward attached to the state troops. He was a zealous patriot and a very brave officer during the en-
tire war and performed very valuable service in harrassing the British when they attempted to raid the eastern counties, extending his operations at this time to all the country
north of the British lines from the Raritan to the Delaware. He resided in a fine house
built by his father near the present site of Weston Station on the Delaware and Bound
Brook R. R. and was buried in the middle of a fifteen acre field on his own farm. He was
the father of Gen. Peter I. Stryker, who was President of the Senate of New Jersey from
the 47th to the 50th sessions and by virtue of that position acted for a few months as gover-
of the state.

He was told by the sergeant that if he was not such a contempt-ible little "runt" they would take him with the rest, and if he gave them any more of his "sass" they would take him anyhow.

"Little Jake" was very sensitive about his size, and told them that if he was little he could handle a musket better than any Hessian they had in the crowd, and this little speech sealed his fate for the time and he was hustled in line at the point of the bayonet and marched off with the rest.

Several times on the way to Princeton he managed to break ranks and run up on the bank at the side of the road and speak his mind, and when they threatened to shoot him he struck his tiny fists together and called them a set of cowardly thieves and dared them to put their threat in execution.

This challenge had such a comical side to it on account of his dwarfish size that it only provoked a smile and he was allowed to have considerable freedom in defying the whole British army, so long as he kept inside the fences.

The squad reached Princeton early in the morning and the prisoners were drawn up in line on the College Campus for inspec-tion by the colonel, who, when he came down the line to "Little Jake," asked the sergeant what he brought that "dirty nosed little brat" over there for, and slapping him across the back with his sword told him to run home to his mother.

Under ordinary circumstances "Little Jake" would have re-sented this unpardonable insult, but the sight of the brilliant uni-forms, and dazzling equipments of the officers had taken all the "wind out of his sails" and for once he was completely awed.

In relating the incident years afterward he said that being un-der size had always been very humiliating until that morning, when he got a great deal of satisfaction out of it as he skipped over the hills to Hopewell.

Jacob Lane Golden was the son of Joseph and Elizabeth Lane Golden, and grandson of Joseph Golden, Sr., the first of the name in Hopewell township.

Jacob's father had died some years previous to the war, and he probably lived at this time with his Uncle Jacob in the old house on A. L. Holcombe's lower farm on the Trenton road.

He was born about 1760, and married about 1790 Peninah, daughter of Richard and Mary Reed of New Market (now Linvale),

Hunterdon county, who was born February 9, 1751, and was consequently nearly ten years his senior.

They resided on the farm where his father had lived before the Revolution, and which is now owned by Clifton W. Blackwell, and is located on the west side of Stony Brook, near John L. Burroughs', and the old house standing near the "Big Spring" is still in good condition, although one of the oldest houses in this part of the state.

This old couple had no children, but brought up as their own child Zilpah Reed Decker, a niece of Mrs. Golden, who had been left motherless in 1782 at the age of one week, and who married first Jonathan Hunt of Linvale, and after his death became the second wife of John Ege.

The writer is indebted to the wonderful memory of this estimable old lady for many reminiscences of the past. She died in 1862 at the age of eighty years.

Jacob L. Golden died March 1, 1827, aged 66, and his widow October 28, 1827, aged 77, and they are buried in the Golden family plot on the farm of A. L. Holcombe.

January 8, 1902.

NUMBER VIII.

The prisoners whose capture was described in our last article were all allowed to return to their homes except Abraham Golden, who, being in his uniform, was held as a prisoner of war and confined temporarily in the basement of the college at Princeton. This was the last his family ever heard of him, and he was doubtless taken with others and incarcerated in one of the vile and loathsome prison pens in New York City, or harbor, where he and thousands of other brave patriots perished miserably.

In March, 1778, his brother Jacob administered on his estate, and the old inventory and other papers in connection with the settlement of the estate are still in existence, and in possession of Mrs. George S. Golden of Hopewell, who has a large number of interesting documents relating to the settlement of the Golden family in Monmouth and old Hunterdon counties.

Abraham Golden married a Miss Waters and had two children, Deborah, born about 1770, and Amos, born 1772.

Mrs. Golden must have died some time before the occurrence of the incidents related above, as there is a tradition in the family that his two little motherless children were in bed with him at the time of his capture.

Deborah, daughter of Abraham, married a Mr. Stout, and removed to Ohio at the time of the great migration during the early years of the last century.

Amos, son of Abraham, married Elizabeth, daughter of Ethan Smith and Ruth Sexton, born January 2, 1773. She was a sister of the mother of Governor Olden, and of Dr. Charles Smith of New Brunswick, who left a legacy to Mrs. Golden, but the bulk of his large estate to his nephew and namesake, Charles Smith Olden, afterward governor of New Jersey.

Amos Golden and Elizabeth Smith were married about 1791, resided on the homestead of his father Abraham, now occupied by A. L. Holcombe, Esq., and had children as follows: Temperance, born 1792; Aaron S., born September 25, 1794; George, born November 27, 1797; Sarah, born December 29, 1800; Deborah, born March 1, 1803; Amos, born 1804.

Amos Golden was killed by falling from a load of lumber, on his way home from Trenton, June 23, 1804, at the age of 32, and his widow, who was familiarly known in her later years as "Aunt Betsy," died June 18, 1864, aged 91, having lived a widow three score years.

She was left a widow at the age of 31, with six small children with but limited resources pecuniarily, but with unlimited faith in the resources of Him who has promised to be the "Husband of the widow and the father of the fatherless" She was a christian mother to them in the highest sense of the term, doing her part nobly, and rearing her little family in the fear and admonition of the Lord.

She gave them the best educational advantages that her slender income would permit, and as they grew up to manhood and womanhood they became widely known as one of the most estimable families of this region, and were among the leaders of Hopewell society eighty years ago.

The youngest son, Amos, did not reach maturity, however, but died October 1, 1815, aged eleven years.

Several members of the family were accomplished singers, and George had the honor of organizing and leading the first choir in the old Hopewell church.*

Temperance, oldest daughter of Amos and Elizabeth Golden, married December 26, 1816, Joseph Wilson of Amwell, removed to Indiana, and settled in Franklin county, near Indianapolis. They had six children as follows: Mary, born April 1, 1818; Jane, born February 6, 1821; Sarah, born August 8, 1824; Elizabeth, born June 1, 1827; George, born April 29, 1831, and James, born August 14, 1836.

Aaron S., son of Amos and Elizabeth Golden, married Dorcas, daughter of James Oakley of New York City in 1823, and resided in Newark, N. J.

They had two children, James Oakley and Elizabeth Ann.

---

*It was the custom in all country churches at the beginning of the last century to have congregational singing led by a chorister, or "Clark" who stood in front of the pulpit, the pastor reading the lines. two at a time, and then the clark leading off in the singing. This was one of the time-honored customs brought over from the fatherland, where hymn books were few and seldom used by any but the pastor and clark. and the writer well remembers when the custom was still in vogue in evening meetings held for prayer at private houses. It was a slow and tedious proceeding, and the frequent interruptions in reading the lines made it exceedingly difficult to sing a hymn through on the same pitch.

Mr. Golden died November 5, 1826, aged 32, and was buried at Newark.

James O. Golden, son of Aaron S., married Julia Hopkins and resided at Elizabeth. They had two children, viz : George, who married Josephine Halsey, and Julia A., who married Hobart Van Doren, all residing at Elizabeth, N. J.

Elizabeth, daughter of Aaron S. Golden, married Prof. John Hardenbrook Black November 1861, and they had two children: Henry Hardenbrook, born July, 1863, died February, 1888, and Dora Golden, who resides at Newark, N. J.

Prof. Black was one of the professors in Oakland College located in Claiborne county, Mississippi,† for some years, and after his return north conducted a school for boys in Newark, N. J., and later at Bellville, N. J.

Prof. Black died in 1874, and is buried at Orange, N. J., and his widow, Elizabeth Golden Black, died February 19, 1888, aged 61 years.

Sarah Golden, second daughter of Amos Golden and Elizabeth Smith, born December 29, 1800, married John Musgrove of Princeton, N. J., in 1825, and resided at Princeton until 1832, when they emigrated to Bureau county, Ill., which was at that time one of the frontier settlements in the United States, and very sparsely settled, the principal population being Indians, who were not at all friendly, the Black Hawk war being at that time in progress.

Black Hawk was defeated in the great battle which took place August 2, 1832, on the banks of the Mississippi, opposite the mouth of the Iowa, and in September the difficulties were settled by a treaty, in which the Sacs and Foxes ceded to the United States thirty millions of acres of the finest lands on which the sun ever shone.

The little village of Chicago had at that time a population of about twenty families, exclusive of the garrison at old Fort Dearborn.

Mr. Musgrove purchased a fine farm of 480 acres, and after the Indian treaty the population increased very rapidly, and a village

†Oakland College was founded in 1830 and David Hunt (who was a Hopewell boy one hundred years ago) was one of its founders and most liberal supporters. Mr. Hunt was the son of Jonathan Hunt, who was a brother of Israel, from near Mount Rose, and a cousin of Wesley Hunt, deceased, some of whose children are now residents of our borough and vicinity. Mr. Hunt went to Mississippi when a young man, married a Miss Calvitt, and became a very wealthy planter. He was a liberal contributor to benevolent objects and gave at one time $50,000 to the Colonization Society.

sprang into existence near Mr. Musgrove, which he had the honor of naming after his native town in New Jersey.

Princeton soon after became the county seat of Bureau county, and was a very important trade centre several years before there was a railroad in the state of Illinois.

Mr. and Mrs. Musgrove had three children, viz : Mary, Emily and Charles. Mr. Musgrove died in 1839, and Mary and Charles, who never married, died in 1859.

Emily married Wm. C. Trimble October 28, 1853, and died in 1869. They had five children, who are all the descendants left of that branch of the family. George, the second son of Amos Golden and Elizabeth Smith, born November 27, 1797, never married, and died August 3, 1833, and is buried in the old Golden family plot on the farm of Mr. A. L. Holcombe.

Deborah, the youngest daughter of Amos Golden, never married. She resided with her mother at Princeton, N. J., and afterward at Lambertville, N. J., until the death of her mother, when she removed to her sister's in Indiana, and afterward to Mrs. Musgrove's at Princeton, Illinois, where she died May 10, 1882, aged 79.

Mrs. Musgrove, who was the last survivor of the children of Amos Golden and Elizabeth Smith, died December 12, 1882, aged 82.

The Golden family of Hopewell were not only one of the pioneer families of this region, but also one of the patriot families of the revolutionary period, all four of the sons of Joseph Golden, who were living at that time, being enrolled in the Continental Army.

Elias, Jacob and William were all in Captain William Tucker's Company, First Regiment, Hunterdon county, and Abraham in Capt. John Stryker's Troop of Light Horse, as stated in my last article.

Joseph Golden purchased December 30, 1734, 200 acres of land of Thomas Houghton described in the deed as the "easternmost part of his tract," being the tract now owned by Messrs. A. L. Holcombe and Charles A. Holcombe, and fully described in former articles as the tract which was surveyed by Thomas Revell, agent for The West Jersey Society, for Thomas Tindall, on February 27, 1696, being the first farm of which we have any record located in the Hopewell valley. This Joseph Golden was known in Monmouth Co., prior to his settlement at Hopewell, as Joseph Golden, Junior, his father being active in business affairs at that time.

Joseph Golden, Senior, was registered as "an Englishman" in the town book at Gravesend, Long Island, in 1698,‡ and soon after this emigrated to Monmouth county, New Jersey, and on December 4, 1704, purchased of James Hubbard, 130 acres of land at Schenck's Mill, near the present site of Marlboro.

In 1709 the Reformed Dutch Church of Navesink, now the Brick Church of Marlboro, was organized, and among the 49 charter members are found the names of Joseph Golden, and Anneke Daws, his wife, and again in 1725, we find the name of Maritje (Maria) Van Dyck, wife of Joseph Golden. These were doubtless the first and second wives of Joseph Senior.**

In December, 1711, and again in 1713 Joseph Golden served on the grand jury in Monmouth county as shown by the records.

On June 13, 1727, Peter Wyckoff of "Flatlands in Kings county, in the Island of Nassau, in the State of New York," sold to Joseph Golden, of the "township of Middletown, in the Province of East Jersey," ninety acres of land, more or less, for the sum of one hundred and eighty pounds, current money of New York, he, the said Golden, to pay the "quit rent," due to the proprietors of said Province, according to the tenor of the patents granted for the same. This deed is still in possession of the Hopewell branch of the Golden family in a good state of preservation.

On even date with the above deed a bond was given to the said Wyckoff for the full amount of the purchase money, and signed by Joseph Golden and Joseph Golden, Junior.

Both signatures are in the handwriting of Joseph Junior, so often met with on public documents after his settlement in Hopewell, Joseph Senior making his mark.

April 9, 1902.

---

‡The tradition in the Hopewell branch of the family, that they are of Dutch decent, may have originated in the fact that both Joseph Goldens, as the records show, married Dutch wives, resided among the Dutch, and could doubtless speak the Dutch language fluently, as they attended church where all the sermons at that time were preached in the Dutch language. They can justly feel proud of their Dutch ancestry, who were true as steel to the principles of civil and religious liberty, and among the staunchest of patriots during the darkest days of the revolutionary period. The Monmouth branch of the family claim that their first Golden ancestor came from southern England, and the records of the family would seem to justify the claim, as William Goulden was one of the friends of Lady Deborah Moody, and with several others accompanied her from England to escape religious persecution, settling first at Salem, Mass.

**Anneke Daws, the first wife of Joseph, was the daughter of Elias Daws of Middletowr, and Maria Van Dyke, the second wife, the daughter of Claes Thomasse Van Dyke, who was born 1696-1700, the granddaughter of Jans Thomasse, who imigrated from Holland in 1652. Dirck Van Dyke, a brother of Claes, was the ancestor of the Hopewell Dykes, through Hendrick 1st, Hendrick 2d, Jeremiah 1st and Jeremiah 2d. Hon. Jeremiah Van Dyke of Hopewell being the sixth generation from Jans Thomasse, the imigrant, and the seventh generation from Thomasse Janz of Holland, who, so far as we know, never came to this country.

NUMBER IX.

The patent alluded to in the deed from Peter Wyckoff to Joseph Golden was granted to twelve proprietors in 1665, the name of William Goulden (or Golding) heading the list.*

This patent covered all the present limits of Monmouth county, except Upper Freehold and a part of Millstone townships.

It also covered portions of Middlesex and Ocean counties, which were subsequently set off from Monmouth.

In the "History of Monmouth County." page 69, the statement is made that William Golding (or Goulder) became a permanent settler in Monmouth county, and with Richard Stout and others, was one of the founders of the Middletown Baptist church ; and local historians are doubtless correct in placing him at the head of the family of Golden in Momouth county, and the father of Joseph, Senior, and the grandfather of Hopewell Joseph.

William Goulden is enrolled among the Massachusetts Baptists who were banished from the colony at the time of the Puritans persecutions, and with Lady Deborah Moody (who was their acknowledge leader), her son Sir Henry, Ensign Baxter, "Sergeant" James Hubbard, John Tilton, Thomas Spicer and others of less prominence, left Massachusetts in the summer of 1643 and came to Gravesend, Long Island.

At the time that Lady Deborah was "admonished" that she must modify her religious views or leave the colony, Governor Winthrop spoke of her as the "Ladye Moodye, a very wise and anciently religious woman, but with very erroneous views on religious matters."

Lady Moody was the daughter of Walter Dunck, Esq., of Aves-

---

*On examining the early records of Long Island and of Monmouth county we have found the name spelled Golden, Goldin, Goulden, Goulder, Golding, Goulding, Golder and Goolder. The family invariably signed their names Golden, and the variations were made by ignorant and careless clerks, justices and others who sometimes spelled the name two or three different ways in the body of the same document.

bury, England, and about 1625 married Sir Henry Moody, of Garresden in Wiltshire, who was one of the baronets created by James in 1622.

Sir Henry died about 1632, leaving her with one son "Sir Henry." She was an ardent Baptist, and, like the Quakers, refused to pay taxes for the support of the established church, preferring to leave her native land and all the associations to which her position as a Baroness entitled her, and seek a home in the new world which had been glowingly pictured as a refuge for the oppressed and persecuted.

Her company, including several families, that of William Golden doubtless among the number, arrived in Boston early in 1640, as in April of that year we find them at Salem, where Lady Moody purchased a large farm of John Humphrey, one of the original patentees.

In less than two years after her settlement she found to her great surprise and dismay, that the Massachusetts colonists, who had so recently escaped religious persecution themselves, were as intolerant as Prelate or Star Chamber of the fatherland, and to avoid further trouble she and her associates chose to seek a home among the Dutch on Long Island, and as she had great influence with the Dutch governor, they were allowed the religious freedom which had hitherto been denied them.

William Golden became a large land owner at Gravesend, and also owned some land on Manhatten Island, and "Golden's Hill" in what is now the heart of New York City, was known as such until it was leveled and graded in the march of improvement to make way for the great metropolis.

In 1656, we find among the freeholders of Gravesend, the names of Richard Stout (ancestor of the Hopewell Stouts), William Goulder, Joseph Goulder and others, whose descendants afterward became the pioneers of old Hunterdon county.

On November 25, 1672, William Golder sold out his right, title and interest, in the Monmouth Patent to Richard Hartshorne, but we find that in 1676, under "grants and conssessions" of the proprietors, that for himself and wife he was granted 240 acres, and the presumption is that at the time of the transfer he received the grant as a part of the consideration.

On September 10, 1686, a patent was granted by Gov. Dougan to James Hubbard, John Tilton, Jr., William Golder, Nicholas

Stillwell and Joachem Gulick, for a considerable tract of land on Long Island, and the "quit rent" exacted was "six bushels of good merchantable winter wheat, to be paid on the 20th day of March, annually, for his majestie's use at the city of New York, forever."

The writer has visited the old Golden homestead in Monmouth county. It is located about three miles from Middletown, and now is in possession of the family of Peter Schenck Golden of Freehold.

The farm comprises 197 acres, and has descended from father to son for several generations.

The old mansion stands on a beautiful eminence on the Holmdel road, and with a recent addition comprises thirty-two rooms, and as the traveler climbs the hill, it presents quite an imposing appearance.

Possibly this is the same tract granted to the patentee, William Golden, by the proprietors in 1676. Indeed it is altogether probable, as Mr. Peter S. Golden of Freehold, a very intelligent and finely educated old gentleman, informed the writer that he heired the property from his father, and he has no knowledge of any other old Golden homestead in that region.

On this farm Elias Golden (named for his grandfather Dawes), the brother of Hopewell Joseph, resided over 150 years ago, and here no doubt they were born about 200 years ago.

It has not only been the birth place, but also the burial place of several generations, and the old cemetery located a few rods from the house, contains many Golden names identical with those of the the Hopewell family, viz: Abram, Elias, Joseph, William, John, etc.

Joseph Golden, Junior, married Jannetje (or Jane) Lane,† and removed his family to Middlebush, Somerset Co., and after sojourning here a short time came to Hopewell.

All the Monmouth families who came to Hopewell about that time and earlier, doubtless came by Amboy and New Brunswick, as there existed quite a good throughfare between those points at a very early day, while most of the so-called roads were merely bridle

---

†The probability is that the wife of Joseph Golden was a daughter of Jacob Lane of Marlboro, Monmouth county, as he mentions in his will a daughter, who married a Golden. Jacob Lane was one of the charter members of the old Dutch church of Marlboro, near which is the old Lane homestead, which has been visited by the writer and on which a Jacob Lane still resides. It is a well known fact that it was the custom at that time to name the the first son for the paternal, and the second for the maternal grandfather, and this custom was observed in Joseph Golden's family, as in his will he mentions first his son Joseph, second his son Jacob, etc.

paths winding through the forests, the only means of transportation being by pack horses, several of which were managed by one man, much the same as the canal mules are managed on the tow path at the present day. Mr. Golden sojourned for a time at Middlebush, Somerset Co., as shown by the records, but we are unable to find that he invested in any real estate there.

Joseph Golden purchased his first tract at Hopewell of Thomas Houghton (father of Col. Joab), on December 30, 1734, and it is supposed settled on it the following spring, as we find that he gave a bond to Mr. Houghton in 1735, for one hundred pounds current money of New Jersey, at "eight shillings per ounce," conditioned for the payment of fifty pounds of like money, on, or before the twenty-fifth day of December, 1737.

Mr. Houghton gave Mr. Golden a receipt for payment in full on this bond, which I will copy in full here retaining the original capitalization and spelling:

"March ye 22the Day 1744."

"Received of Joseph Golden the sume of fifty pounds Lawfull money, with Lawfull interest of the provence of west New Jersey, which was Dow upon a bond Bareing Datse one thousand Seven Hundred thirty five, payable the twenty fifth day of December, in the yeare of our Lord one thousand Seven Hundred and thirty seven. Given under my Hand and Seal this twenty Second Day of March, 1744.

"THOMAS HOUGHTON."

"Witness present, Benjamin Anderson, Wm. Jones."

On July 19, 1750, Mr. Golden purchased the balance of the Houghton tract, the particulars of the transfer being given in "Number 4" of these articles.

It must be remembered that the road now known as the "old turnpike," leading from Hopewell to Lambertville, had no existence at this time, nor until two generations of Goldens had passed away, the whole tract being in one solid block.

They had access to the Trenton road over their own lands, and there was also an old driftway out to Stony Brook over the Parke tract, later Larason's and Hunt's, now the farms of Messrs. D. P. Voorhees, Amos Sked and C. E. Voorhees, and over this driftway the Goldens passed to and from the farm occupied by Joseph's son Elias, and where they carried on extensive mining operations 1760 to 70, of which I shall speak later.

There was an old Indian village located on this driftway which still existed some years after Roger Parke made his purchase in April, 1697, and over this path they went to Stony Brook to fish and hunt. Over this driftway a detachment of Washington's army passed on June 23, 1778, to their encampment on the Golden and Hart farms, where they remained until the morning of the 25th, when they broke camp and started on their march for Monmouth, where they fought and won their great victory on the 28th.‡

About 1745 or 50 Mr. Golden drew up a petition to the surveyors of the highway for a laid out road from the Trenton road long the west side of his farm north, to the north line of Dr. Coxe's 30,000 acre tract, then the north line of Hopewell township.

The survey began on the north end of the line and ran south along lands now owned by John S. Van Dyke, Reuben McPherson, E. S. Titus, D. P. Voorhees and Mr. Montag.

This petition is in Joseph Golden's handwriting and while there are many errors in capitalization and spelling, it is nevertheless a well written document for a plain farmer of 150 years ago. It is signed by all the abutting property owners except Moses Hart, who at that time owned the small farm now owned by Mr. Montag, but better known as the Schenck Moore lot.

I will copy this petition in full, retaining the original capitalization and spelling.

It will be observed that at least two of these petitioners were men who attained great distinction in Revolutionary times.

"To the Survaors of the roads of hopewel, amwel and madenhed, greating—

"We your humble Petisnors requesting that you would favor us with a two rod road for the use and benefit of the Inhabitants of the Township of hopewel, amwel, and others for Mils and Markits and other buseynes, beginning at the Southwestly corner of Menne

---

‡It is said that Jesse and Nathaniel Hart, the two oldest sons of Hon. John Hart, served as guides to Washington on the march from Coryell's Ferry (now Lambertville) to Hopewell, on this occasion, and knowing full well the damage an army would do during an encampment, they guided them to their father's farm, and the farms of their next neighbors, the Goldens. It rained incessantly during the march and while they were in camp, and under the circumstances no better location could have been selected. "Lake Tommy," located on the top of the hill on Mr. Hart's farm, was quite a body of water at that time and furnished an ample supply for the army during their stay. The army ruined growing crops, and burned and destroyed fences, but it can be said to the credit of both families that they never brought in any bill for damages, although many others did whose damages were very trivial compared with theirs.

gulecks Land. Thens along the Line between Joseph Golden and Charles sacston to the corner stone in the greenbriars, one rod on each side of the Line from thens a South Southeaster corse as the Line directs betwen said golden and timothy brush. Jeams hunt, moses hart and Joseph golden, in the main road which Leads one way to trent ton, the other to rockerhil for the use and benefit of the inhabitants and travillers, and for farther Promoting the good of the Publick. we the subscribers do request this road to be Laid and relaid in manner afore said and your Petisnors Prays for a Public road.

"Wm. Phillips, James Mattison, Joseph Golden, James Larason, Minne Gulick, Joab Houghton, Andrew Stout, Edward Hunt, John Hart, Charles Sexton, Aaron Runyan, Benjamin Stout, Moses Randolph."

It may be of interest to state that the above parties owned in 1750, the lands lying between the road leading from Hopewell to the mountain, on the east line and from a point just north of Moore's mill to the mountain on the west line, excepting Wm. Phillips, who resided in Lawrence, and may have wanted more direct access to timber lands in the mountains. Excepting also James Mattison, who owned the farms now occupied by John M. Dalrymple, Esq., and the congregation of the First Baptist church, and Andrew Stout, who resided on the farm owned by Wm. A. Allfather, better known as the Britton Hill farm.

It is a fact worthy of note that every one of these Hopewell farmers signed his name in a bold plain hand which was unusual at a time when a very large percentage of farmers in some localities made their mark.

May 28, 1902.

NUMBER X.

Soon after the location of the public road described in our last article, the surveyors of highway of Amwell township extended it west to Jacob Snyder's mill, now the little hamlet known as Snydertown.

This mill did an extensive business for its size and capacity, not only during the Revolutionary period, but for many years after, being located on a mountain stream with an immense overshot wheel, it could be operated when many larger mills farther down the stream were obliged to stop for want of water.

About the time of Joseph Golden's settlement in Hopewell, perhaps a little earlier, a log schoolhouse was built in the woods about two hundred yards southwest of the present residence of Wm. F. Golden, Esq. This deserves a passing notice, as so far as known, it was the first educational institution in this region, and it was located about the centre of a neighborhood which contained a large number of influential families.

This was known for many years as the "Golden Schoolhouse," and here the Harts, Houghtons, Hunts, Goldens, Larisons, Stouts, Sextons and other large families were graduated in colonial times.

When we say graduated we do not intend it to be understood that their education was finished when they had mastered the "three Rs," but many of the higher branches were taught, and pupils who attended regularly and took advantage of the opportunities offered were well fitted for the responsible positions thrust upon them during the exciting times of the war of independence and the organization of a free government.

About 1740 this was the only school from the Province Line to Harbourton, and it was patronized by families who lived west of the "Great Road" leading from Trenton to Flemington and as far east as the Somerset line.

The Baptist ministers taught in the old log schoolhouse at an early day and the presumption is that Rev. Isaac Eaton taught there from the time of his settlement in 1748 until 1756, when he opened his school in the academy which his father-in-law, David Stout, (known as Amwell David) built for him on the property now in possession of John M. Dalrymple, Esq. This academy flourished until 1767 and became famous in history as the foundation of Brown University of Rhode Island.

About 1780 Rev. Oliver Hart came from South Carolina to Hopewell, and accepted a call to become pastor of the Hopewell church, and, being a man of superior education, became very prominent in school matters, teaching in the old log schoolhouse a number of years prior to the division of the district, and accomplishing much for the intellectual development of the youth of this region.

About 1790–95 the grandmother of the writer attended this school, walking from the farm where Clifton W. Blackwell now resides, west of Stony Brook, and one of her schoolmates who accompanied her was Wilson Price Hunt, who resided where Wm. D. Hill now lives, one and a half miles northwest of Glen Moore.*

The increased attendance at this time made it imperative either to build a larger schoolhouse or divide the district. The eastern families demanded a building near the meeting house, so a new district called Columbia† was then formed and a stone schoolhouse erected in the cemetery, a few feet east of where the Hart monument now stands.

The western half of the district erected an eight-square schoolhouse at the place where the road leading from Moore's mill to Runyan's saw mill crossed the old Bungtown road.‡

This building was used as a schoolhouse until about 1835, and from this time until 1850 it was used as a dwelling house, after which it stood in a delapidated condition until it was finally taken down in 1880.

There is nothing left to indicate to the traveler where either of these four institutions of learning stood.

---

*Mr. Hunt commanded the first commercial expedition across the Rocky Mountains to the Pacific Ocean in 1810–12, reaching the mouth of the Columbia river in January 1812, after suffering untold hardships and privations. He became the hero of Washington Irving's "Astoria," and after his return settled in St. Louis, Mo.

†The village of Hopewell was called Columbia until the post office was established in 1825. From 1800 to 1850 the village contained eight houses exclusive of the meeting house and schoolhouse.

‡This old road was the only direct thoroughfare from Hopewell to Lambertville, until the "Franklin and Georgetown" turnpike was constructed in 1820–22.

They were very plain unpretentious structures, but hundreds of noble men and women, who made their mark in the world, were educated in the old log and stone schoolhouses, and their children and children's children have risen up to call them blessed. Of the old academy it may be said that during its brief existence it "blessed every department of intellectual life and influence."

While it is not our purpose at this time to give a history of the schools of this region, we cannot pass without copying the conditions of a contract entered into about one hundred years ago, between Rev. James Ewing, also pastor of the Baptist church, and his employers when he took charge of the school here.

The conditions of this contract, which was signed by Mr. Ewing and his employers, are as follows, viz :

1st Discipline :

"The employers shall individually support him in keeping impartial order in the school, and in chastising any scholar for immorality, such as filthy or profane language, or action, lying, fighting, wilful disobedience, &c.

"Mr. Ewing engages not to chastise any scholar until it is proven guilty in the face of the school, also the employers to support him in expelling any scholar who may prove incorrigible in wicked ways.

"The terms of tuition as follows, viz :

"For teaching reading, writing and arithmetic to the rule of three, two dollars a quarter ; and for arithmetic beyond that, which he can teach in all its branches, two dollars and a half.

"For English grammar and the general principles of mensuration, three dollars ; for Trigonometry, Navigation, Surveying and Algebra, six dollars a quarter.

"He wishes not to have more than 25 or 30 scholars, and begs the liberty of being sometimes absent for a day, but will make up lost time."

He made a similar contract the next year with the following additions :

"Mr. Ewing engages to lose one half the price of tuition when any scholars are sick or die.

"If desired he will allow an employer to send one scholar in place of another, but will allow no making up of time by sending more scholars than they engage for.

"He will take no signature for less than a quarter, until he has seen all his employers, and if the subscription is filled up with whole quarters, he cannot take parts of quarters.''

The school very frequently had a vacation of a day and sometimes two or three days in a week, unless a competent substitute could be procured, as he was called upon to preach all the funerals in his congregation, besides attending to the other duties in connection with his sacred office.

How, or when he made up his lost time we fail to understand, when we remember at that time, eight hours made a school day, six days a school week, thirteen weeks a school term, and four terms a school year.

Soon after Joseph Golden had purchased the western part of the Houghton 300-acre tract, he had a law suit with the heirs of Col. Daniel Coxe at Pennington, and the record of the proceedings is entertaining reading for those who are interested in the early history of northern Hopewell.

While this record is much too voluminous to be reproduced in full at this time, we will give in part the testimony of two or three of the principal witnesses, the depositions of the others being on the same line but viewed from different standpoints.

As we have stated in a former article the Coxe ejectment suits kept the whole of Hopewell township in a state of suspense and alarm for years, and caused a most distressing state of affairs, many of the settlers being obliged to abandon the farms which they had purchased in good faith and spent the best years of their lives in clearing and improving.

Mr. Golden purchased his tract with the understanding that the Coxe claims had been fully satisfied, and that he was entitled to a warrantee deed without further trouble or expense.

The Coxe heirs refusing to quit claim without further payment, Mr. Golden commenced suit, the trial being held in Pennington in 1754.

There are nine "Interogatories" neatly engrossed on very fine parchment, which is still in as perfect condition as it was one hundred and fifty years ago.

The answers are written out on separate sheets, and the whole proceedings as reported are in possession of Mrs. George S. Golden of Rosedale, in this county.

Mr. Golden kindly loaned them, with many other old colonial documents, to the writer with permission to copy and publish.

The following is the record, the capitalization and spelling being retained as in the original:

"Depositions of witnesses. Taken at Penny Town in the Township of Hopewell, in the county of Hunterdon, and Western Division of the Province of New Jersey, at the House of Jonathan Furman, commonly known by the name of the Red Lyon, on Tuesday and Wednesday the 10th and 11th Days of December, 1754, by virtue of a commission issuing out of his Majesty's High Court of Chancery to us directed for the examination of Witnesses between Joseph Golden, Plaintiff and Daniel Coxe, Wm. Coxe, Robert Lettice Hooper and Richard Saltar, Defendants, on behalf of the Plaintiff."

The first witness called was Col. Joseph Stout, one of the most prominent citizens of the township, who resided on the hill north of Stoutsburg, on the farm known for the past hundred years as the "Weart Homestead."

"Coll: Joseph Stout of Hopewell, in the County of Hunterdon, and Province of West New Jersey, Gent: aged about sixty eight years and upward, Sworn and Examined on behalf of the Plaintiff, sayeth as followeth. That he knew the Plaintiff and Def'dts that he knew Thomas Revel, Thomas Tindal the elder, and Danl. Coxe Esq. & he sayeth further that he supposes that Thomas Revel has been dead about forty years or upwards, and that Thomas Tindal Died near upon the same time, and that Danl Coxe Esq has been dead about fifteen years or above to the best of his memory.

"He further say'th. That he knows the tract of Land commonly called the Thirty Thousand acre tract lying in Hopewell aforesaid, and That he has heard of a certain sett of People, called the West Jersey society, but knew none of them: and that he believes that the aforesaid Thomas Revel was empowered by the said society to sell the whole, or any part of the said Thirty thousand acres of land.

"This Deponent further sayth: That he believes that the purchase was at ten pounds per hundred acres, and that said three hundred acres was included in the said Thirty Thousand acres, joining upon land formerly to the family of Parks,* and further he believes

---

*Roger Parke of "Crosswicks Creek, formerly of Nottingham, England," purchased in April, 1697, 400 acres of land of Thomas Revel, agent for the New Jersey Society. The survey is described by Mr. Revel as beginning at a white oak tree on the north side of Stony Brook at Wissamenson, and at the same time another tract of 100 acres adjoining Thomas Tindal, for his daughter, Annie Parke. This tract now includes the D. P. Voorhees farm, the railroad quarry farm, and also Amos Sked's, C. E. Voorhees', the Samuel Ege farm, and portions of W. W. Kirkendall's, W. C. Velit's and E. S. Titus'.

it was first settled by John Pullen, under the Title of Thomas Tindal, and in possession at the present time of Joseph Golden whose claim is derived from Thomas Houghton, who he thinks purchased it of one of the Tindal's, and further thinks the title was derived to them from Thomas Revel, agent for the West Jersey society.

"This Deponent further sayth : That as to Books or papers in Thomas Revel's life time relating to any affairs of the society, he never knew anything, but many years after Revel's death, this deponent sayth he saw a book which he thought was a record of Deeds of land that the said Revel sold as agent for the society which Sd Book was at that time in the possession of Coll : Daniel Coxe.

"This Deponent sayth : That he knew several persons which he believes purchased of Sd Revel as agent to Sd Society & he thinks the common price to be Ten pounds p hundred acres & that he has seen several of those conveyances & the consideration he believes was Ten pounds p hundred.

"He sayth further that he has heard that Coll : Danl Coxe lay'd claim to all the said Thirty Thousand acre tract by virtue of a conveyance from his father Doctor Coxe, bearing Date one thousand seven hundred and two, and he sayth further that he heard Coll : Danl Coxe say in Publick company in the year 1706 to the best of his memory in answer to question asked by Thomas Revel of the sd Danl Coxe, owned, acknowledged, and say that he had received of Thomas Revel the sum of Three Hundred and Eighty pounds for lands sold by the said Thomas Revel.

"Signed,

"JOSEPH STOUT."

"Taken before us, Jno. Reading, John Emley, Wm. Clayton."

July 16, 1902.

NUMBER XI.

David Price of Hopewell, in the county of Hunterdon and western division of New Jersey, yeo'n, aged about fifty-eight years, was the next witness in the case of Joseph Golden vs. The Heirs of Dr. Daniel Coxe, and after being questioned as to his knowledge of the lands and his acquaintance with the parties in the case, said that :

"About thirty-two years ago being at Coll: Daniel Coxes house, saw a woman come into the house, the Coll: enquiring who it was, Major Lockhart being present, answered it is your friend Tindalls widow. The Coll: answered she shall be well used, whereupon the Major asked the Coll: if he had rec'd the consideration money for the land sold by Thomas Revel to Thomas Tindal, upon which the Coll: took down a Book, and looking into the same Book, answered that he had received Thirty pounds, the sd consideration money for the three hundred acres, only some small matter of interest was still behind and he allowed it.

"Signed,

"DAVID PRICE."

Other witnesses examined were Jasper Smith, Elizabeth Hobbs, Zebulon Stout, Isaac Tindal, Galeace Frazier and Joseph Tindal, all testifying that Dr. Coxe had been fully paid and satisfied of all claims against the heirs of Thomas Tindal, who had purchased it of Thomas Revel, agent for the West Jersey Society in 1696.

Doctor Coxe, Thomas Revel, Thomas Tindal Senior and Thomas Tindal Junior, all died 1712 to 1715, and Thomas Junior devised it by will to his brother, Robert Tindal, in 1715.

Robert Tindal sold it to Thomas Houghton in 1726, and he to Joseph Golden, all the dates of transfers being given in numbers 3 and 4 of these articles.

The last will and testament of Joseph Golden was dated May 29, 1776, and proved before Jared Sexton, surrogate, September 2, 1777.

Dr. Benjamin Van Kirk of Hopewell* attended Mr. Golden in his last sickness and as his last entry in Mr. Golden's account is dated August 1, 1777, his death doubtless occurred at that time.

His son Abraham, who had resided with him on the farm where Mr. A. L. Holcombe now lives, was taken prisoner by the Hessians in December, 1776, the particulars of which are given in number seven of these articles.

Nearly a year had elapsed with no tidings from him, and this had doubtless weighed very heavily on the mind of the old father who had reached nearly four score.

The two little motherless children, who were in bed with Abraham at the time of his capture, were left with the grandparents, and were now not only motherless but fatherless also, as the gallant soldier and express rider never returned, and it was never known under what circumstances his death occurred, nor where his body found a last resting place.

Joseph Golden left a legacy to his widow, but the will does not give her name, and the following is a copy of its other provisions:

"I give to Mary Golden, eldest daughter of my son Joseph Golden, Deceased : 30 acres of land on which she and her mother now liveth, she remaining single and unmarried. If she marries, then I give the 30 acres to Kesiah Golden.

"If they both remain single, they are to have it jointly, their mother having her living there as long as she remains a widow.

"If they both marry, or depart this life, then I give the land to their younger brother Jacob Golden, and to his heirs and assigns forever, he paying his elder brother Joseph thirty pounds at the age of twenty five.

"And concerning the little house, and four acres of land by the brook bank, I give it to all my children, to the use and benefit of mining, all of them to share equally in the expense and profits, my wife to share equally with them in the profit, without any expense to her.

"The remaining part of the plantation I give to my son Elias, he paying legatee to his sisters, and concerning the plantation I bought of Thomas Houghton and on which I now live, I give and bequeath as follows :

---

*The Day Book and Ledgers of Dr. Van Kirk from 1768 to 1815 are still in existence in a good state of preservation, and from 1776 to 1815 his practice extended from Rocky Hill to Harbourton and from Princeton to Wertsville and Ringoes. From 1768 to 1776 he was located in Northern Hunterdon County.

"To my son Jacob Golden, one hundred acres on which he now liveth, he paying legatee to his sisters, his line beginning at the stone between Moses Hart and Peter Mattison.

"I give to my son William Golden that westerly part divided by a line as far as the run whereon he now liveth, he paying legatee to his sisters.

"I give to my son Abraham Golden the easterly part whereon he now liveth, he paying legatee to his sisters.

"I order that the land north of the run be divided equally between my sons, Jacob, Elias, William and Abraham, they paying to their sisters legatee.

"As to the legacies paid to my daughters, my will is that they have one hundred pounds each of them, namely, Anne, Elizabeth and Mary, to be paid to them by their brothers, namely : Jacob Golden, 80 pounds, William Golden, 80 pounds, Abraham Golden, 80 pounds, and Elias Golden, 65 pounds.

"I hereby appoint Jacob, Elias, William and Abraham Golden, executors of this my last will and testament.

"Signed,

"JOSEPH GOLDEN."

"Nehemiah Sexton,
"Jared Sexton,　} Witnesses."
"David Larison,

The mining clause in the above will no doubt excite some curiosity, and will say in explanation that mining was carried on quite extensively on the farm occupied by Joseph Golden's son Elias, at different times between 1750 and the time of Mr. Golden's death, but so far as known they were never reopened after the revolution.

The mining operations were not confined to the farm of Mr. Golden on the west side of Stony Brook, but were also carried on by James Larison on the east side, now the farms of Messrs. C. E. Voorhees and Amos Sked.

Mr. Larison sunk no less than nine shafts on those farms, some of them to the depth of one hundred feet or over, and small quantities of the precious metals were found, but not sufficient to warrant further search at that time, as they had no adequate facilities for pumping or for extracting the ores.

A few years prior to the revolution, one of the most extensive workings on the Larison farm, near what is now known as the old Baryta Mines, had a "cave in" while the workmen were on the outside taking a lunch. They were fortunate in escaping a living grave and unfortunate in losing all their mining tools, which were never dug out, and as they were not replaced by others, their mining enterprises came to an abrupt and disastrous ending.

Mining was pastime on the Golden farm, when compared with the Larison's, as there was no water to contend with and the shafts were as dry in the bottom as at the surface.

Many of these old mine holes are remembered by persons now living; they had "caved in" and been partially filled with stone, until they were huge funnel shaped affairs, and so completely concealed by a dense growth of bushes and briars that a stranger might pass within a few feet of them without being aware of their existence.

In December, 1776, when the Hessians were committing daily depredations through this region, the families in the vicinity of the old mines concealed bedding and other goods in them, and sought them as a place of refuge for themselves when the much dreaded enemy was known to be in the neighborhood.

This tract of land which Mr. Golden devised to his children had not been surveyed since 1696, when it was purchased by Thomas Tindall of Thomas Revell, agent for the West Jersey Society for three hundred acres, and after Mr. Golden's death a resurvey became necessary and it was found to contain three hundred and ninety-two acres.

This was one of many instances illustrating the carelessness practiced in surveying for the West Jersey Society when land sold for fifty cents per acre; but it must also be remembered that the country at that time was an almost impenetrable wilderness outside of the Indian trails, and where there were swamps and marshes in the way the number of chains was often "estimated" and not measured.

An allowance of six acres per hundred was always made for ways, and where small streams were choked and lakes formed several acres were thrown in for good measure.

Mr. Golden's will first mentions the wife and children of his son Joseph Golden, deceased, and in passing will note that we have but little data concerning this family.

In the marriage register in the office of the Secretary of State at Trenton, we find that he married Elizabeth Lane on February 4, 1752, and is called Joseph Golden Junior.

They had at least four children mentioned in the will of their grandfather Joseph, viz: Joseph, Mary, Kesiah and Jacob Lane, and there were two other daughters, viz: Leah, born April 19, 1757, married about 1776 Capt. John Reed of New Market (now Linvale); and Sarah, born about 1755, married October 29, 1782, William Jewell of Hopewell.

It is supposed that Joseph Golden Jr. died in 1766, as there is a receipt among the Golden papers showing that Joseph Senior had paid a Trenton funeral director the expenses of a son's funeral at that time.

After the death of his father the oldest son doubtless went to reside with the Lane family, near Peapack, Somerset county, as a Joseph Golden paid taxes on eighty acres of land in Bedminster township, in 1789, adjoining some of the Lane farms which were numerous there at that time.

The youngest son, Jacob Lane Golden, married about 1785 Peninah Reed, a sister of Capt. John of Linvale, and a brief sketch of their family is given in number seven of these articles.

Elias, third son of Joseph, is mentioned second in the will (as he lived on a part of the tract adjoining the thirty acres) and is left all the remaining part of the "plantation," after reserving the four acres for mining purposes.

This was the farm on which Mr. Joshua J. Hunt now resides, two miles west of the borough, the original tract also embracing the farm now owned by Mr. Clifton W. Blackwell, and the portion of the C. E. Voorhees farm lying on the west side of Stony Brook.

There were 114 acres in the tract when purchased by Joseph Golden, and in 1736 it was occupied by John Hixson.

Elias Golden and his descendants occupied this farm for about one hundred and twenty years, his great, great grandchildren being grown to mature years when it passed out of the possession of the family in 1871.

He had at least two sons, Abraham and David, who were the administrators of the estate in 1795.

David married Deborah, daughter of John Wilson of Amwell township, and raised a large family of sons and daughters on the homestead.

He was widely known in middle life and old age as "Uncle David," and he was always one of the boys among the boys, very fond of a joke and of playing "yankee tricks" on the boys of the neighborhood.

There were several young men and half grown boys among the families of his nearest neighbors, and knowing his fondness for going along the brook on summer evenings bobbing for eels, they hatched a plot by which they could get even with him for some of his pranks, and that the scheme was a howling success in its execution, the sequel will prove.

From the earliest settlement of the country the deep ravine on Stony Brook about two miles west of the borough was regarded by the superstitious as being haunted, in consequence of a tradition that about 1720 a traveler had been waylaid and murdered up on the "great road" about half way between Marshall's Corner and Woodsville and his body buried in the dark hollow along Stony Brook.

During the first century after the country was settled the steep hillsides on either side of the brook were covered with a heavy growth of timber, and there being no houses near at that time, made it a lonely and gloomy place after twilight for those superstitiously inclined, and the boy who had the courage to venture up the dark hollow in the evening after the cows regarded himself as a hero.

Uncle David was authority on ghosts and often entertained the boys with thrilling stories about the traditional spook of Stony Brook among others of a similar nature, but, of course he did not believe in "spooks," although the boys had a suspicion that he believed in them more than he was willing to admit.

Up this hollow the boys resolved to get Uncle David some night after eels, and told him marvelous stories of the big ones that had been caught up there, and finally they prevailed on him to go along and take care of them if anything should happen. Everything being in readiness one of the party provided himself with a sheet, and preceeding the others concealed himself in a clump of low bushes and briars, near the spot where the great drama was to be enacted, and awaited developments.

It was a bright moonlight evening and the old monarchs of the forest which destiny had separated stretched their long arms toward each other across the brook and cast wierd shadows over the scene.

Such gloomy surroundings, associated with the traditional character of the place, needed only the breaking of a dry twig or a rustling among the leaves over in the woods, to cause a peculiar sensation under the hat which must be felt in order to be appreciated.

After the boys had succeeded in getting Uncle David located within a few yards of the clump of bushes, which concealed the "apparition," they retired further down the stream to try their luck, leaving the innocent and unsuspecting victim of the conspiracy waiting for a bite.

He did not wait long, however, before he heard a most unearthly groan just behind him, and looking around saw the shrouded spectre slowly rising out of the bushes, and without waiting to hear the second groan dropped his pole and "lit out" without further ceremony.

The boys, to carry on the joke, followed suit but after running a hundred yards or so, thought they had carried the joke far enough and shouted out, "Come back, Uncle David! come back!" but Uncle David was already far in advance of the others, and having had enough experiences for one night was ready to go home.

The boys said that "he fairly flew over the ground" and losing the path, he plunged into a slough near where Mr. W. W. Kirkendall now lives and lost his hat and both shoes, but he continued to "press with vigor on" until he burst open the kitchen door and stood hatless, shoeless and breathless in the presence of his astonished family.

After recovering himself sufficiently for an explanation, he threw his arms around wildly and declared that there were a "whole lot of spooks up the brook where the old man was buried," but if the boys had only stood by him they would have cleaned them all out.

Uncle David lived several years after his thrilling adventure, but never quite forgave the boys for putting up such a "mean job on him," and they never succeeded in getting him to be their protector on any more bobbing expeditions.

This incident is well authenticated and several children of the boys who took part in the drama are still living, and have often heard the story related as one of the standing jokes of the neighborhood where it occurred, and where Uncle David was a general favorite. At a vendue or raising of the olden time where jokes were free and general good humor prevailed he could always draw a crowd.

August 20, 1902.

NUMBER XII.

The farm located on the west side of Stony Brook described in our last article, and on which David Golden succeeded his father, Elias, was in possession of the Golden family for five generations.

His grandfather, Joseph Golden, purchased it of John Carman about 1758, as Mr. Golden gave Mr. Carman a bond bearing date of January 20, 1758.

Caleb Carman (the father of John) paid taxes on lands in Hopewell in 1722, and doubtless purchased the tract of Thomas Revel, agent for the West Jersey Society.

On December 29, 1736, Caleb Carman made an agreement with Col. Daniel Coxe, to pay him twenty shillings per acre for the tract in settlement of his claims, but Col. Coxe died in 1737, before the deed was given.

Caleb Carman also died in 1745 and by will bearing date August 25, 1745, devised it to his son Jonathan, and in the event of his dying without issue, to his son, John Carman and his sisters.

On December 20, 1745, John Coxe, executor of the will of Col. Coxe, gave to Jonathan Carman a deed for the farm at the price stipulated in the agreement which their fathers had made nine years before.

The Carman family disappeared from this region nearly one hundred and fifty years ago, and so far as we know not one of their descendants have since that time resided in this township, but Mr. Carman was among the pioneers, living just across the brook from Dr. Roger Parke, and the old records locate them both at Crosswick's Creek near Bordentown before coming to Hopewell.

Caleb Carman was the father, or perhaps an uncle, of the Caleb Carman of Bordentown, who figured so conspicuously in revolutionary history, in what was known as ''The Battle of the Kegs,'' and which was made the subject of the very humorous and popular ballad written by Hon. Frances Hopkinson of Bordentown, one of the signers of the "Declaration of Independence."*

The idea of the kegs was first conceived by Mr. Carman and they were manufactured in the cooper shop of Col. Joseph Borden, which was located just in the rear of Mr. Hopkinson's mansion.†

Mr. Carman called to his assistance Joseph Plowman, a pin maker, and a gunsmith named Jackaway and they constructed a spring lock, which they attached to the kegs in such a manner that if they came in contact with an object and rubbed against it the keg would explode.

The kegs were fastened together with ropes, two by two, so that if they struck the bow or stern of a vessel they would swing around on each side and blow a hole through it.

Everything being in readiness, the kegs were filled with powder, and the fleet which was destined to spread such terror and consternation among the British sailors at Philadelphia was launched in the Delaware just below the present outlet lock of the Delaware and Raritan canal.

The kegs were submerged, but the buoys which floated them were visible, making it the strangest war fleet ever heard of in the annals of naval warfare.

Caleb Carman, who is referred to in history as "one of the patriots who never tired of serving his country," volunteered to undertake the hazardous task of piloting them down the river to Philadelphia, were the British war vessels lay in the middle of the stream opposite the city.

He started on the evening of January 6, 1778, and cut loose from them about daylight the next morning just above the city.

It so happened that the vessels which had laid out in the middle of the river for several weeks had been ordered into the docks the day before, to avoid the effects of the ice which was soon expected to form, and the kegs floated by the city without doing any damage except to destroy a small barge, killing four sailors and wounding a few others.

This unexpected explosion caused the greatest consternation among the British sailors and alarm guns were fired immediately,

---

*A portion of this old ballad which was set to the tune Yankee Doodle, and sung by the revolutionary soldiers and the patriots of that period, is to be found in "Barber's Historical Collections of New Jersey," page 102.

†See Evarts and Peck History of Burlington County, page 463.

which brought out not only the British soldiers, but a throng of people who stationed themselves on the tops of the houses in order to witness a novel battle with an invisible foe.

The wharves were lined with soldiers who were under orders to open fire on every chip or stick they saw afloat, and this singular battle continued at intervals until darkness brought it to a close.

The inventors of the "formidable engines," which were constructed for the purpose of destroying the whole British fleet, were greatly chagrined and disappointed that their fleet had come so far short of fulfilling their expectations, but they were entitled to the gratitude of all the patriots of the country, on both sides of the river below Bordentown, as they had made the attempt with the laudable purpose of clearing the river of the British war vessels, which had, for several months, been a constant source of terror to the inhabitants along the river front.

The famous "Battle of the Kegs" is given a place in history as one of the notable events of that very eventful period, and served to immortalize the inventors, if they were not as effective as our modern torpedoes.

David Golden and Deborah Wilson had at least eight children, and although they are well remembered by the writer, the order in which they are given here may not be entirely correct.

Five of them removed to Illinois about fifty years ago, and many of them and their children have been visited by the writer in their western homes.

Anna, married about 1814 Franklin Lewis, and they resided several years at Mendham, Morris county, N. J. Mr. Lewis died in 1832 when she returned to Hopewell and purchased the homestead on Stony Brook, where she resided until 1850, when she sold it to her son, Elias G., and removed to Illinois with her son, George W., with whom she resided until her death in 1868.

She had three children, viz: Elias G., born June 10, 1815; George W., born December 10, 1816, and David G., born May 10, 1823.

Elias G. Lewis married Anchor, daughter of Jonathan Burd, and had two children, Franklin B. and Jonathan B.

George W. Lewis married first Abigail, daughter of Andrew Vannoy, removed to Fairview, Illinois, and had seven children, viz : Sarah A., John G., Andrew V., David G., Emma E., Wilson and Franklin.

George Lewis married second a Mrs. Bound; no children.

David G., youngest son of Anna Golden and Franklin Lewis, married December 23, 1846, Jane, daughter of Abraham J. Voorhees,* and the following spring removed with his father-in-law's family, first to Jacksonville and later to Fairview, Illinois, where David Lewis died in 1849.†

They had two children, a son who died in infancy, and a daughter, Anna Maria, who married James B. Van Arsdale of Rariton, Ill.‡

Elias, son of David Golden and Deborah Wilson, born 1789, married Martha, daughter of Elijah Hart, born 1793, and had one son, Stephen H., born 1822, who married Mary Thompson, and had three children, John, who resides on the homestead near Woodsville, and two daughters.

---

*The Voorhees families of the Hopewell valley are descended from a Coerte Albertse of Voorhees, Holland, and the name, which was originally "Van Voorhees" is derived from their location in Holland which was before the town of Hees (or Hies) hence the name (from before Hees). Coerte Albertse Van Voorhees was born in the early part of the 15th century, and one of his sons emigrated to America with a large family of grown children in April, 1660, in the ship "Bontekoe" (Spotted Cow) Capt. Pieter Lucassen. He purchased November 29, 1660, from Cornelis Dirck Hoogland 9 morgens of cornland, 7 morgens of woodland, 10 morgens of plainland and 5 morgens of salt meadowland at Flatlands, Long Island, for 3,000 guilders, as per page 37 of Liber B. of Flatbush records. He and his wife, Willempe Roelofse Seubering, were members of the Dutch Church of Flatlands in 1677, and his name appears as a magistrate in 1664. His will is dated August 25, 1677. He had six sons at the time of emigration, some of whom remained in Long Island and Monmouth Co., others settled in the valley of the Hudson, and two, Lucasse and Jan, settled in the valley of the Raritan, in Somerset county, early in 1700. They all had large families of sons and they became scattered over all the colonies before the time of the Revolution, and the very large number of the name who served in the Continental army is very good evidence of their loyalty and patriotism. The history of the Voorhees family in a volume of 725 pages was published by Elias W. Van Voorhees in 1888, and enables most of the name to trace their genealogy from Steven Coerte, the first emigrant.

†The journey from Hopewell to Illinois was made in two large farm wagons which were very comfortably fitted out in the barn of the writer's father. They were constructed for sleeping apartments as well as day coaches, and were the "homes" of a party of seven persons for 44 days, in which they traveled about one thousand miles. A copy of the daily diary of Mrs. D. G. Lewis is in the writer's possession, and gives a detailed account of the journey, which on account of its novelty and the continual change of scenery, made it one of great interest and was an experience never to be forgotten. There were few bridges after leaving Pennsylvania, and after storms or showers they were frequently detained for hours waiting for swollen streams to become fordable. Such were the difficulties of a trip to the now central west fifty-five years ago, which can now be made in twenty-four hours.

‡James B. Van Arsdale and Anna M. Lewis were both descended—through different lines—from the first emigrant, Isaac Van Arsdale, who was sent to America in 1645 (either by the government of Holland or by a company there) to inspect the white clays to see if they were suitable for porcelain or pottery ware. Having fulfilled his mission, he was about to embark for home when he received a letter from his father stating that a great pestilence was raging in his native town and that his wife and children had all died during his absence. This intelligence caused him to change his purpose and instead of returning to Holland he settled in Flatlands, Long Island, which at that time was just beginning to settle with emigrants from his native land. He married a Miss Janse (Johnson) and their children, Simon and Gertrude, became the progenitors of two of the largest families in this country. Gertrude married October 18, 1678, Cornelius Peterse Wykoff, who purchased a very large tract of land in Franklin township, Somerset county, about 1703, and all the Wykoff family of this region are descended through her from Isaac Van Arsdale as well as other collateral branches of the Van Arsdale family, many of whom are settled in Hopewell township, and among whom the writer is included, who traces his genealogy to Isaac Van Arsdale through eight generations, all the family records having been preserved during a period of two hundred and fifty years. About thirty of the name of Van Arsdale are found on the roster, as enrolled among the officers and privates in the Continental army from Somerset county alone, besides the large number of the descendants of Isaac Van Arsdale who had lost the name by marriage.

Sarah, daughter of David Golden and Deborah Wilson, never married. She removed to Illinois about 1850 with her brother, Cornelius, and died there at an advanced age.

Deborah, daughter of David Golden and Deborah Wilson, married Ralph Burroughs, son of Philip, and great great grandson of John Burroughs of near London, England, who settled near Salem. Mass, in 1637. Ralph Burroughs and Deborah Golden had three children, David G., Philip and Sarah.

John W., son of David Golden and Deborah Wilson, born 1797, died March 21, 1879, married Pamelia, daughter of Elijah Hart,* and had four daughters, viz: Elizabeth, unmarried; Charity, married John L. Burroughs of Woodsville, and a nephew of Ralph, whose ancestry is given above. They had one son, Charles R., who was a skillful physician, locating first at the New Jersey State Hospital and later in Trenton. Mary married Ralph Phillips and had three children, Elizabeth, John R. and Rena. Emeline married William Large and removed to Illinois.

Cornelius, son of David Golden and Deborah Wilson, married Eliza Dallis and resided in New Jersey until 1850, when they removed to Illinois and settled at Sand Prairie on the Illinois River near Pekin. They had six children, viz: Joanna, married E. E. West; Ephraim, married Lydia Van Duzen; Frank, married Mary Brewer; Jane, married J. B. White; Rebecca, married George Praal, and Sarah married William Pollard.

Elizabeth, daughter of David Golden and Deborah Wilson, never married. She resided on the homestead with her sister, Anna Lewis, until 1850, when she removed to Fairview, Illinois ,and resided with her nephew, George W. Lewis, until her death in 1890.

Letitia, daughter of David Golden and Deborah Wilson, married John Wilson and resided near Trenton, N. J., until about 1852, when they removed to Fairview, Illinois. Their only child, Sarah Elizabeth, married Peter Groom of Hamilton Square, N. J., and removed to Fairview and later to Raritan, Illinois, where she died, leaving one son, John, and perhaps others.

September 24, 1902.

---

*Elijah Hart was the son of Benjamin Hart and Hannah Cook of Trenton and grandson of Major Ralph Hart, one of the earliest pioneers of Hopewell township. Elijah married Elizabeth, daughter of John Lanning of Lawrence.

NUMBER XIII.

Jacob Golden, the second son of Joseph, was a man of considerable prominence one hundred and twenty-five years ago, and resided on the south part of the original Golden tract, the house standing on the Trenton road, one mile west of the borough.

He died in 1811, and in his will, probated September 16, 1811, leaves first a legacy to his wife, Mary, and also leaves his son, John, who was his only son by his first marriage, a small legacy, stating that he had previously received his share of his estate.

He leaves to his son Isaac, the homestead farm and all the personal property, he to pay legacies to his sisters in the order named, viz: Ruth Barney, Frances Drake, Charity Barton, Phebe Houghton and also a granddaughter, Elizabeth Golden.

He appoints his son, Isaac, sole executor, and the witnesses to the will were his neighbors, William Jewell, Amos Golden and Ralph Drake.

John Golden, oldest son named in the will, married Deliverance, daughter of David Labaw and Mary Stout of Amwell.

They had one son, Reuben, who became prominent in business affairs, and one of the pillars of the Baptist church of Harbourton.

He married Rhoda, youngest daughter of Capt. Nathan Stout of Amwell,* and had two children, viz: John S., who married Elizabeth, daughter of Joseph Hart, and had three children, viz: Sarah E., born June 11, 1842, died May 7, 1858; Rhoda S., born

---

*Capt. Nathan Stout was born January 31, 1748, and in 1768 married Esther Ketcham, who was born March 16, 1748, and had children as follows: Mary, born January 1, 1769; Sarah, born July 16, 1770: John, born October 25, 1771; Levi, born June 20, 1774; Zephaniah, born May 9, 1776; Rachel, born July 18, 1778; William, born September 2, 1780; Catherine, born May 14, 1782; Robert, born June 18, 1786; Rhoda, born March 30, 1788; Captain Stout first enlisted in Capt. William Chamberlin's Company, Second Regiment, Hunterdon Co., and when Capt. Chamberlin was promoted to major in 1776, he was made captain of the company, and served with distinction during the war. He was a justice for several terms 1777—1798, and judge of the Court of Common Pleas in 1800. In 1804 he was elected a member of the State Legislature from Hunterdon County, and re-elected for several terms. He wrote the history of the Stout family, completing it in 1823, and died March 10, 1826, aged 78 years.

July 8, 1845, died July 12, 1857, and Joseph H., born September 19, 1848, who married Sarah, daughter of Thomas F. Howell and Marcia Hendrickson, and had two children, Helen Elizabeth and Lester.

Joseph H. Golden is deceased and his family reside in Pennington, N. J.

Esther, daughter of Reuben Golden, married Andrew, son of Abner Hart and Mary Updike* of Harbourton and had three children, viz: Reuben, Mary A. and Georgiana.

Mary A., married Edmund, son of Joseph Rue Burroughs and had three children, viz: Esther, Joseph and Andrew.

Isaac Golden, son of Jacob, married Amy Vannoy and had ten children, viz:

(1) John, married first Mary, daughter of Joseph Moore, proprietor of Stony Brook Mills. She died February 12, 1828, aged 22, and he married second Nancy Reading and removed to Philantropy, Indiana.

(2) Nancy, married Philemon Waters of Hopewell, and had six children, viz: (1) Catherine A. Waters, residing in Hopewell unmarried. (2) Jonathan H. Waters, married Mary A. Frambes of Philadelphia. They resided in Brooklyn and had two children, Kate and Claudine. (3) John G. Waters, married Anna Humphreys of Pennington, and resided in Washington, D. C. They had two children, both of whom died in infancy. (4) Abigail W. Waters, married Reuben Titus, son of Reuben, and resided on a part of the original Titus homestead, east of Pennington. They had five children, viz: J. Elwood, Ambrose, William, Emily and Gertrude. (5) Isaac G. Waters, married Cornelia A., daughter of Noah Reed,† of Lawrence, and resides in Hopewell. They have five children, viz: Edward P., Mary Esther, James Golden, Charles M. and Kate M. (6) Hannah M. Waters, married D. Webster Stout, son of Charles, and grandson of David Stout, known as "Esq.

---

*Robert Updike, the father of Mary Hart, was a revolutionary soldier and a private in Capt. Patterson's Company, 3rd Batallion, 2nd Establishment, New Jersey Continental Line. See history of Opdyke family.

†The history and traditions of the Reed family are among the oldest in existence, claiming to go back to the "confusion of tongues" at Babylon. They were of Phoenician origin, and later were found among the Celts, who came into Europe from the northeast, prior to the historic ages, and when Herodotus wrote of them 440 years before the Christian

(Foot note continued on bottom next page.)

David" of Hopewell. D. Webster Stout and Hannah M. Waters had three children, Charles W., Harry H. and Sadie.

David Stout, Esq., was the son of Andrew, the grandson of David, and great grandson of Jonathan Stout, who was the first permanent white settler in the northeastern part of Hopewell township, locating on the hill one mile north of Stoutsburg, and near the old Indian town of Minnepenasson, about the year 1703.

Of the interesting history of this prominent family of pioneers and patriots, we hope to speak more fully in subsequent numbers of these articles.

Jonathan Waters, the ancestor of the family of Waters in Hopewell, was one of the pioneers of this region, and was born in 1696.

In 1746, when the "Borough of Trenton" was chartered, and comprised within its limits all the territory then included in the townships of Hopewell and Maidenhead (now Lawrence), Jonathan Waters was one of the sixteen members of the common council, Jonathan Stout being the other member from northern Hopewell.

This charter was surrendered in 1750 and Trenton again became a part of Hopewell township.

Jonathan Waters died in 1762, his will being probated September 27 of that year.

---

era, he only knew of them as "dwelling in the extreme northwest of Europe." Later we find among the Reeds the most powerful noblemen of Saxon blood, and the reigning princes of Northumberland, Kent and Wessex in the 6th, 7th and 8th centuries, and the political alliances which existed among them, made them one of the most powerful Clans of that period. During the early wars in Briton, they became scattered and dispersed, being found in England, Scotland and Ireland. They were known in the various places of their abode as the Reds, Redes, Rhedes, Reeds, Rheeds, Rheedes, Reads, Rheads, Reids, their being nearly a score of variations of the name in use by different families at a very early day. Col. John Reed of Cornwall, England, came to America in 1660, but there were Reeds on Long Island in 1652, and Thomas Reed built a house for the Episcopal minister at Middleburg in 1656. John Reed was the first of the name in Northern Hopewell, coming from Long Island about 1706. He was born in 1675, and his wife Elizabeth in 1680. They resided on the hill between Marshall's Corner and Woodsville, where John L. Burroughs, Esq., now lives, purchasing the farm of Thomas Revell, agent for the West Jersey Society. John Reed died in 1731, aged 56, and his wife in 1765. The writer has a copy of the will of John Reed, which is an interesting document, but too lengthy to copy at this time. John Reed and his wife, and other members of this pioneer family, are buried in the "Hunt graveyard" on the farm now owned by John Guild Hunt, about one and a half miles northwest of Glen Moore. The inscriptions on their tombstones could be seen distinctly thirty years ago, but are now nearly obliterated by the ruthless hand of time, and very soon their last resting places will be unknown and forgotten.

We hope to give more Reed history in subsequent articles.

This will is very short and I will copy it in full, retaining capitalization and spelling as in the original copy, which is in the possession of John M. Titus, Esq., of Pennington, N. J., whose great great grandfather, Andrew Muirheid, was a son-in-law of Jonathan Waters, and one of the executors of the will, which is as follows:

"In the name of God Amen. I Jonathan Waters of the Township of Hopewell and County of Hunterdon, and State of New Jersey, being of sound mind, and calling to mind the certainty of death, and that the time thereof is uncertain, Do make and Ordain this my Last Will and Testament in manner & fform ffollowing, viz : Whereas principally and first of all, I recommend my soul into the hands of God that gave it, and my body I recommend to the Earth to be Buried in a christian and Decent manner at the direction of my executors hereinafter mentioned, And as Touching such personal Estate as God hath made me steward of, after my just debts are paid, and all my funeral charges are paid, I give and bequeath, comit, Dispose and order, the same as hereafter followeth. I give all my movables to my son William Waters, and to my daughter Elizabeth, to be equally divided between them two.

"Lastly, I constitute, make ordain and appoint my son William Waters and Andrew Muirheid to be my executors of this my Last Will and Testament.

"In Witness Whereof, I have to this my Last Will and Testament set my hand and seal the second day of January, in the year of our Lord one thousand seven hundred and sixty.

"Signed,

"JONATHAN WATERS."

"Sealed, Signed and published as my last Will and Testament. In presence of Albert Akers, John Davison, Stephen Jones."

Elizabeth, daughter of Jonathan, mentioned in the will, was born in 1722, and married Andrew Muirheid, the son of Sheriff John, who was the first sheriff of Hunterdon County.

She became the mother of four soldiers of revolutionary fame, viz : John, Jonathan, William and George Muirheid, whose courage and heroism are matters of history.

George, when only seventeen years of age, went to Elizabethtown, with three other young men alone. Col. Seeley, who was in command, at first refused them pay or rations, but finally attached them to Capt. Updike's company, where they served out their time and were honorably discharged.

The first record we have of the Waters family in America, is of Anthony Waters of Hempstead, Long Island, who was born in 1630, and died February 14, 1730. He was town clerk of Hempstead in 1663, and when a widower at the age of ninety-two, he married December 12, 1722, Sarah, widow of Joseph Wiggott.

The line of the Hopewell family is (1) Jonathan, 1696; (2) William, 1720; (3) Jonathan, 1750; (4) Jonathan, 1775; (5) Philemon, 1804; (6) Isaac G., 1837, Isaac Waters' grandchildren being the eighth generation in Hopewell township.

The above dates may not be all exactly correct, but approximate the birth of each generation.

October 29, 1902.

NUMBER XIV.

Abigail, the third child of Isaac Golden, married Peter Wilson and removed to Oxford, Indiana.

(4) Susan, married Nathaniel Smith, son of Timothy, removed to Mount Halthy, Ohio, and had seven children, one son and six daughters.

(5) Jacob, married Martha A., daughter of Edward Lanning of Lawrence and sister of Hon. A. Price Lanning.*   They had seven children, viz : George, married Sarah, daughter of Noah Reed, and had five children, viz : Noah R., Jacob, Charles M. R., Sarah M. and Mary E.   Sarah, daughter of Jacob, married W. W. Meredith, a Baptist clergyman of Delaware ; Edward L., married Emma, daughter of Peter Vanderveer Van Dyke of Hopewell.   He died soon after and his widow married John Q. McPherson and resides in Pennington.   Elizabeth, married Chas. Pierson of Lawrence. Ebenezer W., married Anna, daughter of Reuben Savidge, who was a prominent merchant of Mount Rose, in this county.   Ebenezer W. Golden died November 30th, 1899, and his widow and three children, viz : Maude, Jennie and Edward, reside in Hopewell.   Margaret, married Reuben L. Savidge, who succeeds his his father in business at Mount Rose.†   J. Price, married Eliza, daughter of Jefferson Drake, and resides near Hopewell.

---

*Robert Lanning emigrated from Wales and came to New Jersey about 1698, or earlier, his name being found among the grantees of land on which to build a Presbyterian church at Lawrenceville in 1698.   He married a Miss Hart and had sons Stephen, Ralph, Richard, John, Daniel and Robert, who married among the most prominent families of this region nearly 200 years ago.   The genealogy of the family in part is found in Dr. Cooley's "Early Settlers of Trenton and Ewing."

†The family of Savidge (spelled "Savage") is prominent in English history.   Sir John Savage was engaged with Edward I, at the memorable siege of Carlaverock, in Scotland, and there, for his signal service was with his brother Thomas created a baronet.

Sir John Savage, ancestor of the Earl of Rivers, commanded the left wing of the Earl of Richmond's army August 22, 1485, during the wars of the Roses, at Bosworth Field, and was afterward made a "Knight of the Garter" by Henry VII, King of England.

Thomas Savage came in the year 1635 with Sir Henry Vane and several persons of rank and family to New England, where he became speaker of the House of Representa-
(Foot note continued on bottom next page.)

(6) Frances, daughter of Isaac Golden, born 1807, died 1893 at Newark, N. J., aged 86, married 1830 Enoch A. Titus, son of Joab, resided near Pennington and had six children, viz: Mary A., born 1832, married Nathaniel D. Blackwell; Susan S., born 1834, married Samuel Hagamen; Joab, born 1837, married Willie Chatten; George Golden, born 1839, married Julia E. Furman; James Golden, born 1842, died October 1863; Emma K., born 1844, married Samuel Davenport. Of the above sons Joab and George enlisted in Co. D. 3rd Regiment N. J. Volunteers, when the first call was made in April, 1861. Joab re-enlisted in 1862 and was promoted to 1st lieutenant, Co. F., 21st Regiment, N. J. Vols. Both of these veterans are still living, Joab residing in Long Branch and George G. in Brooklyn.

(7) Phebe, daughter of Isaac Golden, married Reuben Titus, Sr., for his third wife. She was born in 1809 and died in 1890, aged 81.

---

tives, representing Boston for eight years, being a major of artillery, and in the early part of King Philip's war was commander-in-chief of the forces.

Samuel Philips Savage, one of his sons, was a native of Boston, and presided at the meeting held in Boston in 1773, which decided that the tea should not be landed. He was a judge of the Court of Common Pleas and died at a good old age in 1790.

The Savages of Chesire, England, are mentioned by "Wingfield York's Herald" among the few distinguished houses that are by prescription right entitled to use supporters to their coat of arms.

The supporters of this family are a falcon billed, and a unicorn arg, as they now appear on the monument of Sir John Savage of Rock Savage, in the same chapel, at the side of the old church at Macclesfield, County Chester. Sir John Savage was grandfather of Thomas, Lord Viscount Savage, and great grandfather of John Savage, first Earl of Rivers.

The Savage chapel at Macclesfield was erected by Thomas Savage, Bishop of Rochester in 1492, Bishop of London 1497, and Arch Bishop of York in 1501, brother of John Savage, King's guards, and nephew of Thomas Stanley, first earl of Derby, and was for many years the burial place of the Savage family. See 2d vol. Burke's "Landed Gentry" corrigenda page 424.

The first genealogical record we have of the Savidge family is of John Middleton Savidge, who, on February 10, 1652, married Elizabeth Dubbin at Hartford. Their children were John Middleton, born December 2, 1652; Eliza, born June 3, 1655; Sarah, born July 30, 1657; Thomas, born September 10, 1659; Hannah, born April 6 (or 16), 1661. John Middleton Savidge, Junior, was the only male survivor of this family, and married May 30, 1682, Mary, daughter of Thomas Ranney. Their children were as follows, viz: John, born February 20, 1683, died in a few days; Thomas, born August 24, 1684; John 2d, born January 30, 1686, died in a few months; John 3d, born August 7, 1688; Mary, born February 11, 1691; William, born May 10, 1693; Elizabeth, born 1696; Abigail, born December, 1698; Sarah, born September, 1700; Rachel, born January 15, 1704; Mercy, born April 10. 1706. The only one of this family of whom we have any record is William, who, on August 7, 1720, married Elizabeth Smith, who was born August 5, 1699, and emigrated from England soon after. They had two children, viz: Anna, born July 2d, 1721, and William, born June 29, 1723. Anna Savidge married Hugh Runyan, born June 20, 1715, who was probably an uncle of Col. Hugh Runyan of revolutionary fame. Anna Savidge Runyan died about 1795, and is buried in the Friends burying grounds on the old Princeton battle field, near Stony Brook. See "Genealogy of the Runyan family."

(8) Philemon, son of Isaac Golden, married Julia A. Griggs, and removed to Walnut, Bureau Co., Illinois, and had six children: J. Woodhull, Gideon G., Philemon, Theresa, Bertha and Wildal.

(9) Mary, married Reuben C. Titus, son of Joab, and had one child, Anna, who married Charles Bechtel of Trenton.

(10) James, son of Isaac, born 1814, died 1836, unmarried.

It will be observed that three of the daughters and one grand-daughter of Isaac Golden, married in one branch of the Titus family, all getting their companions from the old homestead farm of John Titus, who with his wife, Rebecca, came from Long Island about 1709, and were the first of the name to settle in old Hopewell township.

The ancestor of the Titus family in America was Robert Titus of Stansted Abbey, of Hertfordshire, England, about thirty miles northwest of London.

Silius Titus, the noted English politician, born in 1623 and died in 1704, was probably a brother or brother's son of Robert, as the name of Silas was frequently found among the early family of Titus in America.

Silius was an ardent Presbyterian, as were the early family in this country, which also seems to point to his being of the same family.

He claimed to be of Italian origin, and of the same family as the Roman Emperor Titus, whose reign was marked by such great clemency that he did not even inflict the punishment of death upon those who conspired against his life, and who was the instrument in the hands of God in the fulfillment of prophecy in the destruction of Jerusalem by the Romans, A. D. 70.

Silius Titus was captain in the regiment of Col. Ayloffe and took part in the siege of Donnogton Castle October, 1644. (See "Chatterbuck's Civil War in Hertfordshire," page 124).

Silius Titus seems to have been in attendance upon Charles 1st at Hallenby, as on June 4, 1647, he brought the House of Commons word of Joice's seizure of the king, and for this service was rewarded by a life annuity of fifty pounds.

His name appears in the list of the King's household, in the Isle of Wight, which was approved by the House of Commons, November 20, 1647. Titus was an ardent Loyalist and assisted in the King's escape.*

Robert Titus and his wife, Hannah, emigrated to America in the spring of 1635, landing at Boston and settling at Weymouth, Mass.

In the "Genealogy of New England Families" is found the following record, which was copied by the writer :

"Ship Hopewell, Capt. Bunlock. Robert Titus, age 35 ; his wife, Hannah, age 31, and their children, John, age 8, and Edmund, age 5 years."

They had four children after their settlement here, viz : Samuel ; Abiel, born March 17, 1641 ; Content, born March 28, 1643, and Susannah.

Content Titus, born March 28, 1643, is in the line of the Hopewell family, and was known as Capt. Titus, receiving his commission from the crown on December 30, 1689. He settled first at Newtown, Long Island, and during his long life filled many offices of trust and responsibility, retaining his faculties of mind and body to an extreme age. He was ordained a ruling elder in the Presbyterian church at Newtown at the age of 82.

John Titus, one of the sons of Capt. Content, came to New Jersey among the first pioneers of old Hopewell township, settling on Stony Brook, two miles east of Pennington, on the farm now owned by Ira Stout, Esq., the original tract being much larger than at the present time.

Joab Titus, mentioned above, was the great grandson of John, through Samuel and Johnson ; and Reuben Titus, Sr., mentioned above, was a great grandson, through Samuel and Solomon.

The will, dated January 21, 1761, and other old documents of John Titus, are in possession of C. A. Titus, Esq., of Hightstown, N. J., who is a grandson of Joab. Some of them have been copied by the writer, whose great grandmother, Anna Titus, was a granddaughter of John Titus, through his son, John, Jr.

John Titus, Jr., married about 1740, Anna, daughter of Andrew Smith, the pioneer settler of Hopewell township, near Harbourton.

The wife of Andrew Smith was Sarah, daughter of Jonathan Stout, the pioneer of northeastern Hopewell.

*See long account of Titus in "Dictionary of National Biography," published in London in 1898.

The writer has in his possession the old English clock of John Titus, Jr., which was possibly owned by his grandfather, Capt. Content, of Long Island.

Its age is unknown, but it was considered worn out one hundred years ago, and for many years was stored away with other rubbish in the garret. The works are operated by a single leaden weight, which was concealed during the revolutionary war to prevent the soldiers from using it for musket balls. In its place was a small iron pot filled with nails and scraps of iron, which kept the machinery in operation until peace was restored. It is still an accurate time keeper, and has done its duty faithfully for nearly, if not quite, two hundred years.

The Titus family were well represented in the militia and state troops in the war of the revolution, and we will insert just here the following unique advertisement, to prove that at least one of the family was a poet as well as a patriot :

Copied from the Trenton Gazette of May 16, 1779. Hopewell township, Hunterdon Co. "Sixty Dollars Reward." Taken from a wagon in Trenton.

> On the fifteenth day of May,
>   Some time in the night,
> A mare all over black
>   But the near hind foot white.
>
> A curl'd mane and tail
>   And a very bad eye,
> About ten years old
>   And 14 hands high.
>
> She being shod all around,
>   A tender mouth I do tell,
> A slow pace she can go
>   But trots and canters well.
>
> Whoever secures the thief
>   That to justice he may come,
> And likewise the beast
>   That the owner may get her home.
>
> They may call upon me,
>   And I will them repay
> The sum above mentioned
>   And that without delay.
>
> Or half of the sum mentioned
>   For either of the two,
> And that I do promise
>   I will pay unto you.

And also the charges
   That's reasonable and fair,
I will pay without fail,
   And that I declare.

And now my dear countrymen,
   If this prize you will gain,
I your humble servant
   Will ever remain.   —Joseph Titus.

The writer of the above was the son of Joseph Titus of Titus-ville vicinity, and grandson of John, the first settler. Joseph Junior was born September 9, 1757, and was enrolled in Capt. Henry Phillips' company, state militia, and also in the Continental Army as a corporal in Capt. John Mott's company, 1st regiment, Hunterdon county.

He settled on the farm known as the Titus Mills property on Stony Brook, one mile below Glen Moore station and about three miles southwest of Hopewell.

He owned the mills, which are still in the family, the present owner being William M. Titus, Esq.

December 3, 1902.

NUMBER XV.

William Golden (son of Joseph, the old pioneer), born October 7, 1743, spent his whole life on the farm near Hopewell, and was a revolutionary soldier, enlisted in Capt. William Tucker's company, Continental Army, and was also after the war a captain of militia.

He married first, about 1767, Ruth Drake, and they had four children as follows, viz: Amy, born May 11, 1768; Rachel, born September 22, 1770; Jerusha, born August 29, 1772; Pamelia, born October 26, 1774.

After the death of his first wife he married June 28, 1777, Christian Hortman, born August 6th, 1754, and had eleven children, viz: William, born June 19, 1779; Abraham, born October 14, 1780; Andrew, born April 8, 1782; Jonathan, born February 24, 1784; Urie, born January 5, 1786; Enoch, born September 13, 1787; Achsah, born June 30, 1789; Jared, born February 7, 1791; Joseph, born June 30, 1793; Charity, born November 14, 1795; Theodosia, born May 21, 1797.

Capt. William Golden died February 10, 1816, aged 73, and his widow, January 15, 1839, aged 85, and are buried in the old family plot on the farm of A. L. Holcombe, Esq.

We have very little data concerning the family of Capt. Golden by his first marriage, except their names and date of birth, as recorded in the old family bible, now in possession of William F. Golden, Esq., who resides on the homestead which has descended from father to son for so many generations.

Amy, the oldest, married Benjamin Drake and moved to Ohio.

Rachel, married Lemuel Hunt, son of John, who was a brother of "Miller James" Hunt, one of the pioneers of this region, who owned the farms now owned by D. P. Voorhees, Esq. and the railroad quarry farm, west of the borough.

John and James were the sons of Edward Hunt of Long Island, who was among the first to purchase land in Hopewell township, an old deed for the farm above mentioned being in the writer's possession.

Jerusha Golden married John Williamson of Amwell, and Pamelia married Joseph Salyer, who, tradition says, also removed to Ohio, and was among the earliest pioneers of that state.

William, oldest child by the second marriage, born June 15, 1779, married 1811, Catherine, daughter of Captain Nathan Stout of Amwell, a sketch of whose history as soldier and citizen is given in number 13 of these articles.

She was born May 16, 1782. They settled on the homestead farm and had six children, viz :

(1) Esther, born August 24, 1812. She never married and resided on the homestead during her long life, greatly respected and beloved by a large circle of friends and relatives. She died December 4, 1889, and is buried in the family lot.

(2) Abraham, born September 19, 1814, married Sarah, daughter of John Wikoff and Elizabeth Ege of near Ringoes, Hunterdon county, and had one daughter, Helen O., who resides in Hopewell.

Abraham Golden and his brother, William, then a young man of 23, made a business trip to Western Illinois, in the spring of 1839.

They drove the whole distance, taking with them a lot of wagons which they disposed of to advantage to the new settlers of the then border state, and after visiting among friends and prospecting for some time, Abraham was taken sick and died at Mrs. John Musgrove's, at Princeton, Illinois. (Mrs. Musgrove was a Golden and the history of her family is given in number 8 of these articles).

After the death of Abraham, his brother returned to New Jersey on horseback, riding the horse which had belonged to his deceased brother and leading his own.

One can scarcely imagine the sense of dreariness and utter loneliness he must have experienced during that long ride of over one thousand miles over a road they had traveled together such a short time before.

(3) William, born January 1, 1817, married first, Matilda,

daughter of Nathaniel R. Hunt of Lawrence township,* settled on a farm about two miles northwest of Hopewell, and had three children, a daughter and son who died in infancy, and Abram S., who married first, Emma E., daughter of Elias P. Ege of Woodsville, and had two children, William E. and Matilda. William E. married Etta V. Van Fleet and resides in Hopewell.

Mrs. Abram S. Golden died February 19, 1890, and he married, second, Eldora, daughter of Peter Sutphin of Amwell, and resides in Hopewell. They have one son, Newell Hunt.

Matilda Hunt, first wife of William Golden, died May 8, 1853, aged 31, and he married, second, the widow of his brother Abraham.

William Golden was a kind, obliging neighbor and an upright citizen. He removed to Hopewell a few years before his death, and spent the closing years of his life in well earned leisure. His death occurred February 23, 1901, at the ripe old age of 84 years.

His widow resides in Hopewell with her daughter, Helen, to whom the writer is indebted for much valuable data concerning the family.

They have in their possession a highly prized and well preserved Dutch bible, which has descended to them through several generations of the Wikoff family, and which may have been brought from Holland by the first Wykoff emigrants.†

---

*John, the father of Nathaniel R. Hunt, was born January 1, 1761, and was the son of Edward of Long Island, who married Charity Cornwell (afterward called Cornell.) Edward was grandson of Ralph Hunt of London, who emigrated to America in 1652, and was one of the seven patentees to whom Gov. Gen. Richard Nicholl granted the patent for the land on which Newtown was afterward built.

The wife of Editor Savidge of the Herald is the seventh generation from Ralph Hunt, who was known at the time of his settlement here as "London Ralph," to distinguish him from another of the same name.

The first record we have of the Hunt family is of Adam le Hunt, of Nottinghamshire, Eng., in 1295, and, using the exact language of the record, a Ralph le Hunt was "distrained to receive knighthood" about the year 1300.

There was also a Ralph Hunt at Southampton, England, in 1305, and we have many names of Ralph and Thomas Hunt down to the time of the emigration of London Ralph in 1652, but the name was so widely diffused in different portions of the British Isles five hundred years ago that their genealogy cannot be accurately traced.

†This branch of the family came to the vicinity of Ringoes from Monmouth county, N. J., and wrote the name "Wikoff." but they are a branch of the old stock of Long Island "Wyckoffs," who came to Monmouth, Hunterdon and Somerset counties about 1700. The first emigrant was Peter Claes Wyckoff, who emigrated from Holland in 1636, and settled in Flatlands, Long Island, where he was a magistrate of the town 1663-65.

His wife was Gretia, daughter of Hendrick Van Ness. One of their children, Cornelius Peterse, married Gertrude, daughter of Simon Van Arsdale, Oct. 13, 1678, and came to Middlebush, Somerset County, about 1703.

John Wikoff, the father of Mrs. Golden, was born April 11, 1781. He was the son of Daniel and Ursula Wikoff, and, Daniel, born January 1, 1748, was the son of John and Aeltye Wikoff, who were among the pioneers of Ringoes vicinity. John was born February 10, 1709, and Aeltye, August 19, 1710.

(4) Rachel, born August 31, 1819, married Judge Levi T. Atchley of Pennington, who was widely known as one of the most prominent and highly respected citizens of this county.

They had one son and four daughters, all of whom are deceased except the two youngest daughters, Eliza and Katherine, who reside at Pennington.

(5) Amos, born October 27, 1821, married Theressa Reading, a descendant of one of the seven sons of Gov. John Reading of Hunterdon county, and had four children, viz: William, Levi, Judson and Eva.

Mr. Golden resides at Cordova, Rock Island county, Illinois, and is the last survivor of the children of William Golden.

(6) John N., youngest son of William Golden and Catherine Stout, born December 12, 1824, married Emma, daughter of Caleb Farley Fisher, of Ringoes, Hunterdon county, and resided on the Golden homestead.*

They had two children, viz: Katie S., who died at the age of 20, and William F., who married Susan, daughter of Edward S. Durham of Amwell, and succeeded his father on the homestead, being the fifth generation to own the western part of the tract purchased by Joseph Golden, July 19, 1750; the eastern part, purchased December 30, 1734, having passed out of the family many years ago, and being now owned by A. L. Holcombe, Esq.

Abraham Golden, second son of William Golden, Senior, and Christian Hortman, was born October 14, 1780, and when a young man went to Maysville, Kentucky, and married in 1806, Sarah, the sixteen year old daughter of Aaron Houghton and Elizabeth Sexton, and a granddaughter of Col. Joab Houghton of Hopewell, whose history has been given in former articles.

Abraham Golden resided at Maysville, Kentucky, until 1824, when he removed with his family to Morgan county, Illinois, and in 1833 pushed still farther west, and settled in Hancock county, near the Des Moines rapids of the Mississippi, and within a few miles of the town of Commerce, which a few years later became

---

*Caleb Farley Fisher spent the whole of his long life on the farm at Rocktown, Hunterdon county, which his great grandfather, Peter Fisher (who emigrated from Germany), purchased of Thomas Eman, in 1729, paying 54 pounds for the tract of 200 acres. This was a part of the large tract purchased by John Reading and others, of the Indians, for 700 pounds in 1703.

the great centre of the Mormon settlement, when the name of Commerce was changed to Nauvoo.

Mr. Golden was the pioneer of that region, his cabin being the first to be erected on the edge of the prairie near the rapids, and being just after the close of the Black Hawk war, many roving bands of hostile Indians still infested the country.

They were held in check by a semi-military company of the settlers, banded together for self protection, and widely known as "The Illinois Rangers," whose courage and daring won for them a conspicuous place in the early history of that part of the state.

Many of Mr. Golden's sons and sons-in-law were members of this organization, which succeeded finally in driving their treacherous and vindictive foes to the west side of the river.

The point of timber which was at the end of a deep ravine leading to the river, was known as "Golden's Point," and this piece of timber was a favorite scouting place for the savages when they crossed the river from Iowa.

The schoolhouse standing near this point was still known as "Golden's Schoolhouse," when the writer visited it a few years ago.

This whole region was the scene of some very thrilling and exciting events during the period of the Mormon occupation of Nauvoo, and at the time of the assassination of Joseph Smith at Carthage, and the final expulsion of the Mormons in 1847.

When the writer visited Hancock County, in the summer of 1859, these events were still fresh in the minds of the settlers, and when he last visited it in 1899, not one stone was left upon another of the famous old temple erected in 1841-42 and the last trace of Mormonism had disappeared as completely as if it had never existed.

Abraham Golden and Sarah Houghton had children as follows: Aaron Houghton, born 1807, married 1830 Nancy Smedley; Evaline B., born 1809, married 1828, Peter W. Conover; Elizabeth, born 1811, died in infancy; Ure, born 1812, married 1829, Hezekiah P. Bradley; William, born 1814, married 1844, Hannah Mc-Fall; Charlotte A., born 1818, married 1st, 1835, James Robinson, and 2nd, 1850, Henry Benner; Jeanette, born 1821, married 1841, James Wilson; Achsah, born 1823, married 1842, William White; Catharine, born 1828, married 1845, Parmenias Jackman; Charles

P., born December 12, 1831, married December 15, 1853, Margaret A. Fulton, and settled near Nauvoo, where he spent many years of his life engaged in farming.

He has recently retired, and is living in Nauvoo. He is an intelligent, well informed gentleman of over three score and ten years, well preserved physically and mentally, and has reared a large family of children.

Abraham Golden died in 1866, aged 86, and his widow died in 1876, at the same age.

January 14, 1903.

NUMBER XVI.

Andrew Golden, third son of Capt William, born April 8th, 1782, went to Virginia early in life, married, and reared a family, of whom nothing is known by the New Jersey family.

Jonathan, fourth son, married Mary Emrod, and settled on a farm adjoining his father on the west, now owned by John S. Van Dyke, Esq.

Jonathan died in middle life, leaving a family consisting of two sons and four daughters, viz.: Margaret, Sarah, Elizabeth, George Smith, William and Christian.

All of this family, except the youngest, remained unmarried and resided together on the farm where they were born and reared.

They were noted for their honesty, industry and hospitality; their "latch string" was always on the outside for the wayfarer and stranger, and their purse strings were ever ready to unloose at the story of want or suffering.

The whole family toiled early and late, none of them were perhaps ever twenty miles from the place of their birth, (except the oldest daughter who spent several years in Philadelphia) their wants were very few and simple, they indulged in no luxuries, and barely the necessities of life, when viewed from the standpoint of the present generation.

It would seem that such a life of untiring industry and unswerving honesty, deserved to be rewarded by at least a competency sufficient for the infirmities of age; but the fates seemed to be against them and when it rained their tub was invariably "bottom side up."

Those who survived to old age had to battle with adversity, and they had the sincere sympathy of all their friends who had known them in better days. They are buried in the family plot, but no inscription marks the last resting places of parents or children. Christian, the youngest of the family, was gifted with more than ordinary beauty and intelligence, and quite early in life went to Philadelphia with her older sister and attended school. While in Philadelphia she married Heber C. Kimball, who became identified with the Mormon church, and they removed first to Illinois, and finally to Salt Lake, Utah.

They had three children, viz.: Jonathan G., Elias S., and May who married a Mr. Moffat who was not of the Mormon faith and they removed to Montana.

The sons of Christian Golden married and became prominent as elders and teachers in the Mormon church, and a few years ago visited the home of their Golden ancestors at Hopewell.

They are well remembered as gentlemen of education and refinement whose dignified and courteous manners won for them many friends during their brief sojourn here.

Urie, daughter of Capt. Golden, married John Hart, who for many years kept the hotel located near Washington's Crossing, known as the "Bear Tavern." He was a son of Philip Hart and Hannah Palmer, and a great grandson of John Hart, one of the very earliest pioneers of Hopewell township, whose name appears on an agreement, signed August 26, 1703, nearly two centuries ago.

The children of John Hart and Urie Golden were: Hannah, who died at the age of 18; Catherine, married Howard Dazell; Sarah, married Bayard Updike; John, married Rosa Updike; William, Theodosia, Harriet, Washington, Joshua.

Enoch, fifth son of Capt. Golden by his second marriage, was a carriage manufacturer in Philadelphia many years and later in Trenton, N. J.

He married Elizabeth Ball and had children as follows, viz: Henry, Emeline, who married a Mr. Dennis; Christian, married Asa Burroughs; Phebe, married George Akerman; and Clara, married Daniel Hogencamp.

Achsah, daughter of Capt. Golden, married Amos Sine and resided in Philadelphia.

Jared, sixth son of Capt. Golden, married first a Miss Mathews and had one child, Charity.

After the death of his first wife he removed to Illinois, married a second wife, and had two daughters. (1) Phebe, who married Warren Olds, and had two children, Ellen and George, who reside at Albany, Illinois.

(2) Mary, married a Mr. Trent, and had two children, Robert and Phebe, and after Mr. Trent's death married a Mr. Mears, and had two children, Ella and Lottie.

Charity, the daughter of Jared Golden by his first marriage, remained in New Jersey, until after the death of her grandmother Golden, when she went to Cordova, Illinois, and became the wife of her cousin, Henry Marshall, by whom she had three children, viz : Christiana, wife of Simon Trent ; Andrew, who married Josephine Wilson, and Kate, wife of Charles Tavener.

Charity, tenth child of Capt. Golden, born February 14, 1795, died October 7, 1878, married September 7, 1816, John Marshall of near Pennington, N. J., who was born May 10, 1793, and died April 27, 1832,* leaving her with nine children, six sons and three daughters, the oldest being only fifteen years of age.

In the spring of 1842, when her youngest child was ten years of age, she emigrated with this large family to the vicinity of Cordova, Rock Island Co., Illinois. Here she purchased a large tract of unbroken prairie, so near the Mississippi that during the times of great freshets portions of it were overflowed.

Six sons and two of her daughters settled on this tract, and at one time all except one were on adjoining farms.

---

*The first ancestor of the Marshall family of Hopewell township, of whom we have any knowledge, was Conrad Marshall, born 1729, and died 1813.

He settled on a farm on the top of the "Witchamenting" mountain, two miles northwest of Pennington, on the farm now owned by Azariah Phillips, Esq., and had one son John, and perhaps others.

John Marshall, born 1762, died 1803, was twice married, one of his wives being Rebecca, daughter of John Hart, and granddaughter of the first John Hart of Hopewell township.

His children were: Philip, William, John and Rebecca. Philip married Sarah, daughter of James Wilson of Amwell, and had James Wilson Marshall, who immortalized himself by discovering the first nugget of gold in the then almost unknown valley of the Sacramento, and inaugurated a tremendous rush of events such as had no parallel in the world's history. His discovery made more changes in the map of a continent and added more wealth, power and prestige to the nation in one decade, than any other event of the century.

Philip Marshall had also four daughters, Abigail, who married Smith Ely; Rebecca, married Thomas B. Carr; Mary, married Martin L. Reeve, and Sarah, who married Peter C. Hoff. All the above were prominently identified with the religious, social and business interests of Lambertville, N. J., and are now deceased.

William Marshall married Catharine, daughter of Elijah Larison, of Hopewell, was a merchant at Marshall's Corner for many years, and represented his district in the State Legislature from 1830 to 1836.

He removed to Cordova, Ill., over sixty years ago, and had a large family, many of whom occupied positions of responsibility in the state of their adoption.

The other children of John Marshall were John, who married Charity Golden, and Rebecca, who married Jonathan Titus, and became the mother of several children, among whom are William M. Titus, of Titus' Mills, near Pennington.

They were a most remarkable family, not only for their industry and thrift, but also for their activity in church and state. They were of the type of pioneers who have done so much toward building up and strengthening society in that part of the state which was then on the border of civilization.

Mrs. Marshall was truly a "mother in Israel," possessing to a remarkable degree all those sterling qualities of mind and heart, which fitted her to train up her large family in the way they should go; and such was their respect for her judgment, that when the writer visited them in 1859, and they were in middle life, "mother" was always consulted before undertaking any enterprise of unusual importance. At the time of her death she had nine children, fifty-nine grandchildren and thirty-one great grandchildren, of whom two children, fourteen grandchildren, and ten great grandchildren had died, leaving seventy-three living descendants. "Her children rise up and call her blessed," were the words of the text selected for her funeral sermon, and in the language of her biographer, "No more appropriate words could have been chosen, and in the hearts of those whom she has so long cherished and guided by her loving counsel, she leaves a monument more lasting than mortal hands can rear."

Her children were (1) Mary A., born June 17, 1817, died April 10, 1890, married Andrew S. Ege, son of George of Hopewell, N. J., and they removed with Mrs. Marshall's family to Cordova, Illinois, and had seven children, viz: Emma, married Isaac Bates; George, married Sarah M., daughter of Elijah Ege; John M., unmarried, residing at Guthrie, Oklahoma; Adeline, married Andrew D. Ege and resides near Cordova. Rev. Charles M., a Baptist clergyman, born November 5, 1849. He received his collegiate education at the University of Chicago, from which he received his degree of A. B. in 1878, and at the Baptist Theo. Seminary at Morgan Park, (near Chicago) from which he graduated receiving his degree of B. D. in 1882.

He served as pastor of Baptist churches at Chatsworth, Aledo, and Washington, in Illinois, and near St. Cloud, Minnesota. He also served as principal of schools at Erie and Milan in Illinois, and now resides at Rock Island, Illinois. He was married in 1882, to Miss Kate J. Huntington, daughter of Charles R. Huntington of Chicago. Four sons were born to them, viz: Lucius, Marshall, Charles and Stanley. Charles was drowned in the Mississippi river while skating in 1896; Marshall died in Rock Island in 1901. Both Rev. and Mrs. Ege have been especially useful in social and religious work in their various places of residence.

Mary, unmarried, residing with her brother, John M.

William Marshall, youngest child of Andrew S. and Mary A. Ege, was born December 16, 1855. He attended the common and graded schools until he had fitted himself for teaching, and entered the University of Chicago in 1877, and graduated with the degree of Ph. B. in 1881. In 1886 his Alma Mater conferred upon him the degree of Ph. D. He was engaged for eleven years in the work of the Young Men's Christian Association as secretary of the branches at Muscatine and Burlington, Iowa, where the writer had the pleasure of visiting him a number of times.

In 1893 he returned to his chosen profession of teaching and became Professor of German and Science in an Academy at Osage, Iowa. In 1898 he was principal of the High School at Mason City, Iowa, and is now in the service of the U. S. Government as a teacher on the Rosebud Reservation, South Dakota. He was married in 1883 to Miss Loie A. Davis, daughter of Charles A. Davis, Esq., of Burlington, Iowa, and has five children, viz: Raymond, now in college at Ames, Iowa; Eloise, Harriet, Howard and Arthur. Mrs. Ege was for a number of years a teacher in the schools at Burlington, Iowa, and their present work among the Sioux Indians affords abundant opportunity for their varied talent and experience.

(2) John Marshall, born April 1, 1819, married first, Mary E. Cool, and had eleven children, viz: Elizabeth, Charity, Harmon, Jerome Edward, Samuel, Jonathan, Clara, Robert, Horace and Minnie. He married second, Mrs. Mary Skelton, and a few months ago was still living in Cordova, aged 83 years.

(3) William G. Marshall, born August 4, 1820, married first, Catharine, daughter of John Phillips, formerly of Hopewell, and had two children, who died in infancy. He married second, her sister, Elizabeth, resided at Cordova and became very wealthy.

(4) Henry, born May 20, 1822, record given above.

(5) Elizabeth, born April 5, 1824, married Isaac Crosby, and had ten children, viz: Amos, Clarissa, Sarah, Horace, Cecilia, Charity, Ella, Harriet, Isaac and Charlotte.

(6) Sarah Marshall, born September 9, 1826, married J. Evans

Smith, son of Geo. W. Smith, Esq., of Woodsville, N. J., and had eight children, viz : Phebe, Ella, Julia, Judson, John, Alfred, Jacob and Elizabeth.

(7) Jacob H. Marshall, born November 22, 1828, married Sarah Cain, and had two children, Mary and Ruth.

(8) Theodore Marshall, born August 12, 1830, married Derinda Williamson and had three children, viz : Lucilla, Charity and Bertha.

(9) Jared Marshall, born July 8, 1832, married Amanda Rockwell, and had eight children, viz : Edwin, Anna, Emma, Albert, Charles, Grant, Louis and Grace.

February 11, 1903.

NUMBER XVII.

One of the long forgotten pioneer families of northern Hopewell, which figured in some of the exciting events of the revolutionary period, was that of James Hunt, whose name is written "James Hunt Senior" in some of the old records; but who was widely known as "Miller James," to distinguish him from his neighbor, "Deacon James," who resided less than a mile from him on the farm now occupied by Mr. Morgan D. Blackwell, and who was the son of Wilson Hunt, who resided in the house which is still standing near Marshall's Corner and now occupied by William D. Hill, Esq.

Miller James owned the tract west of the borough, the northern part which is now owned by D. P. Voorhees, Esq., and the southern part known as the railroad quarry farm. There is nothing to indicate the spot on which the old house stood at the time of the revolution, as the location of the buildings has been a cultivated field for nearly sixty years. They are remembered, however, by many now living, and stood about two hundred yards north of the corner of the Stony Brook road, near the old baryta mines, and about the same distance west of the dwelling now standing on the quarry farm.

Miller James Hunt was the son of Edward Hunt of Maidenhead, now Lawrence township, in this county, and the grandson of Captain Ralph Hunt of Long Island, for whom Thomas Revell surveyed a large tract of land lying on both sides of the "Kings Road" between Lawrenceville and Princeton January 7, 1694, the survey being recorded in "Book of Surveys" in the office of the Secretary of State at Trenton.

Capt. Hunt settled on the tract about that time, and at once became identified with all the religious and political activities of the period, as the public records will show. His name is found on the first list of grand jurors of Hunterdon County, and also among the county officers, and in 1698 he was one of the Presbyterian society which purchased land for a church at Maidenhead.

In 1722–1723 he was collector of the County of Hunterdon. (See History Hunterdon Co., page 263). In Riker's "Annals of Newtown" we find the name of Ralph Hunt among a party of Englishmen who emigrated to Long Island in 1652. He was also one of the party who purchased Middleburg in 1656, his share of the purchase being one pound. January 7, 1662–3, he was chosen one of seven men to conduct the affairs of the town. In 1663, he, with other leading men, was denounced for resisting Dutch authority, aiding to form a junction with the Connecticut colony.

In February, 1663–4, he was chosen, with six others, in the name of his majesty, Charles II, to town office in Hastings (the new name of Middleburg), for the ensuing year. In 1664 he was admitted as a freeman of the colony of Connecticut, and was chosen a surveyor to view the "Indian reserved lands," which the town was to purchase. April 21, 1665, he was commissioned lieutenant of the military in Newtown (the new name of Hastings), by Governor Nicholl, and from November, 1666 to April, 1668, was the town overseer.

December 4, 1666, he was a freeholder of Newtown named in the list, and the same year was also "overseer" of Edward Jessop's will. January 4, 1666–7, he was one of the eleven land holders who agreed to enclose their lands in a single field for cultivation. March 1666–7, after having been appointed by the town to get a draught of boundaries, he became one of the patentees of "Newtowne, in the West Riding of Yorkshire, upon Long Island." April 2, 1667, he was chosen constable. About 1668, his house and barns, with all his effects, were destroyed by fire, together with the corn which he had collected for rates. January, 1667–8, he was chosen permanent surveyor, and in 1670 elected town overseer.

In 1671, the first church edifice in Newtown was erected on a "gore" of land appropriated for the church by Ralph Hunt. The site is at the corner of Main street and Jamaica Road, the corner house recently owned by Peter Duryea.

On September 6, 1673, he was sworn to office as a "Shepen," or magistrate, upon the reinstating of Dutch authority. He died early in 1677, and his biographer gave a glowing tribute to his high character and usefulness as a man and citizen.

His children were : (1) Ralph, (2) Edward, who died in 1716

after a life of eminent usefulness ;* (3) John, of Newtown, L. I.; (4) Samuel, (5) Ann, who married Theophilus Phillips†, and (6) Mary.

Reference has been made to the Hunt family in several of the articles of this series, and in a foot note to article 15 will be found the earliest records of the family in England, in the 13th and 14th centuries, going back to Ralph le Hunt of the year 1295.‡ We might add that in tracing the families down to the 17th and 18th centuries, we find very many of the old names which are still favorites in the Hunt family, and the collateral branches. In a history entitled "The Family of Hunt," published in 1860, from which we have largely copied the above items, we find names identical with those of the New Jersey family, in the New England families, although they emigrated at widely different periods from various localities in the British Isles, and claimed no relationship whatever.

Thomas Hunt, gentleman, of Chalneston in the Parish of Roxton, England, in his will dated September 6, 1546, after first bequeathing his soul to God, the Virgin Mary, and all the saints in heaven, and directing that his body be buried in the chancel of the church, where his father and mother are buried, then makes bequests to his wife, Alice, and children, William, Thomas, Sapborowe, Roger, Annie and Barbara. (The name of Roger was known as George in the generations following).

Thomas Hunt, yeoman, of West Horsley, England, by his will dated July 15, 1598, makes bequests to wife Joana, and to "brother John and his son John, also Nicholas, brother of Edward, William, son of brother John, the elder, Edward and Thomas son of William." If the last mentioned may be taken as a sample of the wills of that period, we need not be surprised that they frequently led to legal complications, and that several old estates still remain unsettled.

Many of the Hunt family in England have distinguished them-

---

*This is the Edward Hunt, who, about 1670, married Sarah, daughter of Richard and Joana Betts, from whom a large number of the Hunt families in Hopewell are descended.

†Theophilus Phillips and Ann Hunt had children as follows, viz: Theophilus, born May 15, 1678, settled at Maidenhead ; William, born June 28, 1676, settled in New York ; and Phillip, born December 27, 1678, who also settled at Maidenhead. This Phillips family furnished many brave officers and men for the Continental army, and deserves far more than this passing notice, but we hope to be able to refer to them again.

‡The coat of arms of the Hunt family is described as consisting of a shield of three mastiff's heads, surmounted by the figure of a mastiff chained, and the motto, "Faithful to the End."

selves, not only as soldiers and statesmen, but also in the field of science and literature. In this country they have been eminent in every department of human effort, and in the war for American Independence they were found on the side of the struggling colonies, and the bravery of many of the Hunt family of New England, New York and New Jersey, on the battle fields of the revolution, gave added strength and lustre to the achievements of an honored ancestry.

The house in which Miller James Hunt resided was the scene of the only capture of a detachment of British soldiers ever made in the vicinity of Hopewell. It was accomplished about the middle of December, 1776, by the old hero, Col. Joab Houghton, who had heard that they were expected in the neighborhood, and hastily summoning a small band of militia, captured the Hessians and hustled them off to Lambertville, were they were placed in charge of a detachment of Washington's army, who were guarding Coryell's ferry, while the main body of the army were at Newtown, Pa., and Cornwallis was at Pennington. A very brief sketch of this affair is given in Barber and Howe's "Historical Collections," and alluded to in article number 4 of this series.

The farm on which Miller James Hunt resided was bequeathed by Capt. Ralph Hunt, of Maidenhead, to his son, Edward, in his will dated November 5, 1732, and which is on file in the office of the Secretary of State at Trenton.

He makes a bequest first, to his wife Elizabeth. To his oldest son, Edward Hunt, he left 150 acres of land in Hopewell, described as the tract "formerly known as the vacancy."

He left to his second son, Ralph Hunt, his tract of land on the north side of the King's Road in Maidenhead, he to pay his sister, Jemima, (not of age) a legacy, when he comes to the age of 22; also to pay his brother John, (not of age) a legacy, when he comes to the age of four and twenty years; also to pay his sister, Keziah, a legacy, when he comes to the age of six and twenty years.

To his third son, Samuel, he left his land lying on the south side of the King's Road, in Maidenhead. He also left his sons Ralph and Samuel, each a tract on the great meadows on the present line of the Delaware and Raritan canal.

To his daughters, Elizabeth, Kezia and Jemima, he leaves all his "moveable" property, each to have a one-third share.

The closing clause of the will reads —"I hereby nominate and appoint Major Lockart and Theophilus Phillips, together with my wife, Elizabeth, the executors of this my last will and Testament."

Theophilus Phillips mentioned above was the oldest son of Theophilus Phillips Senior, of Newtown, L. I., and his mother was Ann, daughter of Ralph Hunt, also of Newtown. For some unknown reason Mr. Phillips refused to serve as one of the executors, as on the back of the will we find the following entry: January 20, 1732, "These articles do certify to whom it may concern, that I, Theo. Phillips, of Maidenhead, nominated as one of the executors of the last will and testament of Captain Ralph Hunt, do relinquish the same. "Given under my hand and seal,

"THEOPHILUS PHILLIPS."

Witnesses: Joshua Anderson, James McKinly.

The above date, January 20, 1732, is old style, the new style not being adopted by British Parliament until 1751. If this was not taken into account it would seem that Mr. Phillips relinquished his office before his appointment.

The tract which Capt. Hunt describes above as "formerly known as the vacancy," was surveyed in part by Thomas Revell, agent for the West Jersey Society, for Roger Parke of Crosswicks Creek, in April, 1697, "for his daughter Anne Parke."

The survey commenced at a stake in Roger Parke's corner, near the old mines, and followed the old Wissamenson Indian path, (which in some old deeds is written "Wisomoncey," "Wosamonsa" and "Witchamenting") northeast thirty-seven chains, to a stake which stood near the present residence of Mr. James Shelby; thence northwesterly on the south side of the hill twenty chains; thence again northeasterly twenty-two chains to Thomas· Tindall's line (now Mr. A. L. Holcombe's) which was surveyed by Mr. Revell for Mr. Tindall February 27, 1696, and thence along said Tindall's line northwesterly eight chains to a stake, and thence west sixteen chains and two poles to Roger Parke's, now Amos Sked's line, and thence south along said Parke's line to the place of beginning.

It will be observed that this survey did not include the hill, now Mr. Montag's, and the railroad quarry, nor did it include the north side of the Hunt tract as afterward surveyed for Capt. Ralph Hunt.

It is not known that Annie Parke ever married, or that she ever occupied this tract, but it is known, however, that a small band of the Lenni Lenape, did occupy it at intervals and whenever it suited their convenience to do so, for several years after the Parke family occupied the tracts on the west and north. Their wigwams occupied the vacant land not included in the Annie Parke purchase, and they lived on the most friendly terms with the Parke family.

Roger Parke, who was popularly known among the pioneers as "Old Doctor Parks," studied the Indian practice of medicine with the old squaws and medicine men, and the early settlers came to him for many miles around, his treatment being much the same as that practiced by Dr. Jacob Tidd in later years, who, it is said had many of the recipes of Doctor Parke.

David Hunt, son of "Miller James," who spent his whole life of three score and ten years on this tract, is authority for the statement that the young Indians, in shooting at random for the purpose of testing their nerve, and the strength and elasticity of their bows and strings, could, by elevating their arrows slightly, drive them across the valley from their wigwams, just north of the present residence of Mr. D. P. Voorhees, to the present line of the railroad, a distance of over two hundred and fifty yards. The timber at that time had been cut off in the valley, but the hillsides were still covered with a heavy growth.

About 1725–30, the red man bid adieu to the Hopewell valley forever, and started on his long and weary pilgrimage toward the setting sun, and when Edward Hunt made a settlement with the heirs of Col. Coxe in 1746, the whole tract, as now embraced in the two farms, was included.

March 25, 1903.

NUMBER XVIII.

This tract of land bequeathed to Edward Hunt by his father, Capt. Ralph, November 5, 1732, was a part of the thirty thousand acres lying above the falls of the Delaware which was conveyed by eleven Indian Chiefs to Adlord Bowde, agent for Doctor Daniel Coxe of London, by deed bearing date March 30, 1688.

The record of the above is to be found in the Book of Surveys, page 103 in the office of the Secretary of State. Doctor Daniel Coxe never resided in this country, but his son, Col. Daniel Coxe, resided in Trenton many years, and the large proprietary tracts here and in the northern part of Hunterdon County made the family immensely wealthy.

Col. Coxe died in 1737, before Edward Hunt obtained his deed, but on July 16, 1746, John Coxe, one of the heirs, and surviving executor of the will of Col. Coxe, gave him a deed for the farm, the consideration being one hundred and eighty-three pounds, twelve shillings, proclamation money, for the tract of one hundred and fifty-three acres, besides the usual allowance for "ways."

The survey commenced at a corner in the Stony Brook road near the old mines, and from thence north seventy-eight chains, along the line of David Stout,* who at that time owned the farms now owned by C. E. Voorhees, Esq., Amos Sked and the part of the E. S. Wells tract known as the Samuel Ege farm.

---

*David Stout, who owned the farms on Stony Brook, was the fifth son of Jonathan, the pioneer settler of Northeastern Hopewell, and was born at Hopewell in 1706.

About 1726 he married Elizabeth, sister of James Larison, and had four sons and five daughters.

All who are familiar with the Stout history have noticed the fact that the author, Capt. Nathan Stout, was very sparing in his compliments, but that he made an exception in favor of David, and on page 11 gives a glowing tribute to his memory.

We cannot at this time, for want of space, give a history of the family of David Stout and Elizabeth Larison, but will only say that the oldest son, Jonathan, married Rachel Burroughs, and that probably one of his daughters, Mary, married David Hunt, the son of Miller James.

Job Stout, one of the sons of Jonathan, married Rhoda, daughter of Abner Howell, and had a large family, the complete record of which is in the writer's possession, and will
(Foot note continued on bottom next page).

No other abutting property owners are mentioned in the deed, but the north line was the same as at present ; while in the survey of Thomas Revell for Anne Parke in 1697, described in our last article, the northern part of the tract on which the Indian wigwams were located was not included, which was doubtless in accordance with the wishes of Doctor Parke.

The east line was the old Tindall tract (afterwards the Golden's) and the Moses Hart lot (now Mr. Montag's) and from thence following the old "Wisomoncey or Wissamenson Indian Path," to the place of beginning, and is described as "the tract whereon the widow Merrill lately dwelt."

This dilapidated old deed, written on very heavy parchment, is in the writer's possession, and has a very venerable appearance.

In the will of Edward Hunt, dated October 28, 1757, and on file in the office of the Secretary of State, his first bequest is to his son James, to whom he gave this farm of 150 acres of land in Hopewell, describing it as "the farm on which he now liveth, he to pay his sister thirty pounds." His next bequest is to his three grandsons, viz : Benjamin, Daniel and Nathaniel, the sons of his oldest son Edward, "lately deceased," to whom he gives his farm, describing it as "the plantation on which I now dwell," and also provides for granddaughter Elizabeth, daughter of Edward.

He provides for the education of the above grandchildren and also that "they shall be brought up out of the yearly income of the estate."

"Item, I give and bequeath to the old, or first Presbyterian congregation of Hopewell and Maidenhead ten pounds for the sup-

---

probably appear later. Job Stout removed to Mays Lick (now Maysville) Kentucky, in 1788–90, and was either accompanied or followed soon after by his father, who was then well advanced in years.

The writer has in his possession an account of a trial held at Mays Lick in 1794, in which Jonathan Stout figured prominently as one of the judges, and in which one of the parties to the case wilfully perjured himself, and died in less than forty-eight hours after its occurrence, from remorse of conscience, which produced a nervous condition closely resembling the terrible disease of hydrophobia.

Mr. Stout had refused to administer the oath and had advised him to settle the small matter in dispute, warning him of the consequences of swearing falsely, as he feared he would do.

The warning however, was not heeded, and he was sworn by Mr. Young, another of the justices present, and seemed stricken with death immediately after giving his testimony.

The report of this trial was circulated all over the country at the time, and being well authenticated made a most profound impression.

David Stout was an invalid for several years before his death, and the high-backed chair in which he spent his declining years, is one of the most prized treasures of the writer's "better half," who is a great, great granddaughter of its former owner.

port of the gospel ministry." "Item, I give and bequeath to my daughters Sarah Anna, Angelica and Elinor each twenty pounds when they come of age."

He appoints his son-in-law, Isaac Laning, and Edward Hunt, son of his brother Ralph, his executors. The witnesses were Joseph Reed, Joseph Scudder and Rev. John Guild.

Only ten days after the date of the above will Edward Hunt assigned the Coxe deed to his son James, the assignment, written on the back of the old parchment deed is as follows, viz: "Know all men by these presents that I, Edward Hunt, of Maidenhead, within named, for the better assuring, conveying and confirming unto my son, James Hunt, of Hopewell, a certain tract or plantation lying in Hopewell, mentioned in the within written instrument, as conveying to me by Mr. Coxe Do by these Presents assign unto my son James, the within written deed. Together with all my right, title and interest therewith in any wise appertaining or belonging as fully to all intents and purposes, conveying and confirming the sd plantation to my sd son James, to him, his heirs and assigns forever, as fully, clearly and absolutely as I might or could in any other form whatsoever, and freely and clearly discharging from me and my heirs of all debts, dues and incumbrances, excepting only the paying of thirty pounds to his sister." "In witness whereof, I have hereunto set my hand and seal this seventh day of November in the year of our Lord, one thousand seven hundred and fifty-seven," signed Edward Hunt, in presence of Henry Cook and Rev. John Guild.

Immediately under the assignment is found the following receipt, "May ye 3, 1758. Then received of the above mentioned James Hunt the sum of Fifteen pounds on account of the above assignment. I say received by me, Isaac Laning."

The above James Hunt known as Miller James was born in 1724, and died March 22, 1802. His wife Rachel, who was probably a sister of his nearest neighbor Jonas Wood,* was born in 1726, and died June 18, 1774. They are buried on the south side of the Hunt burial plot on the farm of J. Guild Hunt, near Marshall's Corner. They were married about 1746, and had children as follows:

---

*Jonas Wood was a private in Capt. David Stout's company of provincial forces from Hunterdon County, Col. John Johnson's regiment, enrolled May 9, 1757, discharged June 1, 1757.

(Foot note continued on bottom next page.)

(1) David, born 1747, died April 11, 1817, married and resided on the homestead.

(2) Hannah, born 1750, married a Mr. Hawk, who was probably the William Hawk who in 1787 resided on the "societies tract," near High Bridge Iron Works, and later removed to the "Lake country," of New York state.

(3) Rachel, born 1754, died June 7, 1832, married Stephen Blackwell, born 1756, died December 3, 1831. They resided on the the farm now owned by Chas. Durling, Esq., near the borough, the farm at that time also including the farm of D. W. Housel, Esq., now residing in the borough.

(4) Deborah, born 1756, never married.

James Hunt was a popular business man, kind hearted and benevolent in disposition, and during the time of the revolution, and at intervals for many years after, operated the grist mills on Stony Brook now known as Moore's mills. He probably rented them of the owner, Francis Blackwell, who had purchased them in 1771, and 1779 sold them to his brother Rev. John, who also owned them for a short time.

These mills had at least nine different owners during the first

---

He was also a private minute man Hunterdon Co. Militia, and also sergeant in Capt. Henry Phillips' Co., 1st Regiment, Hunterdon Co., 1777.

For many years he resided on a lot at the corner of the Stony Brook road near the old baryta mines, and from entries found in old account books was a wheelwright and cabinet maker of considerable prominence.

His large shop stood on the corner of the road and appears to have been quite a business centre many years before the revolution.

The blacksmith shop of Thomas Merrill also stood somewhere in the vicinity, as the old accounts show, but its exact location cannot be definitely determined, although it may have stood on the same corner. As long ago as any now living can remember the old shop of Mr. Wood was used as a barn. It blew down about fifty years ago, and was rebuilt by Mr. Stephen Blackwell, about one-half its former size for the use of his tenants.

The old house, which was quite large and accommodated two families, was burned down in 1890 and never rebuilt, the barn was taken down, and now there is not a vestige left of the home of this worthy old family, who flourished during the revolutionary period, and for many years before and afterward.

The old veteran, Jonas Wood, in his old age resided with Stephen Blackwell, Senior, and Miss Martha Phillips, now living in the borough, who is a granddaughter of Mr. Blackwell, has in her possession a stand which Mr. Wood, while living there, whittled out with his penknife, and it is a valued keepsake.

From the account books of Dr. Benjamin Van Kirk we find that he attended Mr. Wood at Stephen Blackwell's in 1790, and as no later entries are found the supposition is that he died about that time.

Mrs. Rachel Wood, wife of Jonas Wood, was a member of the Presbyterian church at Pennington in 1785, as shown by the records, and Mr. Wood was a subscriber toward the salary of Rev. John Cross in 1731, when Mr. Cross officiated as stated supply of the Pennington church. This Jonas Wood was probably the father of the revolutionary soldier, as there were at least three of that name living at the time of the emigration from Long Island to Hopewell township.

century of their existence, and it is our purpose to give something of their history in a future article. These mills were frequently raided by the British soldiers when they were quartered at Trenton, and during the short time that Cornwallis was at Pennington in December, 1776, they were visited by foraging parties nearly every day, who carried off everything that was portable, but they did not burn and destroy as they did in the years following.

Cornwallis had driven Washington and his little band of patriots across the Delaware on December 8, and not finding any boats in which to follow him, returned as far as Pennington, where he remained until the 13th, to give his men an opportunity to recuperate before resuming his march to New Brunswick. He considered New Jersey a conquered province, and while there confined his operations principally to compelling, (by threats if other means failed) all the inhabitants he could find to swear allegiance to King George III., promising them the protection of the crown.

In a foot note to article number seven is given a copy of one of these so-called ''Protection Papers'' which failed to protect when most needed, as explained at that time.

During this period, while the British were making a house to house canvass, Mr. Hunt's family heard that they were expected to pass along the Hopewell road on a certain evening, and did not light up the house, hoping that, as it was located quite a distance from the public road, it might be passed by undiscovered. The British were shrewd enough, however, to always employ a Tory guide who was familiar with every highway and byway of the territory they intended to traverse, and all families who were suspected of being in sympathy with Washington's band of patriots were visited, no matter how secluded their places of residence.

Before the evening was far advanced, Mr. Hunt's family heard the soldiers outside, and they were ordered to open the door or it would be broken down. Knowing full well that this threat would be put in execution, Mr. Hunt opened the door and admitted his unbidden and very unwelcome visitors, who ordered him to light a candle at once. One of Mr. Hunt's daughters made the attempt, but the fright and excitement made her extremely nervous, and observing this the officer snatched the candle out of her hand with an oath and proceeded to light it himself. Mr. Hunt was then informed that he was their prisoner, and that he must accompany

them to Pennington, where Cornwallis would administer the oath
of allegiance to the King of Great Britain.   Mr. Hunt's daughters,
although fully grown, failed to comprehend the full force of the ob-
ligation about to be imposed upon their father.   Their mother had
been taken from them by death only two years before, and the terri-
ble dread of their father being held a prisoner in the British camp
and the possibility of his never returning to his home, made their
grief uncontrollable.

When the party started off for Pennington with their father, the
daughters followed, crying and screaming at the top of their voices.
The officer in charge cursed and threatened but all to no purpose ;
the grief and excitement had made them hysterical, and his threats
only aggravated their overwrought nerves until they were on the
verge of collapsing.   Finding that his threats were of no avail, and
thinking doubtless that their screams ringing out on the night air
would be heard for a long distance and arouse the whole neighborhood, and that they might be waylaid before they reached Pennington, he released Mr. Hunt, telling him that he was "too old to be
good for anything and he could go home and take care of his
babies."

The writer is reminded of another incident which took place
about the same time, of an ardent patriot who escaped without taking the prescribed oath, after being taken prisoner.

Mr. Jonathan Bunn was captured at his house (which is still
standing about one mile northwest of Pennington) and taken before
Cornwallis to have the oath administered.   Seeing that he had on a
new pair of shoes Cornwallis informed him that they must be given
to one of his aides, whose shoes were in a very shabby condition.
It being about the middle of December and the weather very cold,
Mr. Bunn bravely remonstrated, telling Cornwallis that a man in
his position ought to have too much humanity to send a man out to
freeze his feet in such extreme weather, and suggested that he send
a man home with him to bring back the shoes.   Cornwallis admir-
ing his courage consented to this proposal, sent an escort back with
Mr. Bunn, and in the parley over the shoes the oath was forgotten.
After procuring the shoes the escort galloped back to Pennington,
and Mr. Bunn skipped for the Woosamonsa mountain, where he remained during the temporary stay of Cornwallis at Pennington.

Mr. Bunn was enrolled as a minute man in Capt. Henry Phillips' Company, State Militia, and also enlisted in Capt. William Tucker's Company, First Regiment, State Troops, and did good service in his country's cause after this event. His great grandson, Mr. George Bunn, still occupies the old mansion, which is one of the very few old colonial landmarks remaining in this region. This has remained practically unchanged for a period of nearly one hundred and seventy years, and has the distinction of being the house in which Rev. Gilbert Tennent frequently preached at the time of the organization of the "New Side Presbyterian church" in 1741.

A history of this "New Side" movement is to be found in Rev. Dr. Hale's historical discourse, page 109.

April 23, 1903.

NUMBER XIX.

Reference was made in our last article to the capture of Miller James Hunt by a detachment of Cornwallis' army while at Pennington, in December, 1776; and soon after this occurrence, the British made them another visit which proved far more disastrous.

The day previous to their second visit, a man who claimed to be a great friend to them, as well as to the cause of liberty, came to Mr. Hunt's, notifying them that the enemy would be in the neighborhood the following day and advised them to conceal all their silverware and other valuables in a safe place. While discussing the matter some member of the family suggested that the heap of wheat in one of the up stairs rooms might be a safe place for small articles of value. Their visitor said it was a happy thought, as the soldiers would never think of searching for jewelry and silver spoons in such a place. Accordingly all their precious keepsakes and valuables were entrusted to the pile of wheat by the unsuspecting family. The next day they were visited by the soldiers, who to the great consternation and dismay of the family, proceeded at once to the second story and appropriated all the hidden treasure, proving conclusively that they had been basely betrayed by their pretended friend, who doubtless received a share of the booty for his cleverly conducted scheme.

As stated in a previous article James Hunt had charge of the Stony Brook mills (now J. H. Moore's) during, and for several years subsequent, to the revolution, and when the mill was kept running during the night, and frequently during the day he left it in charge of his trusted slave known as "Black Sam." One of Mr. Hunt's friends suggested to him that he was placing entirely too much confidence in Sam's integrity, as he was in a position to show his colored friends a great many favors without his master's knowledge. Although Mr. Hunt's confidence could not be easily shaken, he gave his informant permission to test Sam's honesty, telling him to black his face and try the plan of working on his sympathies.

One night soon after this, Sam heard a knock at the door of the mill, which was always fastened at night by pulling in the latch string. Sam opened the top door just far enough to peep out in the darkness, and heard a very pitiful story of a destitute family, without bread or the means of procuring it. "Hab you see Massa Jimmy?" was Sam's inquiry. The man replied that he had not, and that he had already walked several miles and could not possibly go a mile further to Mr. Hunt's residence, adding that he knew it would be all right with Mr. Hunt, for he never would turn a poor man away without giving something to relieve his necessities. "Dat am so," replied Sam, "and I feels berry sorry, but de meal am Massa Jimmy's, and ef he say so you kin hab him, but you no git him off ob Sam." After coaxing and pleading for some time in vain, the would be customer went away fully convinced that Mr. Hunt's confidence was not misplaced, and that in an extremity he would stand a much better chance in appealing to "Massa Jimmy's" sympathies than to "Sam's."

At the time of Mr. Hunt's settlement here in 1748, and for some years after, the channel of Stony Brook was completely obstructed by fallen timber and bushes, and the smaller streams emptying into it had no well-defined outlet, but spread themselves over the lowlands now owned by Messrs. C. E. Voorhees and E. S. Wells. The now beautiful meadows were at that time covered with small lakes and impenetrable swamps and marshes, which the early settlers never attempted to explore, except in winter when frozen. Trunks of trees are still found in places buried three or four feet below the surface and some of them as sound as when they fell, probably hundreds of years ago, and were covered with the sediment which came down from the hillsides. This swamp furnished a shelter for abundance of large game such as wolves, bears and panthers, and was a favorite hunting ground for the Indians who had their wigwams on the hill to the north.

The earliest settlers made a great effort to exterminate the wolves and panthers, and, as early as 1739, the Justices and Freeholders of Hunterdon County voted 40 pounds for killing wolves and panthers, but it was totally inadequate, as the following account will show. "72 full grown wolves at one pound each. 19 young wolves at 5 shillings each. 16 grown panthers at 15 shillings each." Some persons objected very strongly to voting any money for such purposes, fearing that the board of Freeholders would bankrupt the county with their extravagant appropriations.

Black bears continued to be quite numerous for several years, but as they were very timid and cowardly, they were not at all feared or dreaded, for unless they were cornered where there was no possibility of escape, they would always retreat at the approach of man as rapidly as their awkward and shambling gait would allow. They seldom visited the clearings except at the blackberry season, when they were frequently seen helping themselves to the fruit of which they were especially fond.

On one occasion two of the daughters of Mr. Hunt, who were perhaps not over twelve or fourteen years of age at that time, had quite an adventure, which goes to illustrate the dangers to which the early settlers were exposed. They were out walking near the old mines not over three hundred yards from home, and when about to climb a fence near the corner of the woods, they were nearly frightened out of their wits by seeing a bear jump up directly in their path. He had evidently been sound asleep, and as he saw no avenue of escape, he raised himself erect on his hind feet and with mouth wide open and arms extended prepared to hug the nearest girl without waiting for the formality of an introduction. There was no time for ceremony, and one of the girls, seizing a piece of an old rail, thrust it in the wide-open mouth endwise. The rail proved to be badly decayed, and very dry and dusty, crumbling in his mouth, choking and strangling his bearship almost to suffocation. The would-be "hugger" had troubles of his own to contend with, and while he was coughing and clawing to clear his throat of the dust and rotten wood, the girls lost no time in jumping the fence and making good their escape.

This bear story is well authenticated, the writer's informant being the granddaughter of one of the girls who played such a heroic part in the drama, and who was also one of the noisy trio who secured their father's release from the British soldiers as described in our last article.

David Hunt, son of Miller James, born 1747, married 1770, (I think a daughter of Jonathan Stout of Hopewell; afterward of Maysville, Ky.) She was born in 1749, and died February 21, 1834, and his death occurred April 11, 1817. They had children as follows, viz: Mary, born February 2, 1771, died December 10, 1852. Deborah, born March 22, 1774, died October 22, 1839. Rachel, born August 23, 1778, no record of death. Amos, born August 13, 1781, married Hannah Waters. Moses, born February 4, 1784, died October 14, 1852.

David Hunt was an only son, and the dependence of his father, and although thoroughly loyal to the patriot cause, did not enlist at the beginning of the war. He was enrolled as a minute man in the militia, which included all the able bodied men between the ages of 15 and 50 years, and whenever additional men were needed for active service a draft was made on the militia for one month, six months, or one year, and the man on whom the lot fell stood ready to leave his plow or workshop at a moment's notice, shoulder his musket, and march to camp or battlefield.

When the first draft was made David Hunt was one of the number on whom the lot fell, and his father's heart was almost broken at the thought of giving up his only son so soon after the death of his wife. Mr. Hunt's first impulse was to secure a substitute for David, but on reflection the kind-hearted old man changed his mind, and said to one of his neighbors, that while he did not see how he could spare David, at the same time if he procured a substitute it would have to be somebody's son and that would be as hard for them as for him. The substitute was not hired, and David went to war-serving his time as Corporal in Captain William Tucker's Company, First Regiment, from Hunterdon County and returned safe and sound. From the stories he loved to relate in his old age, one would judge that war was his greatest delight, and that he always plunged into the thickest of the fight.

In the garret of the writer is a part of an old British musket, which it was claimed David Hunt captured from a British soldier. It was purchased by the father of the writer after Mr. Hunt's death, a percussion substituted for the old flint-lock, and was an excellent fowling piece for the times. After being used by five generations of the Hunt and the writer's families, the stock was accidently broken, and as it had become a chronic kicker it was never repaired.

Amos Hunt, son of David, born August 13, 1781, married Hannah Waters, and built a house on the northern part of the tract, where he resided; and after his death it was purchased by John A. Moore, who many of our readers will remember as one of the most successful farmers of Hopewell township.

Moses Hunt and his sisters, none of whom ever married, occupied the old homestead on the southern part of the tract which, about 1833, was purchased by Amos Hoagland, and descended from him to his son, John Stout Hoagland, and also to his grandson, Simpson, who occupied it for some years after the death of his father, and then sold it and became a resident of Hopewell.*

Amos Hunt and Hannah Waters had but one child, Mary, born July 30, 1818, who married Stephen C. Blackwell, born June 10, 1815, who resided on the adjoining farm afterward owned by Stephen H. Titus, and at present the proprty of his son, Edwin S. Titus, of the firm of Holcombe & Titus, of our borough.

Stephen C. Blackwell and Mary Hunt had two daughters. Sarah Frances, born March 20, 1841, and Helen Matilda, born July 31, 1844. Mary Hunt Blackwell died December 15, 1845, and after her death Mr. Blackwell removed to Delaware, and very seldom revisited the scenes of his boyhood.

Mr. and Mrs. Blackwell were among the most intimate friends of the writer's parents, and the social visits of the families are

---

*The large and influential family of Hoagland in Hunterdon and Somerset Counties are descended from Christoffel Hooglandt, of Haarlaem, Holland, whose will is dated March 13, 1676, and recorded in Liber (3), page 83, in the surrogate's office in New York City.

He married June 23, 1661, Katrina Kreiger, also of Holland. They were married in New York City and had several children, whose births are also recorded. Some of his children settled on the branches of the Raritan in Hunterdon and Somerset Counties about the year 1700, where they purchased large tracts of land, some of which is still in possession of their descendants. Christopher's son Dirck (or Derrick), born 1662, was doubtless the grandfather of Amos Hoagland, who was born August 21, 1741, married Mary, daughter of John Titus of Hopewell, who was born November 6th, 1752. They settled on the Neshanic, near Reaville, and had children as follows: Sarah, born October 8, 1775, who married Jacob Williamson and removed to Ohio; Hannah, born December 10, 1777, married Wm. Williamson; Jonathan, born June 6, 1779, never married, resided in New York City; Andrew, born July 6, 1780, married Mary, daughter of Elijah Carman, near Copper Hill, and had Aaron C., Elijah C. and others, who resided near Flemington; Rebecca, born November 6, 1785; Amos, born November 17, 1787, married Sarah, daughter of John Stout of Hopewell, and finally settled on the Hunt tract as stated above; Mary, born April 4, 1790, who never married.

Amos Hoagland and Sarah Stout had children: John Stout, married Rebecca A., daughter of Joab Mershon; Mary, unmarried; Elizabeth, wife of Schenck Moore, and Simpson, who died a young man.

John Stout Hoagland and Rebecca Mershon had children as follows: Sarah M., wife of Richard Lowe of Neshanic; Simpson, who married Anna M., daughter of John Hart, and resides at Hopewell; Hannah, second wife of Richard Lowe; Mary E., wife of Henry C. La-Rowe, of Brooklyn, and Malvina, who died in childhood.

John Stout Hoagland will be remembered by many as a very public spirited, enterprising citizen, and is especially remembered by the writer as a kind obliging neighbor, and a warm and valued friend.

If there was sickness or death in the neighborhood, he was always among the first to offer his services, and the last to leave the afflicted family, after he had done all in his power to assist and comfort, regardless of his own personal loss or inconvenience.

The loss of such a man to a community is irreparable, and there are many, who, with the writer, will always cherish the memory of his many deeds of love and kindness among his neighbors.

among the most pleasant recollections of his early childhood. Mrs. Blackwell was a victim of that dread disease consumption, and her sad death at the early age of 27, leaving behind her two little infants, cast a heavy gloom over the community in which she was so greatly loved and esteemed. Her eldest daughter married William H. Moore, Esq., of Pennington, and she too died in early life leaving two children, Charles H., and Sarah Francis, wife of George H. Curlis, son of the late Col. William B. Curlis of Pennington.

Helen Matilda, second daughter of Mary Hunt and Stephen C. Blackwell, married John Blackwell of Hamilton Square, N. J., and died soon after, leaving one daughter, who became the wife of a Mr. Burroughs.

June 3, 1903.

NUMBER XX.

In the preceding articles of this series frequent reference has been made to the Stony Brook mills at Glen Moore, which are now owned by Joseph H. Moore, Esq., and which have been in possession of the Moore family for a period of one hundred and five years, having been purchased by his great grandfather in 1798.

Some of our readers have expressed a desire to know more of the early history of these mills than has heretofore been published, and something of the families of their various owners. This old mill was the pioneer manufacturing industry of this region, and is historic as well as ancient, having been in possession of the American and British troops alternately, during the revolutionary period, affording aid and comfort to both armies from its stores at different periods of the great struggle. The red coats appropriated as legitimate spoils of war all its supplies that were in sight, but never molested its owners nor made any attempt to destroy it, as they did the mill at Rocky Hill on the morning of January 4, 1777, on their retreat from Princeton. The exact time of the erection of the first mill cannot be definitely determined, but we have an official record to prove that it was included in the list of taxable property of Hopewell township in 1722, and in 1723, when the Stony Brook road at the old baryta mines was surveyed, it was known as Philip Ringo's mill.

The record of the survey of the old road is as follows, spelling and capitalization preserved :

New Jersey, County Hunterdon, 1723, March ye 20. ''Then Mett the Commissioners for ye sd. county & layed out A road of two Rods wide within ye township of Hopewell, beginning at a white oak tree in Roger Parks, his lande, from thence down to Stony Brook thence downe ye same to the ford att Philip Ringos Mill.''

Samuel Fitch
Philip Philips
23d March   John Ely
Then entered the   John Dean
above road by me,   William Cooke
Alexander Lockart
Recorder

The survey of this road, which is recorded on page 39 of the minutes of the Court of Common Pleas for the County of Hunterdon, in the clerk's office at Flemington, establishes the ownership of the mill at that time, as there is no question as to the location of the Dr. Roger Parke tract. The record of this tract is found in "Revell's Book of Surveys"—reversed side—page 14, and it is described as being "on the north side of Stony Brook at Wissamenson." This tract now comprises the farms of Messrs. C. E. Voorhees, Amos Sked, W. W. Kirkendall, W. C. Velit, the part of E. S. Wells' tract known as the "Samuel Ege farm" and portions of the E. S. Titus and Edward Beihl farms.

As there has recently been considerable agitation and discussion in reference to the width of the road from Hopewell to Marshall's Corner, as originally surveyed, we yield to the impulse to publish it at this time, although it had been our intention to reserve it for a future article. The original capitalization and spelling is preserved :

New Jersey, County Hunterdon, March ye 18, 1723. Then Mett the Commissioners for ye said County and layed out a Road four rods in breath, within the township of Hopewell. Beginning at ye division line of East & West Jersey at, or near, the division line of John & Abraham Van Horn* from thence along A line of Marked trees to Joseph and Benjamin Merrills, thence along the same line betwixt them and James Hide, thence along the same line betwixt

---

*The Van Horns were merchants in New York City, and owned large tracts of land between the Province Line and Millstone River. now in Montgomery township, Somerset County. That the road did not start exactly on their corner, is shown by the bend in the road at the village of Stoutsburg. The Merrills owned the land on the north, and James Hyde on the south, including the eastern part of the borough of Hopewell. Jabez Gervas owned the Baptist parsonage farm, and John Parke and Robert Tindall lying between the mountain road (Greenwood avenue) and the road running from M. Montag's to the mountain. Henry Oxley owned the F. P. Van Dyke farm, and lands east and south, and William Merrill, Jr., the railroad quarry farm. John Houghton owned the farm on the north side of the road, and between Stony Brook and the Trenton road, and John Hendrickson the south side, now the stock farm of E. S. Wells at Glen Moore, the road ending at Marshall's Corner.

James Heide & William Merrill and thence by James Hide and John Parks, and thence by Jabis Jarvis and Robert Tindall. From thence along by Henery Oxley & William Merrill and thence along by a line of Marked trees to Stony Brook, from thence along betwixt John Houghton & Johanis Hendrickson, into the Kings Road that leads to Trenton.

	William Bryant,
	John Dean,
	Philip Philips,
March 23	Samuel Fitch,
Then entered the	William Cook,
above draught of	John Ely,
a road. pr me	Commissioners.

Alexander Lockart, Recorder.

Philip Ringo, who owned the Glen Moore mills was not only an enterprising business man, but also prominent in political affairs, for we find by the records of old Hunterdon County that he was assessor in Maidenhead, (now Lawrence) township, in 1717—18. In 1721 we find him in Hopewell, and representing the township in the Board of Freeholders, and if he erected the mill it must have been between 1718 and 1722. He seems to have been a popular official, as he was a justice from 1723, to 1745, and after his removal to Amwell, about 1730, he was chosen to represent that township in the Board of Freeholders, and was one of the judges for the county in 1754. He also built a mill about one mile south of Ringoes, which was said to be the first in Amwell township, erected about 1730. In 1736 he resided on a farm just east of the village of Ringoes, afterward known as the Young farm.

John Ringo kept the hotel at Ringoes at that time,· having settled there in 1720, when the country was a wilderness, building his house where the Indian paths crossed. It is supposed that Philip and John were brothers, but the relationship existing between them cannot be stated positively. "Ringo's old Tavern" was widely known, and was one of the landmarks of the Amwell Valley for three generations. It was destroyed by fire in 1840.

Philip Ringo's will was dated April 21, 1757, and proved May 23, 1757, so that the date of his death is established very nearly. He makes bequests to his wife Catharine, and to his sons, Albertus, Henry, Cornelius and John. He leaves them farms in Hopewell and Amwell. To different members of his family he leaves silver and gold buttons and buckles, some of which he specifies as "being now attached to my britches."

He also makes a bequest to "grandson Philip, son of my son Henry," gives him great English Bible and shoe buckles. Leaves his son Albertus his large Dutch Bible and Testament with silver clasps, and also pair of gold sleeve buttons, and one set of silver buttons. Gives to his son Cornelius, son of his second wife, (who is not yet of age,) "the farm adjoining Rudolph Harlin's land, when he comes of age, excepting thereout a burying yard on the westermost corner for the use of the family forever."

The Ringo family left no male representatives, and the family name has long ago become extinct; but their memory is kept green by the beautiful little village which bears the name, and which for many years was the most important business and political centre in the whole Amwell Valley. The Ringoes post office enjoys the distinction of being the only one so named in the world.

The next owner of the Glen Moore mill property, of which we can find any record, was Joshua Anderson, who on July 30, 1751, obtained a quit claim deed for the mill tract, from John Coxe executor, and sole acting executor of the estate of Col. Daniel Coxe, as a part of his thirty thousand acre tract in Hopewell. How long Joshua Anderson had been in possession of this property before securing the Coxe deed does not appear.

In many instances lands in Hopewell were purchased of Thomas Revell, agent for the West Jersey Society, as early as 1696 to 1700, and were not quit claimed by the Coxe heirs until 1750 to 65, for reasons which have been clearly stated in previous articles of this series. This Coxe deed for 33½ acres is on the east side of Stony Brook, and is the same tract which Anderson conveys to Hon. John Hart, and his brother Daniel, and is described as including the mill, etc., and is signed October 4, 1751, by Joshua Anderson* in the presence of his neighbors, Joseph Parke and James Larason. On December 26, 1751, Joshua Anderson sold the tract adjoining the mill tract on the east side of Stony Brook, and lying be-

---

*This Anderson family was very prominent in the early affairs of the township, the name of Cornelius appearing very frequently among its officials. Cornelius, Sr., left a will dated December 6, 1765, and mentions wife "Caterin," and sons Thomas and Cornelius. Cornelius, Jr., left a will dated September 29, 1791, and mentions his sisters, Francina, wife of William Larison, Zilpha Waters and Thisbe Britton, also his brother's children, Andrew, Reuben and Amos, and their sister, Pamelia Palmer, who was the wife of Edmond Palmer. He also mentions Sarah Hudnut, daughter of his sister Catherine. Appoints his brothers-in-law, Daniel Drake and William Larison, or the survivors of them, executors. Penelope Anderson, the daughter of his brother, Thomas, married Capt. Ralph Hart and became the mother of Mary, wife of Esq. George Smith, and is not mentioned in the will of Cornelius.

tween the mill tract and the Stony Brook road at the old mines, to Joseph Parke, who is described in the deed as a "Victualler."

Previous to the transfers of these tracts in 1751, the mill appears to have been in possession for a time of Nathaniel Ward, of whom but little is known unless he should be identical with the Nathaniel Ward of Middlesex County, who was a very large real estate speculator, and a very public spirited citizen. We are inclined to the belief however, that he was a son of Joshua Ward, who was one of Hopewell's taxpayers in 1722, and is mentioned in the will of John Houghton, Sr., dated January 24, 1709. He gives to his sons John and Joseph, 320 acres of land on Stony Brook in Hopewell, which is described as between Joshua Ward and Samuel Allen, divided by a line from Stony Brook to Thomas Smith's land.

Thomas Smith owned the farm of Wm. D. Hill and the part of the Dr. Macauley farm on the west side of the Trenton road at Marshall's Corner, at that time ; and in 1722, John Houghton owned the tract between Stony Brook and the Trenton road, afterward the William Larison, and still later the Asa Titus farm, now owned by E. S. Wells.

We have no positive proof that Samuel Allen owned the Jno. L. Burroughs and Joshua Hunt farms in 1709, but think he did, and if so, it would locate the Joshua Ward farm as the tract on which E. S. Wells now resides.

Large tracts of land changed hands very frequently at that early date, and deeds were written on small pieces of parchment and never recorded, as it required a trip to Burlington on horseback through the woods to have them recorded, and on their return they would sell them again in a few days if they had a tempting offer. From 1695 to 1710, nearly all the tracts were bought for speculation, but from 1710 to 1730 the great majority were bought for settlement and improvement.

In 1722 Johannis Hendrickson paid taxes on 149 acres, being the tract on which Mr. Wells now lives, and on November 12, 1735, sold it to John Hunt, describing it as "the plantation on which John Hendrickson now dwells," containing 149 acres, and bounded on the east by Stony Brook, and south by Thomas Runyan.* It is our purpose to give something of the history of these farms and their owners in subsequent articles.

---

*Thomas Runyan purchased the farm on which Mr. Enoch A. Titus now lives, in 1708. See foot note to article number five of this series.

We have in our possession, the copy of a petition for the relay of a public road, which we will insert here as an item of interest, giving the names of many of the people of the township living on, or near the road at that time. The absence from this list of the names of many others who are known to have been residents of this locality, at that time, can only be explained on the theory that they thought enough signers had been obtained to secure the needed improvement, and no effort was made to increase the list. It will be observed that the name of Nathaniel Ward does not appear on the list, although the road leads to his mill, and would be considered a benefit to his property. He may have thought, however, that a better road to Trenton would take more custom from his mill than it would bring him, as many would pass him by and go to Trenton.

"Petition for a relay of the public road leading from Trenton to Nathaniel Ward's mill, in Hopewell. The road being in a perilous condition we ask to have it altered and laid out in a more convenient place, filed December 10, 1745. Samuel Hunt, Joseph Golden, John Hunt Sr., Thomas Tindall, Cornelius Polhemus, Joseph Furman, Jeremiah Smith, John Reed, Cornelius Anderson, Vincent Runyan, Jonathan Hunt, Hezekiah Bonham, Edward Cooper, John Hunt, Thomas Burroughs, Sackett Moore, Joseph Baldwin, Nathaniel Davy, William Snead, Timothy Temple, Ichabod Leigh, Francis Vannoy, Eliakim Anderson, Abraham Anderson, Cornelius Vannoy, Cornelius Anderson Jr., Samuel Ketcham, Abraham Moore. Application made to Benjamin Green, Daniel Lanning, Richard Phillips, and Wilson Hunt, Surveyors of the Highway."

July 22, 1903.

NUMBER XXI.

Our last article closed with the copy of the petition for the improvement of the road from Trenton to Nathaniel Ward's mill in Hopewell. It is not known whether the petition was acted upon at that time or laid over, but it is a matter of record that only seven years had elapsed before the road was again brought to the attention of the authorities, and this time in a manner that doubtless secured the necessary improvement. The following is a copy:

"May 15, 1752, Hunterdon County, S. S. We, the Grand Jury, now sitting in, and for the County of Hunterdon, Oyer & Terminer, Do present the overseers of the road of the Township of Hopewell for not repairing a certain road called "Roger's Road," leading from a Stone School House by Daniel Hart's mill* to the Province Line, being the road leading to Brunswick."

"SAMUEL STOUT, Foreman."

The above was the piece of road leading from Marshall's Corner through the borough of Hopewell to Stoutsburg, which was laid out as a four rod road in 1723, the original survey being given in our last article. The old "Stone Schoolhouse" stood at Marshall's Corner, where Mrs. Ferris now has her garden and was erected about 1720. The father of the writer attended school there in 1820-25, when it was taken down and rebuilt on the site of the present structure, the one now standing being the third stone school building erected in that district.

As there has been considerable discussion at different times as to the origin of the name of the road leading from Trenton to the county line at Stoutsburg, we will say that it was originally given to the road leading from Trenton to the settlement on Stony Brook made by Dr. Roger Parke about 1700; which previous to that time was designated in the oldest deeds as the "Wissamenson and Wissomencey Indian path." As early as 1708 deeds for farms

---

*This was Philip Ringo's mill, now J. H. Moore's at Glen Moore. It was purchased by Daniel Hart in 1751.

between Trenton and Pennington are described as bounded by "Rogers Road;" and the will of William Cornwell, dated 1747, describes his land as lying between Stony Brook and "Rogers Road." This is the farm adjoining the borough of Pennington on the north, now the property of B. F. Lewis, Esq.

We will insert in this connection a copy of the original survey of the road from Ringoes to Marshall's Corner, the closing paragraph of which calls the Trenton and Hopewell road "Roger Park's Road." The capitalization and spelling is the same as in the original record :

"1722 March 31

"We, the commissioners for the county of Hunterdon have layed out a Road of four rods in Breadth as follows. That is to say, beginning att a white oak tree near the end of John Knowles, his lande, by the side of Yorke Road going to the Rarinton, from thence Along by the line of Marked trees with a Blase and three notches, to a black oak tree standing upon Nathan Allen's land by the side of the road that leads from Malayelick hills, to the falls, and so along the said road to another Black Oake standing upon Mr. Thomas Lambert's land, and so along by a line of Marked trees as above said to the cleared land of Joseph Hixson's,* and so through the said cleared land betwixt the house and barn, and so along by A line of Marked trees as above said, to John Reeds land, and so along the said land to a Hickory tree marked as above said, and so along by a line betwixt Thomas Smith's land and John Houghton's, and from thence along a line of marked trees as above said, to a Hickory tree standing near Samuel furman's Corner by the side of Roger Park's his road.

"Signed by us this twenty eighth day of March Anno Domini, 1722.

Philip Ringo	George Green
Charles Clark	John Holcombe
John Burroughs	His
	Thos. ᴇ Burroughs
	Mark

---

*The first trading point north of the falls at Trenton was doubtless established at New Market, now Linvale, as early as 1700, if not previous to that time. There is but little doubt that Joseph Hixson was the first Indian trader in this region, locating at the junction of the Malayelick Indian path with that leading to the wigwams on the Neshanic below West's mills, and to the junction of the North and South branches of the Raritan.

This place on the Raritan was called by the Indians Tuck-a-rama-hacking, and here they had a considerable tract of cleared land on which the squaws raised corn and beans for succotash.

It will be noticed in the foregoing road survey, that the only cleared land mentioned between Ringoes and Marshall's Corner is Joseph Hixson's at New Market, and it was probably cleared by the Indians long before his settlement there.

"Then entered ye above road the day and year above written by Mr. Alexander Lockart recorder for the county of Hunterdon."

The property owners mentioned in the above survey were located on the line of the road as follows: John Knowles was one of the first settlers at Ringoes and was the first collector of taxes for old Amwell, receiving his appointment in 1723. Nathan Allen of Allentown, N. J., purchased May 29, 1702, of Experience, widow of Benjamin Field, of Burlington County, N. J., 1650 acres, being a part of the Field tract of 3000 acres, which extended from Ringoes south to the village of Rocktown. Thomas Lambert settled about 1679 at the Falls of the Delaware, and the village of Lamberton, now a part of South Trenton, was named for him. He owned a large tract of land at New Market, now Linvale, and also around Woodsville.

Joseph Hixson owned lands on both sides of the road between Linvale and Woodsville, purchased no doubt of Mr. Lambert. John Reed owned the tract now owned by John L. Burroughs, Esq., between Woodsville and Marshall's Corner, the tract at that time extending to Stony Brook on the east. John Houghton as stated in our last, owned the farm adjoining Marshall's Corner on the north, including all the land from Stony Brook to the above road, now owned by E. S. Wells and the part of the Dr. Macauley farm east of the road. Thomas Smith owned the farms of William D. Hill and J. Guild Hunt, and also the part of the Dr. Macauley farm lying west of the road, the tract being purchased by Thomas Smith, son of Andrew Smith, February 25, 1698.

To Andrew Smith may be given the honor of naming Hopewell township, and a short sketch of his history may not be out of place just here as he was the progenitor of a distinguished family in the early history of the township. In the deed of Cornelius Empson of Brandywine Creek, now Wilmington, Delaware, to Andrew Smith dated May 20, 1688, the tract is called "Hopewell," and when on February 20, 1699, application was made by the inhabitants north of the falls of the Delaware for a new township, they requested in the petition that it be called "Hopewell." There were three Andrew Smiths in succession, among the early settlers of Hopewell township, all of whom distinguished themselves; but in the published histories of the family they have not included the first Andrew, giving the credit of naming the township to the second.

The will of the first Andrew Smith was dated January 16, 1703, and is not recorded, but is on file with the inventory of his estate, in the office of the Secretary of State at Trenton. He resided within the boundaries of old Hopewell township in the vicinity of the pres- ent site of the Hospital for the Insane now in Ewing township. In his will, which was proved March 7, 1703, he leaves a legacy to his son Andrew Smith, who married Sarah, daughter of the first Jona- than Stout of Hopewell, and soon after the death of his father moved to the northern part of the township, and settled on the farm adjoining the Hopewell poor farm, now owned by Oliver G. Woodward.

The will also mentions daughters as follows: Sarah, wife of John Parke; Mary, wife of William Schooley, and Elizabeth Smith; also mentions John Fidler, servant, who also came to the vicinity of Harbourton and purchased a farm near Andrew Smith Jr. He appoints his son Thomas Smith, and daughter Elizabeth, executor and executrix, and signed his name in presence of William Hixson, Caleb Wheatley and Joshua Ward, all of whom resided in the vi- cinity of the falls at that time. The executors bond was signed by Thomas Smith, George Willis and Emanuel Smith.

The last named was the brother of Samuel, the author of "Smith's History of New Jersey," published in 1765, and was doubtless a nephew of Andrew; and George Willis was the father- in-law of Emanuel. The bond was witnessed by Ralph Hunt and Joshua Anderson, and the appraisers were Robert Pearson, Thos. Tindall, and Roger Parke, the father of John Parke who married Sarah Smith mentioned in the will.

All these parties resided at or near the falls in 1703, but several of them came to northern Hopewell soon after, and we hope to give something of their history in subsequent articles of this series. The following is a copy of the petition for a new township to be called Hopewell.

"Court in session. February 20-21-22, 1699. Justices on the bench:

Mahlon Stacy,	John Adams,
Francis Davenport,	John Wills,
Peter ffretwell,	Joshua Newbold,
William Biddle,	Ralph Hunt.

"Petition of some of the inhabitants above the ffalls for a new township to be called Hopewell, as also a new road and boundaries of Sd town and upon file.

"To begin at Mahlon Stacy's Mill and so along by York Road until it comes to Shabbaconk creek, and up the same until it meets with a line of partition that divides the thirty thousand acre tract from the fifteen thousand, and thence along the line of the Societies 30,000 acre purchase to the Delaware River."

This boundary is very nearly the same as the original survey of the thirty thousand acre tract for Dr. Daniel Coxe of London, purchased of the Indian Sachimachers by deed bearing date, March 30, 1688. Recorded in Liber B. Part 1, on file in the office of the secretary of State at Trenton.

The old township line commenced at the Assanpink, while the old Indian purchase of Dr. Coxe commenced "two miles above the ffalls mill." The two lines intersected about a mile southeast of the present village of Ewingville and then followed the line of Dr. Coxe's purchase to a point near where the Province line crosses Stony Brook west of Princeton, and thence north four miles and thirty-two chains to the hills north of Minnepenasson* and from there by a direct line west by north to Ateokin's wigwam on the Delaware, and so down the same to the mouth of the Assanpink at Trenton. The north line of the township was subsequently surveyed and re-surveyed, until finally the present zigzag line was established.

The name "Hopewell" adopted by Andrew Smith in 1688, may have originated in the fact that many of the early English emigrants were safely carried across the boisterous Atlantic in the "ship Hopewell," of which Capt. Bunlock was the commander. However, the more plausible theory is that the township, like many others, received its name from the locality in England where many of the settlers resided previous to their imigration.

There was doubtless great joy among the residents of the Hopewell valley when the wheels of Philip Ringo's Stony Brook mill were first set in motion, as previous to that time they had wended their way through the forest to Col. Trent's mill on the Assanpink. The mill of Capt. John Harrison on the Millstone at

---

*Minnepenasson was on the south side of the hill just north of Stoutsburg, and east of the residence of David Moore, Esq., and Ateokin's wigwam was the present site of Lambertville, where the Old Neshaminy Indian path crossed the Delaware, the path running from there to the wigwams on the Raritan near Bound Brook.

Rocky Hill was not erected until 1717, or about the same date as Mr. Ringo's on Stony Brook. The mills near Princeton, now the property of Hon. Joseph H. Bruere, were built by Thomas Potts of Bucks County, Pa., in 1714, previous to which Col. Trent's mills were the only source of supply for that region.

The erection of the mill at Glen Moore was an event in the lives of the old pioneers equaling in importance the building of the first railroad through the valley one hundred and fifty years later; and their emotions must have been akin to those of their descendants who saw the first iron horse cross Stony Brook on the morning of January 16, 1873. With our present facilities for reaching Trenton by rail and a good macadam road, and also the convenience of having the staff of life brought daily to our doors, it is difficult for us to realize that our forefathers, who first settled this valley, were obliged to transport all their grain for mill or market on pack horses, either to tide water on the Delaware at Trenton, or to the Raritan at New Brunswick.

If this statement needs confirmation we will give the evidence of Mrs. Jemima Howell, the wife of Joseph Howell who was born near the Ewing Presbyterian church in 1725, and died in 1824, aged ninety-nine years, and who, by the way, was the great great grandmother of our townsmen, Messrs. David L., Nelson D. and Charles H. Blackwell. Mrs. Howell stated that she could distinctly remember when there were only three or four houses in Trenton, and when pack horses were used by the farmers to carry their grain to market, which was the sloop landing at Lamberton, and when Broad Street, Trenton, as now located, was only a foot path through the woods to Col. Trent's mill.

This mill was erected by Mahlon Stacy in 1680, and was built of hewn logs one and a half stories high with the end to the street. It was located on the South side of the Assanpink creek where it was crossed by Kingsbury, now Broad Street, Trenton. When we remember the fact that the horse path leading to it from Hopewell, was often obstructed by fallen trees, the streams not bridged and often impassable, we can faintly imagine the difficulties with which the old pioneers had to contend in their struggles to subdue the wilderness and found a home for themselves and their descendants.

September 9, 1903.

NUMBER XXII.

The old mill of Mahlon Stacy referred to in our last, was a very primitive affair, and totally inadequate to supply the necessities of a rapidly increasing population. In 1690 the mill was purchased by Col. William Trent, of Philadelphia, who took down the old building and erected on its site a two story stone building, equipping it with better machinery, and from that time the "Falls" began to be called "Trent's Mills." In 1719 the name was first written "Trent's town" and was called "Trentown" by the old people within the memory of the generation now living.

Some idea can be formed of the patronage of this mill during the period between the years 1690 and 1710, when we consider the fact that no other mills were in existence on the north and east, and the only one east of the Delaware, and south of Trent's was that of Thomas Olive, which was located on Olives Creek, where it empties into the Rancocas three miles below the city of Burlington, and over twenty miles from Trent's by the old path. In Evart's and Peck's history of Mercer County, page 664, the statement is made that those were the only mills in the state for some years after their erection.

It may not be generally known that these pioneer mills had no "bolting cloths," and that even as late as the revolutionary period, all the bolting in the country mills was performed by hand. The old pioneer went to mill on horseback, carrying one bag of grain before him on the horse he rode, and generally leading one or two horses behind him, each loaded with a large sack ; and after riding from ten to fifty miles to reach the mill, he waited until the "grist" was ground before turning his steps homeward, and then the meal had to be sifted by the good house wife before it was ready for baking.

The finest of the dust thus sifted through the cloth was called "flour," and could only be used for "Sunday bread and cookies," while the seconds were called "meal," which was considered good enough for the week-day supply of bread and pan cakes. The corn meal was used largely for mush, and no table in town or country was considered well equipped without a bountiful supply of mush and milk, which was used much as the breakfast foods of the present day—minus the sugar —and reversing the order, mush and milk being often used as the last meal of the day. This dish was not used by our fore-fathers in preparing the stomach for the more substantial dishes to follow, but more frequently as a full course, dessert included.

With the lack of facilities for procuring flour it is no wonder that "plumping mills" were very much in evidence in the earlier days of the pioneers, and were considered indispensable adjuncts to every farmer's outfit. The distance to mill was often great with no road to reach it, and as the mills were built on the smaller streams to save expense, they were frequently "held up" by drought in summer, and ice in winter, so that the great ponderous wooden wheels outside absolutely refused to budge, and consequently the plumping mills were often brought into requisition. These contrivances consisted simply of a large stump neatly hollowed out, and a convenient sapling bent over, to which a large block of hard wood was attached, which served to crush the grain. The fineness of the flour depended on the strength, patience, and endurance of the one - generally a slave—who manipulated the "plumper," and the texture of the cloth through which it was bolted after the plumping process was completed.

In article number 20 of this series, is given the transfer of the Glen Moore mills from Joshua Anderson to Hon. John Hart and his brother Daniel, dated October 4, 1751. They continued to operate them until July 4, 1766, when they sold them to John Wikoff, Peter Wikoff, and Isaac Wikoff, merchants of the city of Philadelphia. This deed is signed by Daniel Hart, John Hart, and Deborah, his wife ; and it is a noteworthy fact that John Hart signed this deed just ten years before he affixed his signature to the immortal document which made him famous in history, and which proclaimed "Liberty and Independence" to the down trodden and oppressed colonists.

It has been our purpose in writing the history of these old mills to give only short sketches of the families of their owners, and although the life and distinguished services of Hon. John Hart demand more than a passing notice an extended article would seem to be unnecessary in this connection. A few articles devoted exclusively to the history of this distinguished family is among the possibilities of the future, and with this apology we will proceed to give the record of his family, and a very few facts connected with his business life, which have been overlooked by his biographers, who have confined their labors to a record of his distinguished services to his country.

In tracing the ancestry of the Hart family of old Hopewell township, it has been found by the most diligent and accurate genealogical students in the country, that the published histories of the family are incorrect, and the following record has been proved to be the correct one.

First generation—John Hart of Newtown, Long Island, who probably first settled in Massachusetts, will proved 1671, names children as follows, viz: John, William, Samuel, Sarah, Susan. Second generation -- John Hart of Newtown, carpenter, died 1712-13. He was a resident of Maidenhead, now Lawrenceville, about 1700, but whether he died there or returned to Newtown is not known. His name is written in old documents "John Heart Senior."

By his marriage with Mary———he had children as follows, viz: John, Ralph, Nathaniel, Edward, Joseph.

This record proves absolutely that the "White Harts" and "Black Harts," so called, were of the same household, and not of separate families, as stated in the published histories. See "New York Genealogical and Biographical Record" Vol. 25, page 170, October 1895.

Another proof that they were all brothers is found in the will of Nathaniel Hart of Hopewell, a copy of which, written on fine parchment and dated January 21, 1742, is in the writer's possession; from which is copied the following, viz:

"Item. I order & nominate, appoint and constitute, Elizabeth, my wife, together with my brother Joseph Hart & John Hart son to my brother Edward to be only and sole executors of this my last will and testament."

This is conclusive proof that John and Joseph were brothers of Edward, the father of Hon. John, and not of separate families, as it has been asserted in the former histories.

Hon. John Hart was the son of Capt. Edward, who was the fourth son of John of Newtown, Long Island. Capt. Edward was very prominent both in affairs of church and state, and either in

1715, or 1746, organized a corps of volunteers called the "Jersey Blues," for the first time so called.

Sanderson in his "Biography of the Signers," says that he took part in the battle of Quebec, in 1759, but this is incorrect, as Capt. Hart died in August, 1752, or previous to that time, as proved by the records.

There is no record of the birth of Hon. John Hart, nor of the birth of his wife, but he was baptized in the Presbyterian church of Lawrenceville on February 10, 1714, and died May 11, 1779, and the record states that he was "about 67, at the time of his death." His will was dated April 16, 1779, and approved May 26, 1779.

The following family record of the children of Hon. John Hart was copied by the writer several years ago from a manuscript written by Hon. John S. Darragh of Beaver, Pa., for the Historical Society of Pennsylvania, and is on file in the rooms of the Historical and Genealogical Society of Pennsylvania, No. 1300 Locust Street, Philadelphia. Mr. Darragh was a son of Deborah, grandson of Jesse Hart, and great grandson of John, the signer; and copied the record from the old family bible of John Hart which was, at that time (1860) in his possession, The bible also contains the record of the death of the wife of Hon. John, doubtless written by himselt, and is as follows: "October 20, 1776. Departed this life in the 55th year of her age, Deborah, wife of John Hart, who left 12 children and 22 grandchildren behind her."

The record of their children is as follows: Sarah, born October 16, 1742; Jesse, born September 19, 1744; Martha, born April 30, 1746; Nathaniel, born October 29, 1747; John, born October 29, 1748; Susannah, born August 2, 1750; Mary, born April 7, 1752; Abigail, born February 10, 1754; Edward, born December 30, 1755; Scudder, born December 30, 1757; a daughter, born March 16, 1761; Daniel, born August 13, 1762; Deborah, born August 21, 1765.

Of the children named above, ten married and had families, and all the sons left New Jersey within about ten years after the death of their father. They settled in western Pennsylvania, West Virginia, and Kentucky, and had an interesting history, some of them becoming very successful in business and others distinguished as politicians and statesmen.

The homestead farm of Hon. John Hart was beautifully located, and comprised the fine farms now owned by William I. Phillips, Prof. Edgerly, and William B. Van Pelt, Esq., and also all that part of the borough of Hopewell lying west of Greenwood Avenue, and north of Broad Street.

The old mansion in which his large family was born and reared, is among the things of the past, not a vestige remaining except a few of the old hearthstones of the large fireplace, around which the family gathered on the long winter evenings, and discussed with their neighbors—the Stouts, Houghtons, and Goldens—the exciting and thrilling events through which they passed during the times which "tried men's souls."

Of the distinguished services of Mr. Hart much has been written, but of his business life very little is known. The fact of his name being so frequently seen on public documents is evidence that he had a great many "irons in the fire," in addition to the care of his large farm and family. Previous to his entrance into public life as a politician, he was much in demand in the settlement of the estates of his neighbors, and in the discharge of his duties in the minor offices, which invariably fall to the lot of every enterprising and public spirited citizen.

After his election to the Colonial Legislature in 1761, and his superior talents came to be more widely known, his life was devoted almost exclusively to public affairs ; and his private business, including his large farm, was left to the care of his sons Jesse and Nathaniel, who remained on the homestead. From 1751 to 1766, he owned a half share of the Stony Brook mills at Glen Moore, and at the time of the revolutionary war, and probably several years previous, he owned a two third share of the grist mills and fulling mills at Rocky Hill, which did a large business, his son-in-law, Col. John Polhemus, owning the other one third share.

On the morning after the battle of Princeton there occurred at this mill a skirmish with the British which, like the battle of the preceding day, resulted in a victory for the Americans. A portion of the British army was encamped at Ten Mile Run, only a short distance from the residence of the great great grandfather of the writer,* and they sent down a detachment of the 55th Regiment,

---

*The person alluded to in this connection was Hendrick DeHart, who was with General Washington at that time and participated in the battle of Princeton the day previous. Two of his little sons, Henry and Uriah, had a narrow escape from being exposed to the fire of Morgan's riflemen that morning. They had just been to the mill at Rocky Hill and were
(Foot note continued on bottom next page.)

with orders to burn the mill at Rocky Hill, and destroy the bridge over the Millstone. Fortunately the corps of Col. Daniel Morgan's riflemen with one piece of cannon was encamped near the mill to recuperate after the hard fought battle of the day before, and the approach of the enemy was discovered in time to defeat their purpose.*

They opened fire on the surprised red coats at short range with such deadly effect that they were utterly routed, and fled in every direction in great precipitation and confusion, leaving several dead and wounded which they made no effort to take with them. The dead were buried by Col. Morgan's men and the wounded carried in the mill and cared for.

Col. John Polhemus, in his diary, says that he was detailed with a rear guard to bury the dead and care for the wounded at Princeton after which he obtained leave to visit his home and mill at Rocky Hill, where he, and his father-in-law had 400 bushels of wheat, and a large quantity of flour stored at that time, and it was a very fortunate circumstance that the enemy was discovered just in time to save mill and contents from destruction.

Not over half an hour after the affair at the mill, Mr. Peter Van Derveer, Senior, (the grandfather of the Peter Van Derveer who spent his life of 96 years on the same spot, as many of us remember,) said that he saw several British soldiers approaching his place on a run. When they came to the brook just in front of his house, they found the ice too weak to bear them and in great haste they procured some rails which they laid on it and thus crossed over. His house stood within a few feet of the brook, and they went there at once and found that Mrs. Van Derveer had just taken a pot of

on their way home, going up the hill on the east side of the river, when they saw the British soldiers approaching and turned aside in the woods until they had passed.

Uriah, who was the great grandfather of the writer and well remembered by him, said that although only a small boy at the time, he recollected very distinctly seeing his mother take the copper kettle and go toward the spring, which was a considerable distance from the house. He followed along and saw her sink it in the spring, after which she took the gold ring from her finger and hid it under one of the stones in the walk.

How our hearts thrill with emotion when we think of the dangers and perils to which our heroic grandmothers were exposed, and the trials through which they passed, in their efforts to protect their families as best they could, and preserve the homes of the brave husbands and fathers who were fighting their country's battles, and defending the homes and firesides to which, alas, many of them were never permitted to return.

*Morgan's Corps of Militia was known as "Morgan's Rangers," and consisted of 700 men and one piece of cannon. His corps of riflemen was a terror to the British, and the pride of the continental army.

Among all of old Hunterdon's valiant sons none have done her more honor than General Daniel Morgan.

mush from the fire for the morning meal of the family.   They told
Mrs. Van Derveer that they had nothing but hot bullets for their
breakfast, and they scooped the hot mush out of the pot with their
hands and eagerly devoured it.

Mr. Van Derveer had not expected to be molested and had not
made any effort to conceal himself, and he was very much surprised
and disgusted when told that he was their prisoner, and was ordered
to march on in the lead, in double quick time, without a mouthful
of breakfast.   Their only motive no doubt was to prevent him from
giving the alarm and starting a party in pursuit.   Their objective
point was the Sourland range and after they considered themselves
safe from pursuit Mr. Van Derveer was allowed to escape and return home.   Whether the excitement, exposure and fatigue incident to his forced march hastened his death is not known, but he
survived only a few months after his thrilling experience, and died
the same year — 1777 — aged 56 years.

On September 6, 1779, Jesse Hart, Nathaniel Hart and Edward Hart, sons of Hon. John, together with Levi Hart, son
of his brother Daniel, executors of his last will, advertised in the
Trenton Gazette as follows :

"For sale.   The two third share of three undivided lots of land at
Rocky Hill, with the grist mill and Fulling mill, being a part of the
estate of John Hart Esquire at Hopewell."

October 28, 1903.

NUMBER XXIII.

Daniel Hart, second son of Captain Edward, and brother and business partner of Hon. John in the Glen Moore mill property, re_sided on the fine farm now known as the "Glen Moore Stock Farm," owned by E. S. Wells, Esq., the old house standing a few yards east of the present mansion.

The families of Capt. Edward and his brother, Major Ralph, were known among the pioneers as the "Black Harts," from their dark complexion to distinguish them from the children of the other brothers, John, Joseph and Nathaniel, who were known from their fair complexion as the "White Harts." All the above families carried down the old family names, John, Edward, Joseph, etc., which made it difficult to designate them, as in naming their children a middle name was a luxury seldom indulged in by our forefathers.

Through the kindness of Joseph H. Moore, Esq., of Glen Moore, we have in our possession all the old deeds for the farm on which Daniel Hart resided, from the settlement of Johannis Hendrickson, previous to 1722—down to the time of Mr. Moore's grandfather. Daniel Hart purchased it of Jonathan Hunt, on April 15, 1748, about three years prior to his purchase of the mill property on the east side of the brook, the date of which is given in our last article.

On March 10, 1784, Levi Hart, "only surviving son and heir of Daniel Hart, deceased," sold the homestead farm to Benjamin Cornell, of Pennington, N. J., the deed being also signed by Mary, wife of Levi, who was a daughter of Elnathan Hunt.

The children of Levi Hart and Mary Hunt were as follows, viz : Daniel, who died in 1795, when a young man. John H. married Elizabeth, daughter of Capt. Timothy Titus, born August 4, 1782. Charity, married Nathaniel Bryant. Sarah, married Nov. 12, 1799, John Stout.

John H. Hart and Elizabeth Titus were married about 1806,

and when their children were very young, two of them not over one
and three years of age, they removed from Hopewell to the vicinity
of Seneca Lake, New York, settling on a tract of land near the present town of Romulus, the farm being still in the possession of one
of his descendants, Mrs. Mary E. Seely, only daughter of Daniel
Hart and granddaughter of John H. Hart. Levi Hart, at that time
about 55 years of age, accompanied his son John H. to his new
home in the wilds of New York, and also his daughters, Charity
and Sarah, with their husbands.

There was quite a large colony of Hopewell families who emigrated at the same time, their mode of conveyance being large canvas covered wagons without springs drawn by oxen. Much of the
country traversed being a wilderness without a road worthy of the
name, and no bridges, they made the journey in the depth of winter,
when the streams and marshes were frozen solid, several families
going together for mutual help and protection.

Colonel, (afterward Judge) William Cooper of Burlington,
N. J., having become possessed of large tracts of land by the extin-
guishment of Indian titles in the region known as the "Lake Country" of New York state, had induced hundreds of New Jersey families to emigrate and settle there in colonies. This extensive tract
lay nearly in the geographical centre of the state, and was an unbroken wilderness, needing only the industry, thrift and enterprise
of these sturdy, fearless patriots of the revolution, and sons of New
Jersey's pioneers, to develop its vast resources, and cause it to blos-
som as the rose.

Through Col. Cooper's glowing representations of the possibilities of this fertile region, the township of Hopewell lost very
many of its best and most enterprising citizens, not only farmers,
but physicians, teachers, merchants and mechanics of every description, and their descendants are today found among the most wealthy
and distinguished families of the Empire state. Through this extensive emigration many of the records of the old families, who were
very prominent here in colonial and revolutionary times, have been
lost beyond recovery.

To this wilderness, remote from any civilized settlements, Col.
Cooper himself emigrated in 1790, carrying with him his one-year-
old son, James Fenimore Cooper, who, reared amid the wild scenes,
rude experiences, and exciting incidents of frontier life, was destined to become one of the most illustrious authors and novelists

that America has ever produced, a Jerseyman by birth and blood, whom our little state is justly proud to own.

John H. Hart and Elizabeth Titus had children as follows, viz: Titus, who married Emma Hanley of Hector, Schuyler county, New York. Daniel, married Hannah Alvana Fortner. Eliza, married Joshua Covert of Greece, Monroe county, New York, left no children. Mary, married John R. Smith, left no children. Enoch, married Catharine Hoagland of Aurora, New York. Amanda, unmarried.

Titus Hart and Emma Hanley had children as follows, viz: Helen, Anna Smith, residing at Trumansburg, New York, to whom the writer is indebted for a sketch of the family since their settlement in New York, and Caroline Hanley, who married Frederick A. Dimick of Trumansburg, New York. They have two children, Emma Katharine and James Hanley Dimick.

Daniel Hart and Hannah A. Fortner had children as follows: Mary E., married S. Alfred Seely, a wholesale lumber dealer of Spencer, New York, now deceased. Their children are Grace Alvana, Charles Alfred, and Hart Irving. Edgar M. Hart married Arinda Trembly and has one daughter, Edna M. To Mr. Edgar M. Hart and his sister, Mrs. Seely, the writer is indebted for information concerning the family of their grandfather, John H. Hart.

Enoch Hart, son of John H., by his marriage with Catharine Hoagland, had children as follows, viz: Carolyn Hart Bachman, deceased; Margaret Hart Ritter; Eliza Hart of California; John Hart, a veteran of the Civil War residing at Fayette, New York; Charles M. Hart, of Union Springs, New York; Elizabeth Hart, Syracuse, New York; Louisa Hart Hendrick of Montour Falls, New York; Ida Hart Goodyear of Toledo, Ohio.

John Stout, who married Sarah, daughter of Levi Hart, and emigrated with the Hart family to New York, returned in a short time to his native state and settled at Rocky Hill, Somerset County, N. J., where he followed his trade of a blacksmith, and was a highly respected and eminently useful citizen.

John Stout and Sarah Hart were married November 12, 1799, and had children as follows, viz:

Levi, died when a young man. Rebecca, married Franklin Wright, a lawyer of Petersburg, Virginia, who at the time of their marriage was a topographical engineer employed in the construction of the Delaware and Raritan canal across the state.

Isaac, married Hannah, daughter of Elnathan Moore of Flemington, N. J., and sister of Hon. Charles B. Moore of Kingston, N. J.

Zebulon, married Deborah Conover of Penn's Neck, near Princeton, N. J.

John, born at Rocky Hill, May 21, 1809, married Eliza A., daughter of Arnold Farmer of New Brunswick, N. J.

Frances, married Alexander Van Dyke of Rocky Hill.

Sarah A., married Thomas Skillman, a well known merchant of Rocky Hill of forty years ago.

Mary, married Dr. Nelson Stryker, a prominent and successful physician of Monmouth Junction, and the father of N. DeWitt Stryker, now a resident of the same place.

John Stout and Eliza Farmer settled at Monmouth Junction, N. J., and had one son, Arnold Farmer Stout, born December 19, 1836. John Stout senior, also removed from Rocky Hill to Monmouth Junction where he died about 1830, aged 62. His widow survived him a few years and died at the age of 75.

A. Farmer Stout married September 8, 1859, Miss Anna E., daughter of John Van Zandt, Esq., of Blawenburg. They had two sons and one daughter, viz: Frank W.; Jennie, wife of Samuel H. Lake, Esq., of Kingston, N. J., and Augustus V., who is engaged in business with his father. Arnold F. Stout is a prosperous merchant of Monmouth Junction, prominently identified with its interests, and enjoys the respect and confidence of all classes in the community. Mr. Stout is one of the very few great great grandchildren of Daniel Hart, now living in New Jersey.

During the two centuries which have elapsed since the first pioneer erected his little cabin in the Hopewell valley, there have been few atrocious crimes committed within the present borders of the township, and there are very few persons now living who have ever heard of the tragic death of Daniel Hart. It occurred in the old house, which stood near the present country home of E. S. Wells, Esq., of Glen Moore, and a sketch of the event which took place about the close of the revolution is published now for the first time, not for the purpose of giving our readers the details of a heinous crime, but with the feeling that the history of the early settlement of the valley would not be complete without some reference to the incident.

Mr. Hart had a young slave named Cuffee, whose laziness was a great trial to his patience and one morning before leaving the house he called Cuffee to get up, informing him that if he was not out on his return he would come up stairs and pull him out of bed. Not finding him up on his return, he proceeded to put his threat into execution, when the negro caught hold of him and began stabbing him with a large penknife, which some of the family had seen him carefully whetting up the day previous. He clung fast to Mr. Hart all the way down the stairway and out of the door, continuing to stab him in the face and neck, and when they reached the outside he seized an ax, which lay at the wood pile, and with it wounded him so severely that he lingered in great agony until near the close of the day, when he expired.

The villian made his escape at once to the heavy woodlands which at that time covered the hill south of the Hopewell Baptist Meeting House (as the locality of our borough was then called) where he concealed himself in a heap of brush. He was seen by a person who was crossing the hill at the same time, and as soon as the alarm was given a party of the neighbors of Mr. Hart armed themselves with shot guns and started in pursuit. As they neared the present residence of Mr. Schomp, south of the borough, some of the party started some wild game, at which they could not resist the temptation to shoot. This alarmed the fugitive, who was in the woods only a short distance away, and he then fled in the direction of Rosedale Mills.

On reaching the residence of Mr. Enoch Drake, who lived on the road leading from Mount Rose to Pennington, and who was a friend of the Hart's, he made the excuse that he was looking for a stray horse and borrowed a halter, with which he ended his wicked career by hanging himself in the woods near Honey Brook, on the farm now owned by S. D. Irwin, Esq., of Pennington, and near the present residence of David M. Voorhees, Esq. The place of his suicide is still known locally, as "Cuffee's Hollow," where after a long search his body was found by his pursuers.

The following verses written nearly or quite 125 years ago, are published for the first time, as a relic of the revolutionary period, and also for the reason that they give a very graphic description of an event which created great excitement among the settlers of old

Hopewell at the time of its occurrence. The manuscript is in possession of Enoch Drake, Esq., of Columbia Avenue, and has been in the possession of the Drake family for many years. While the author of the verses is unknown, it is fair to assume that they were composed by Mr. Joseph Titus, who was a neighbor of Mr. Hart, and who was much given to expressing himself in ryhmes. Two of the daughters of Mr. Titus, Hannah and Phebe, married Philemon and Elijah Drake, and the verses doubtless came into the possession of the Drake family through that channel.

In article No. 14, of this series, will be found the record of Mr. Titus as a soldier, and also some verses written by him for the Trenton Gazette in advertising a stolen horse in 1779.

The verses below were written about the same time, and in comparing them the striking resemblance in language and style will be apparent.

"Good people all to me give ear,
    A doleful story ye shall hear,
Of a sad murder that was done,
    Within the bounds of Hopewell town.

One Monday morning, as they say,
    Hart's wicked negro did him slay,
He took a knife to win the prize,
    And like to put out both his eyes.

The savage wretch had heart like steel,
    And no compassion did he feel ;
He violent hands on him did lay,
    And with an ax his master slay.

While he lay gasping on the ground,
    His life blood swiftly running down,
The doctor's help he then did crave,
    But all his skill could not him save.

He cried for mercy, as they say,
    The biggest part of all that day ;
Before the setting of the sun,
    His life was gone, his work was done.

We leave the dead into the grave,
    And follow after the black slave,
The innocent blood that he had spilt,
    Shall bring on him a heavy guilt.

Soon as the murder he had done,
    Then from all people he did run;
He took himself off to the wood,
    And there he thought on little good.

The neighbors then for him did look,
  And found him down by Honey Brook,
Hung with a rope upon a limb,
  No mortal eye did pity him.

The next day they did then prepare,
  A fire to burn his body there,
They chained it to the self same limb,
  And there they made an end of him.

All negroes who have life and breath,
  Take warning of his wretched death,
Don't take an ax or use a knife,
  To destroy your master's life."

Captain Timothy Titus (referred to above as the father of Elizabeth, wife of John H. Hart,) was born in 1746, and married about 1778, Patience Hoff. His father and grandfather were both named Timothy. The first Timothy was born in Newtown, Long Island, and emigrated to Hopewell Township about 1700. His father was Capt. Content of Newtown, Long Island, a sketch of whose history is given in No. 14 of these articles. The father of Content was Robert, who emigrated in the spring of 1635, in the ship Hopewell, Captain Bunlock.

Robert's parents were Silius and Constantia, of Roman descent, and residents of Hertfordshire, England, in 1600 or earlier. Silius died in 1637, and Constantia in 1667. Silius was doubtless the father of the Silius Titus who was in attendance upon Charles the first at Hallenby, and on June 4, 1647, performed a service for which he received a life annuity of fifty pounds. For a long account of Titus, see "Dictionary of National Biography," published in London in 1898.

Captain Timothy was enrolled as Lieutenant in Capt. Henry Phillips' Company, First Regiment, Hunterdon County, N. J., May 10, 1777, and was promoted to Captain. From records in the writer's possession it appears that he was still in the service in 1781, and probably continued until the close of the war. He was a brave and fearless officer and on one occasion, when surprised by a detachment of British cavalry, who were determined to capture the bold and intrepid soldier, his courage never wavered for an instant, and by resorting to a clever ruse he not only escaped, but won a bloodless victory and sent them flying in every direction, thinking that he had a whole regiment at his command. The incident happened not far from his residence, which was in the vicinity of Bake's mills, on the road leading from Pennington to Harbourton.

An account of his thrilling and exciting adventure was written in verse many years ago, by Mrs. Elizabeth Burroughs Roberts* of Romulus, New York, and are in part as follows :

"Those three same Mr. Hart's I knew,
    Daniel, John, and Levi too,
But that's not all I wish to tell,
    I knew the Titus' as well.

Both names were Timothy, father and son,
    In Jersey state near Harbourtown,
The younger was a Captain bold,
    I'll tell it you as I've been told.

The British lay at Trenton town,
    One day the Light Horse galloped down,
To take a prisoner for their own,
    Found Titus in the woods alone,
He saw their drift, and quick as thought,
    His courage to his aid he brought.

He called his men with loud huzzahs,
    And threw his arms with wild hurrahs,
So artfully did he deceive,
    He made those haughty foes believe,
Their only safety was in flight;
    They wheeled and fled with armor bright,
And hastened back to town so quick,
    They never knew the Yankee trick.

December 9, 1903.

---

*Mrs. Roberts was a daughter of Mr. Joseph Burroughs, who resided on the road between Harbourton and Washington's Crossing, and she married Mr. Phillip Roberts.

Mr. Burroughs emigrated to Seneca Falls, New York State, with his family in 1812, making the journey in a canvas covered wagon, as stated by Mr. W. H. B. Roberts, who is now a resident of Ithaca, New York, and is a grandson of Joseph Burroughs, and a son of the author of the verses.

Mrs. Roberts had another son, Professor Isaac P. Roberts, who was connected with Cornell University of Ithaca, New York, for several years, and is now a Professor in the Leland Stanford University of Palo Alto, California.

NUMBER XXIV.

In article No. 22, we gave a sketch of the transfer of the old mill property on Stony Brook, from Hon. John Hart and his brother Daniel to the Wikoff brothers of Philadelphia, on July 4, 1766. These Wikoffs were doubtless of the same family as Jacob, who married Sarah, daughter of Hon. John Hart, and were of the Monmouth County branch of the family, the ancestry of whom is given in a previous article of this series. These brothers were also the owners of large tracts of unimproved lands in northern Hunterdon and Sussex Counties, in this State, and in Bucks and Northampton Counties in Pennsylvania, and advertised two thousand acres for sale in the Trenton Gazette, on February 20, 1782. They owned the Glen Moore mills for a short time only, and on May 31, 1771, sold them to Francis Blackwell of Hopewell, who owned them about eight years, and on August 6, 1779, sold them to Rev. John Blackwell, a Baptist minister residing at Hopewell, but not a settled pastor.

This old mill deed of Blackwell to Blackwell, is in the writer's possession, is beautifully written on fine parchment, in the bold clear hand of Rev. John Blackwell, and after the lapse of a century and a quarter, is perfectly legible, and can be read with as much ease as any of the type written documents of the present day. In this deed he styles himself "Rev. John Blackwell of Hopewell, party of the second part, etc." By this instrument, Francis Blackwell conveyed the two adjoining tracts of land lying between the brook on the west and the "Great road leading to Rocky Hill" on the east, and from the mill to the Stony Brook road and the old mines, (excepting the lot of Jonas Wood on the corner). The upper tract containing 28¾, and the lower, or mill tract, 33¾ acres.

The consideration was fifteen hundred pounds, and the conveyance included the "mills, dams, wheels, gates, buildings," etc., and is described as the property conveyed to Francis Blackwell, by the Wikoff brothers, as above stated. The deed is signed by Francis Blackwell, in presence of Capt. Nathan Stout of Amwell, and Capt. Stephen Blackwell of Hopewell, the latter being a son of Francis, Sr., brother of Francis, Jr., and the great grandfather of our townsmen, David L., Nelson D., and Charles H. Blackwell.

The Blackwell family is of English origin, and that the name was one of considerable importance in England appears from the fact that no less than six towns in that kingdom bear the name of Blackwell.* Robert Blackwell, the progenitor of the family in America, is first found engaged as a merchant at Elizabethtown, N. J., in 1676. The same year he married for a second wife, Mary, daughter of Capt. John Manningham, of Manning's Island in the East River. He established his residence on that Island, and became the owner of the farm and Island, which eventually took his name, and which has been known for about two centuries as "Blackwell's Island." He died in 1717, and of his children, Robert the eldest, married Elizabeth, daughter of Francis Combes, of Newtown, Long Island.

They resided first at Newtown, and at the time of the great migration of Long Island families to Hopewell Township, about 1700 to 1710, Robert Blackwell and family were found among them settling on a farm adjoining his Newtown friend and neighbor, John Titus, (who came at the same time) about two miles east of Pennington; and near the confluence of Honey, and Stony Brooks.

Robert Blackwell, Jr., and Elizabeth Combes had children as follows, viz : Robert, Anna, Francis, Thomas, Jacob, Mary, Elizabeth.

Francis Blackwell of the above family born January 14, 1713, died November 11, 1791, married first, Elizabeth Cornell, by whom he had eleven children as follows, viz : John, born February 5, 1738 ; Elizabeth, born August 13, 1739 ; Thomas, born January 9, 1741 ; Martha, born November 17, 1742 ; Francis, born July 20, 1746 ; Jacob ; Elijah ; Jemima ; Stephen, born 1756 ; Amy ; Deborah.

Francis Blackwell married second, Sarah Burroughs who bore him five children, viz : Daniel, born February 14, 1780 ; Franey, born May 11, 1781 ; Actia, born October 17, 1782 ; Jonathan, born May 23, 1784 ; Nathaniel, born November 3, 1785.

---

*For coat of arms of the Blackwell family and also a sketch of the early family in America, see "Riker's Annals of Newtown." Page 354.

The writer is also indebted to Mr. Samuel H. Blackwell, cashier of the First National Bank of Princeton, N. J., who has in his possession, a large amount of data concerning the first Blackwell families of Hopewell Township.

Three of the above named sons by the first marriage, were soldiers of the revolution, Jacob, in Capt. Joab Houghton's Company, First Regiment, and Elijah and Stephen in Capt. Carle's troop of Light Horse, Elijah being also commissary of issues. Of the children of the second marriage, Col. Jonathan served with distinction in the war of 1812, and his biographer gives a glowing tribute to his memory as soldier and citizen.

Rev. John the eldest of the above family, was a student in the classical school of Rev. Isaac Eaton at Hopewell, and Rev. Morgan Edwards in his "Materials for a History of the Baptists," published in 1792, says of Mr. Blackwell, that "He had his education at the Hopewell school, obtained holy orders in the Hopewell church, July 23, 1764, and took the oversight of the Upper Freehold Baptist church in 1782,* that he resigned in 1788 to go to Hopewell, where he has a good plantation, and a commodious new house where he lives comfortably with his wife, Sarah Thomas, and their children, John, Lewis and Sarah."

The records show that Rev. John Blackwell was baptized into the fellowship of the Hopewell church, May 22, 1762, and was called upon to exercise his gifts for the ministry August 20, 1763. The records of the Upper Freehold church at Imlaystown, Monmouth County, state that Mr. Blackwell was a very acceptable pastor, and baptized thirty-one persons into the membership of that church. That he was a man of fine education and attainments, some of his well written and scholarly sermons still in existence abundantly prove, and in addition to his ministerial duties, he taught in the schools of the neighborhood at different times.

---

*The church of Upper Freehold is located at Imlaystown, Monmouth County, N. J.

The first pastor was Rev. David Jones, who was educated at Hopewell, and became one of the most noted and eminent ministers of the Baptist denomination. He was in the Revolutionary army under Washington as chaplain, and again during the campaigns against the Indians northwest of the Ohio, in 1794—96.

When the second war with Great Britian broke out in 1812, although seventy-six years of age, he once more volunteered his services and risked the fatigue and exposure of the march, the camp and the battle field, that he might minister comfort and consolation to the brave and noble men who were fighting their country's battles. The autograph of this consecrated old hero of the cross may be found in a Latin grammar in the writer's possession, which has been handed down through five generations of the family. It was used in Rev Isaac Eaton's school at Hopewell—1756-1766, and contains also the autograph of Micajah Phillips, another prominent minister of revolutionary times.

After a lapse of nearly one hundred and fifty years, we look upon the names of these distinguished men with a feeling akin to reverence and are glad that the boys of that period possessed the same inherent propensity to scribble their names on the margins of their school books as they do at the present day. Were it not for those names written in an idle moment, the little book would have had but little significance, but now it takes us back to the time when Mr. Eaton's school was an instrument of great good in this valley. So far as known this is the only book now in existence which was in use by the students there.

He was also an energetic man of affairs, engaged in various business enterprises as miller and farmer, before his call to upper Freehold, and after his return had a general store for several years on the corner of Broad Street and Greenwood Avenue, on the site now occupied by Mr. Simpson Hoagland. During the closing years of Rev. Oliver Hart's ministry, and until the settlement of Mr. Ewing, he kept the records of the old church, and frequently represented the church in the associations. His wife, Sarah Thomas, was doubtless a daughter of John Thomas, and a sister of Rev. David Thomas, A. M., "Who," says Benedict, in his history of the Baptists, "was educated at Hopewell, and became one of the most eloquent and successful ministers of his day, and one of the founders of the Baptist church in Virginia."

Rev. John Blackwell and Sarah Thomas had three children who lived to maturity, viz : John T., Lewis and Elizabeth.

John T., born 1772, died April 4, 1831, aged 59, married Susan, daughter of Deacon James Hunt, of Hopewell, and resided at Hopewell until about 1800, when they removed to Flemington, N. J. John T. Blackwell was appointed a Judge of the Court of Common Pleas, February 8, 1804, and we learn from the History of Hunterdon County that he served the County either as Clerk or Surrogate from 1810 until 1829. John T. Blackwell and Susan Hunt had seven children as follows : Clarissa, Sarah, James H., Oliver H., John P., Jemima and Elizabeth.

Many of the above named children lived to old age, but none of them ever married except John P , who married Miss Maria George of Flemington, doubtless the daughter of Charles George, Esq., who was the founder of the Hunterdon Gazette in 1825, and its editor until 1832. John P. Blackwell and Maria George had children as follows, viz : Susan, Charles, Thomas, Wilson and Henry. This family all removed to New York City and all are now deceased except Henry, who resides in the West. James H. Blackwell, son of John T., was appointed postmaster at Flemington by President James Monroe in 1820 and held the office until 1830.

Dr. Oliver H. Blackwell, son of John T., resided in Flemington and was a physician by profession, but never practiced within the memory of the writer and died in 1877, aged 80 years. Lewis, son of Rev. John Blackwell, married and settled in Philadelphia. He died May 29, 1810, aged about thirty-six.

Miss Anna Sutphin of our borough, who is a great granddaughter of Rev. John, has in her possession a letter written by Mrs. Margaret Blackwell, widow of Lewis, to his sister, Mrs. Elizabeth Stillwell, on the day of his funeral.   She expresses her deep sorrow in her sore bereavement, and writes that he was laid to rest in the cemetery of the Second Baptist church of Philadelphia by the side of their only child—a little boy, who had died a short time before his father.

Elizabeth, daughter of Rev. John Blackwell, married Cornelius, son of Capt. John Stilwell of Woodsville, N. J., and had two daughters, viz: Sarah, the second wife of Deacon Benjamin Drake of Hopewell, and Elizabeth, born June 20, 1814, died Jan. 20, 1903, married Richard Stout Sutphin, and had two daughters, Adelia, who married Henry D. Sutphin of the borough, and Miss Anna referred to above.

Capt. John Stilwell, alluded to above, was a revolutionary soldier in Capt. William Tucker's Company, First Regiment, Hunterdon County, and also served for a time in a company of artillery.

He married Sarah Stevenson of Hunterdon County about 1760, and they had ten children who lived to maturity.   The following order may not be exactly correct:

Daniel, married and resided about two miles north of Linvale, Hunterdon County.

Hannah, married John Johnson, and removed to Sussex County.

William, never married.

Augustine, born November 1, 1769, married and resided about two miles northwest of Hopewell, on the farm now owned by Garret Hunt, Esq.   His children were Anna, born November 10, 1800, married Gabriel Hortman of Snydertown, N. J.   Sarah, born August 4, 1804, married John Hixson, and Stephen H., who occupied the homestead and reared a large family, among whom were John, residing in Amwell Township near the homestead; Simpson D., a merchant at Linvale, William C., of our borough,* and Caroline, who was the first wife of Israel P. LaRue.

*Albert, son of William, is the only great great grandson of Capt. John, bearing the Stilwell name.
    He is the eighth generation from lieutenant, afterward Sheriff Nicholas Stilwell, tobacco planter of Manhattan Island, in 1639, and the tenth generation from Rev. John Still, an episcopal clergyman, who about 1580 was appointed by Queen Elizabeth, the Bishop of Bath and Wells, in Somersetshire, England.
    The family went to reside at Wells and they became known as Still of Wells, Still O'Wells, and finally as the Stilwell family.   The Bishop died in 1607, and is buried in the Cathedral of the city of Wells.

Elizabeth, daughter of Capt. John, married Edmond Roberts of Pennington.

Mary, married Cornelius Duzenbury of Mt. Airy, Hunterdon County.

Sarah, born January 6, 1780, married first, Samuel Brown, by whom she had four children, viz: Andrew, born November 6, 1801; Susannah, born March 12, 1804; Charity, born December 13, 1805; and Keturah, born February 2, 1809, married Joshua Ketcham and had one son, Samuel B. Ketcham, Esq., now a resident of Pennington. Samuel Brown died May 18, 1812, aged 34, and Sarah married second, Joseph M. Van Cleve, son of Col. John, and had one daughter, Elizabeth, who married Joseph B. Horn, who now resides on the homestead farm of his father-in-law, and at the ripe age of four score, is still active and vigorous and the writer is indebted to him and his daughter, Miss Ella, for records of this branch of the family.

Charity, daughter of Capt. John, born November 8, 1784, became the first wife of Joseph M. Van Cleve, and the mother of John S. Van Cleve, and Phebe, wife of David L. Titus, all of whom are are now deceased.

Phebe married Samuel Van Cleve, son of Col. John, and became the mother of Rev. Crook Stevenson Van Cleve, a distinguished Methodist clergyman, who was well known to many of our readers.

Cornelius, whose family is included above in the records of Rev. John Blackwell's family.

February 17, 1904.

NUMBER XXV.

It had been our intention to give a more extended sketch of the old Stilwell family in our last article, but space would not admit of more than a brief foot note, giving the earliest record of the family in Somersetshire, England, the origin of the name and its evolution from Rev. John Still bishop of Wells, to "Still of Wells," "Still O'Wells" and Stillwell.*

We learn from the traditions of the family that in the early part of the seventeenth century three brothers, John, Jasper and Nicholas Stilwell, who claimed royal blood from their connection with the house of the Stuarts—escaped from the persecutions of the Star Chamber (or High Commission Court) by flight, emigrating first to Holland. In 1638 Nicholas emigrated to America, and settled on Manhattan Island, and in 1639 his name is enrolled in the Court records as "Nicholas Stilwell, the tobacco planter." His tobacco plantation, or "Bowerie," was located in the vicinity of Turtle Bay, at a place named by him Hopton, in honor of the family of his first wife.

Some of the courses in the old deed for this plantation are exceedingly interesting. There is a sort of fascination in reading of a "creek running into Kipp's Bay, where they cross on the stones," and it has a very romantic sound when we read further of a large stream emptying into Turtle Bay "where the beech tree hangs over the water." All these places have long since been obliterated in the march of improvement, and it is difficult for us to imagine that "where they cross on the stones" was at the foot of Thirty-fourth Street, and "the beech tree" at the foot of Forty-seventh Street on the East River. From there the line extended back to the "Indian trail," which subsequently became known as the "Old Boston Post

---

*See "Life and times of Nicholas Stilwell," an intensely interesting history of the earliest settlements on Manhattan and Long Island, published in 1878, by Benjamin Marshall Stillwell.

Road," leading from the foot of Broadway up through the centre of the Island to Westchester County.

During the Indian outbreak in 1643, Hopton was destroyed, and Nicholas prudently chose a new residence nearer the Fort, purchasing a house and lot on the north side of Beaver Street, where the stores number twenty-three and twenty-five, Beaver Street now stand. The tobacco plantation he continued to own until April 18, 1653, when he sold it to Lubbert Von Dincklage, who the deed goes on to state was a Dutchman. This statement would seem to be entirely superfluous, as the name in itself would be sufficient to indicate his nationality.

Nicholas Stilwell married in England, Abigail, daughter of Robert Hopton, and sister of Sir Ralph Hopton. They were of royal lineage, and on one occasion Sir Ralph saved the life of the Queen, by taking her on his horse with him and conveying her to a place of safety. Nicholas and Abigail had two sons both born in Holland Richard, born 1634 and Nicholas born 1636. Nicholas married second, in New York, Anne Van Dycke of Holland, by whom he had six children, viz: Anne, born 1643 ; Abigail, 1645 ; William, 1648 ; Thomas, 1651 ; Daniel, 1653, and Jeremiah, 1661.

At the time of the Indian outbreak in 1643, Nicholas Stilwell was elected Lieutenant of a military company, organized among the settlers for mutual protection, and in 1649–50, he purchased another tobacco plantation, this time at Gravesend, Long Island, the agreement reading as follows, viz :

"October 16, 1649. Lieftenant Stillwell bargained, and agreed with George Homes, for his whole plantation for ye use of his Sonne Richard, ye said Lieft. Stillwell has to pay for yt, unto ye said George Homes, ye somme of nine hundred pound weight of good merchantable tobacco in leaf. One hundred pound weight to be paid at ye Christmas tyme twelve months, which will be in ye yeare 1650. Ye said Lieft. Stillwell to have all ye crops upon ye said land, and also housings, houses, ye garden, and all ye priveleges, and appurtances in any way pertaining thereto. For ye said summe of tobacco, as above specified, ye said George Homes is to bring him one freight of goods from ye Fort, in his boat to ye plantation aforesaid. Ye said George Homes has in his agreement excepted one bedd of parsnipps."

An entry on the margin reads as follows, viz : "Lieft. Stillwell has paid William Golding* by George Homes his apportment, the eight hundred weight of tobacco, November 22, 1650, as expressed, and Geo. Homes is satisfied therewith.''

This farm, which is situated on what is called the Coney Island road, was still in the family about twenty years ago, being owned by Mr. C. J. Striker, who inherited it from his mother. who was a lineal descendant of the first Nicholas.

In 1664 Nicholas Stilwell selected a site for a home on the eastern shore of Staten Island, below the narrows, upon which his brother John had settled twenty-five years before, and called it Dover.† Here a block house was erected as a protection against the Indians, and here he settled with his younger sons, Thomas, William, Daniel and Jeremiah; also his sons-in-law, Nathaniel Brittian and Samuel Holmes. Before moving to Dover he had served a term as High Sheriff and had a stormy career during the conflict between the English and Dutch, the details of which we cannot enter into at this time. At Dover he spent the declining years of his eventful life in peace and quiet, and died December 28, 1671, surrounded by his children and grandchildren. His will dated December 23, 1671, is recorded in the Surrogate's office of New York, Liber 1, of Wills, page 168.

Among the most prominent descendants of Nicholas Stilwell, we might mention Hon. Silas M. Stilwell, whose distinguished service in Congress is a matter of history. He was a son of Rev. John, one of the most noted preachers of his day.

Rev. Richard Stilwell, a grandson of William, was one of the founders of the Baptist church in America, and was known as the "silver tongued preacher of Staten Island." He was pastor of the Baptist church on "Golden's Hill," in New York City, in 1724.

General Garret Stilwell's and Col. Richard's names, as well as several others, are on the roster of officers and men in the continental army.

The Nicholas Stilwell who settled at Woodsville about 1750, was doubtless descended from one of the grandchildren of the first Nicholas, who had settled in the vicinity of Middletown, Monmouth County, about 1680, where a large number of their descen-

---

*The ancestor of the Golden family of Hopewell and the owner of Golden's Hill in 1724, now in the heart of New York City. See article 9 of this series.

†Dover was for many years the most important and populous settlement on Staten Island, but for the past 150 years its location has been almost forgotten.

dants are still found. In examining the records in the office of the Secretary of the State at Trenton it is found that there were several Nicholas Stilwells contemporary about one hundred and fifty years ago, all from the same old stock, one of them living in Cape May County and another at the same time in Sussex, but the bulk of the family in Monmouth. Until the contrary is proven, we shall hold to the view that the Woodsville Nicholas was a son of Daniel and came to old Hopewell Township with the Monmouth colony about 1740–50.

On August 27, 1761, Nicholas Stilwell sold to Adam Ege, twenty acres of land on Stony Brook, about a half mile east of Woodsville. This tract was doubtless woodland, and adjoined other lands of Adam Ege on the north.

The will of Nicholas Stilwell is dated August 20, 1801, and mentions his two sons, John and Daniel, and daughter, Rachel Humphreys. He also leaves a legacy to his "sister, Else Milnor." He mentions his two little black girls, "Jin and Peg," whom he orders bound out to good places, "and if convenient to do so, they are to be taught to read the bible." When they arrive at the age of twenty-one years they are to have their freedom. The executors of his will are his sons John and Daniel, and the witnesses his neighbors, Andrew and Burroughs Smith, who resided a half mile west of Woodsville, now known as the Robert Hunt farm adjoining the Stilwell's.

John Stilwell married Sarah Stevenson, and a brief history of their family was given in number 24 of this series.

As one of old Hopewell's most prominent citizens in the early part of the last century was of this old Stevenson family, and a number of our leading families have descended from the same stock, we will give a short sketch of the ancestry of this family in this connexion.

William Stevenson, the father of Mrs. John Stilwell, was the son of Edward Stevenson and Charity Field, and was born about 1696. He married in 1721, Hannah Hicks, who was born in 1704. Their children were Robert, Edward, John, Thomas, William, Augustine, Cornelius, Mary, Deborah, Charity, Susannah, Phebe, Sarah.

Of this family John Stevenson, born March 28, 1728, married 1754, Elizabeth Throckmorton, the ceremony being performed in Christ P. E. church of Middletown, at Shrewsbury, and they soon

after removed to the vicinity of Ringoes, Hunterdon County. Their
children were as follows, viz: Hannah, born January 26, 1755,
baptized in the old Shrewsbury church, and died February 23, 1755.
Robert, born February 9, 1756, resided in Philadelphia, and died in
1791. William, born October 19, 1757; married Rowland Newton, and also resided in Philadelphia, where he died without children, and his large fortune was divided among his nephews and
nieces in Hunterdon County. John, born February 12, 1760, married June 13, 1782, Catherine Corshon, and had one daughter, Margaret, who became the wife of Samuel Wyckoff, son of Daniel Wyckoff and Ursula Craig of Monmouth County, afterward settled in
Hunterdon. Daniel Wyckoff was born in 1743, and his father,
John, in 1709, whose ancestry is briefly sketched in article 15 of
this series.

Samuel Wyckoff and Margaret Stevenson had children as follows, viz: Elizabeth, married Andrew Dunn, son of Isaac of Hopewell.* John S. married Sarah Hoff; Ursula, married Elijah Fish;
Hannah, married Judge John Conrad; Catherine, married Cornelius L. Wynkoop; William, married Cornelia Carroll; Rowland,
married David Bishop Skillman; Daniel, never married, and Sarah,
who married Dr. Benjamin Snowden of Bucks County, Pa. All of
this large family resided in this township at, or near Pennington, except the first two, and the last, and the widow of Judge Conrad still
survives at the age of 92, residing with her only daughter, Mrs.
Joseph C. Bunn of Pennington. Her brother William, who is several years her junior, is also living, and resides at Ivyland, Bucks
County, Pa.

John Stevenson, the grandfather of Mrs. Conrad, was one of
four revolutionary patriots who at the age of 17 went to Elizabethtown on service alone. They were at first denied pay and rations, but

---

*Isaac Dunn was one of the aristocrats of old Hopewell in the early part of the last
century. He was born February 15, 1761, near New Market, Middlesex County, where he
spent his early childhoood. He was a revolutionary soldier, and when less than twenty
years of age he came to Hopewell, and married Jerusha, daughter of Thomas Blackwell.
They had two sons and nine daughters all of whom married except the youngest daughter.

Mr. Dunn was a member of the New Jersey assembly, and was a deacon in the old
Baptist church as early as 1808, and was one of the delegates at the Philadelphia association held on October 4, of that year. He was one of the few who drove out to church with
his chaise and colored driver, and with his silk stockings and gold knee buckles, he created
quite a sensation among the plain old fashioned farmers of that period. He was one of the
charter members of the Hunterdon County Bible Society in 1816, his colleagues from Hopewell Township being Rev. John Boggs, Abraham Stout, James Stevenson, Joshua Bunn and
John Carpenter.

Col. Seeley finally attached them to Capt. Updike's company, where they served out their time and were honorably discharged. Those who accompanied Mr. Stevenson were George Muirheid, Uriel Titus and John Taylor.

Mr. Stevenson was an active member of St. Andrews Episcopal church of Ringoes, now located at Lambertville, and he resided one mile south of Ringoes, owning the flouring and fulling mills on the Rocktown road. His sister, Hannah, born December 3, 1761, married Andrew Muirheid, (son of Andrew), of Harbourton. They left no children.

Capt. James, son of John Stevenson and Elizabeth Throckmorton, born October 16, 1763, married Feb. 17, 1795, Susan, daughter of John Price Hunt, who at that time resided on the farm now occupied by William D. Hill of Glen Moore.

On March 6, 1801, Mr. Stevenson purchased of Moses Quick the farm now owned by John L. Burroughs on the road from Marshall's Corner to Woodsville, and resided there until a short time before his death, when he removed to Pennington. Mr. Stevenson was very prominent in the county, holding many offices of trust and responsibility, and was known as one of the strongest characters of his day, very decided in his opinions and a very fluent talker. Uncle Jimmie's opinions carried great weight among his acquaintances, as he was known to be very well informed on all the current topics of the day, and he could always draw a crowd of attentive listeners.

On the evening of Dec. 30, 1839, he visited his old friend Roswell Howe, a prominent teacher residing in Pennington, and on his arrival at home he complained of feeling unwell and expired immediately. His sudden death was a great shock to the community in which he had been so eminently useful, and he was greatly lamented by a very large circle of acquaintances.

James Stevenson and Susan Hunt had two children, John Hunt, born February 20, 1796, died August 27, 1827, and Elizabeth, who died at Princeton in 1867, unmarried, and is buried beside her parents at Pennington.

April 6, 1904.

NUMBER XXVI.

The old farm where James Stevenson spent so many years of his life, is an historic old spot, and deserves more than merely the passing notice given in our last. Something of its earliest history is given in a foot note to article number 13, of this series.

On May 5, 1756, it was purchased of the heirs of Col. Daniel Coxe, by Benj. Pelton of Long Island, and then included the farms of Joseph B. Horn and N. Stout Voorhees. Benjamin Pelton's will dated September 30, 1775, devised it to his heirs, and on July 5, 1776, Adam Ege, as surviving executor, sold 57½ acres on the west side of the road to Charles Sexton, Jr., brother of Hon. Jared, the Surrogate, Legislator and Judge of 1777 to 1785. This farm is now owned by Joseph B. Horn, Esq., and we have the record of all the transfers from Charles Sexton to the present owner, which we hope to publish in a subsequent article.

Benjamin Pelton's widow died in 1780, when 120 acres of the middle part of the tract descended to her grandson, John Pelton, who on May 2, 1796, sold it to Moses Quick for 1050 pounds in gold, and John united his fortunes with the great tide of emigration then flowing toward Sussex County and central New York State.

During the revolution, and earlier, the old Pelton place was kept as a hotel, and as it was located on the great thoroughfare from tide water navigation at Trenton, to the northern part of the state, it was a noted stopping place for the immense trains of wagons loaded with produce from Hunterdon, Warren and Sussex Counties. That part of the state contained a population of forty thousand as early as 1790, and was increasing very rapidly with families from the eastern and central portions of the state. We hope to give some details of the great traffic over this road in a subsequent article.

The old house which occupied the site of the present mansion of Mr. John L. Burroughs, was a long and low old colonial structure, very substantially built of stone, having one door and three windows in front, and dormer windows in the roof. It had a basement or cellar kitchen in the rear, in which was enacted the famous

''Sam'' Pelton adventure, which tradition has handed down for nearly one hundred and fifty years. During the early settlement of the country, there was a considerable traffic carried on in stolen horses, and it was very rarely that the property was recovered or the thieves apprehended.

Sam Pelton, only son of Benjamin, was a wild and reckless youth, fond of excitement and adventure, who attended the races near his old home on Long Island, and had the reputation of furnishing some good horses for the sporting fraternity of this famous resort. As his associates were not of the best, he was regarded with suspicion by the old settlers, who thought that he knew something of the route over which some of their favorite horses had mysteriously disappeared. Accordingly when the report became circulated that Sam Pelton was keeping a horse in the cellar of the old house, they organized a posse of neighboring farmers who determined to investigate, and if the report was found to be correct, to bring him to an account.

Knowing him to be a fearless character, of great strength and daring, they advanced very cautiously until they reached the cellar door, and hearing that he was inside they demanded his surrender. Finding that he was not disposed to yield without a struggle, they opened the door, which was no sooner ajar, than Sam made a sudden dash for the centre of the posse, throwing himself against them with tremendous force, striking out right and left, and shouting at the top of his voice, ''Clear the road for Sam Pelton!'' The besieging party were not prepared for such an attack, and were so amazed and dumfounded at his daring, that they made no effort whatever to stop him, and while they stood in breathless astonishment wondering what was going to happen, Sam had mounted one of their horses which stood outside, and without a parting salute left this region, never to return. When his would-be captors had recovered sufficiently to realize what a tremendous rush of events had transpired in a remarkably brief period, they were chagrined and disgusted beyond all expression. In playing the role of detectives they had not only made a most dismal failure, but their prisoner had escaped with one of their best horses and all the equipments. Within the memory of the writer, Sam Pelton's escape was still the standing joke of the neighborhood where it occurred, and when the old people gathered around the fireside to recount the traditions of their ancestors, the Sam Pelton episode was never forgotten.

The expression, "Clear the road for Sam Pelton," became proverbial at once among the old settlers, and after the lapse of a century and a half, has not become entirely obsolete. At a vendue or other gathering of farmers, it was frequently heard as late as fifty years ago, when a person wanted to pass through a crowd, and as they stood good naturedly aside, the remark was often heard, "By all means give Sam plenty of room."

In digressing to give a sketch of the above incident, we omitted to mention Crook Stevenson, the youngest brother of James, who resided first, I think, in Philadelphia and later in Trenton. He amassed quite a fortune, and lived in grand style for those times. While spending his vacation at the seaside in the summer of 1820, he was accidently drowned at, or near Long Branch. The inventory of his estate is on file in the office of the Secretary of State of Trenton, and is dated September 7, 1820. The administrators were William, James and John H. Stevenson.

Augustine Stevenson, son of William, and uncle of James, was a member of the Provincial Congress in 1775. He married November 14, 1770, Caroline Willett, who was born May 5, 1750. She was a daughter of Samuel Willett, of Black Stump, Long Island, whose father was John, and grandfather, Col. Thomas Willett, of Flushing, Long Island. Caroline Willett Stevenson's will, dated October 10, 1810, mentions daughters, Elizabeth and Susan Runyan, grandson Augustine Runyan, and Caroline, daughter of her son Robert. She also mentions sons, Augustine and William Stevenson, and her son, Willett Stevenson's children. Her executors were her son-in-law, Daniel Coxe Runyan, her son Augustine Stevenson, and George Muirheid.

Reference was made in our last article to Roswell Howe, Esq., of Pennington, as an intimate friend of James Stevenson, and it had been our intention to give a short sketch of Mr. Howe at that time, but space would not admit.

Mr. Howe was a teacher of unusual prominence, and nearly three score years of his life were passed as a successful, and greatly beloved instructor of youth in this county. Nearly one hundred years ago, when but a youth, he was known as the "Yankee Schoolmaster," and rose very rapidly in his profession, soon making many warm friends among the most prominent people of the locality. He was born in Ridgefield, Conn., in 1792, came to Lawrenceville in 1812, and soon after married Miss Rebecca, daughter of Philip Hendrickson, Esq., of Lawrence Township. Mr. Howe remained at Lawrenceville about twenty years, and it was the birth place of all his five children, who were as follows, viz : Mary, wife of Sheriff John Muirheid of Pennington; Frances, wife of Augustine M. Vankirk, architect and contractor, also of Pennington ; W. Keith, William and Harriet L., who still survives, residing in Philadelphia. To this intelligent and accomplished lady the writer is indebted for some of the facts of this sketch.

In 1836 Mr. Vankirk erected the building afterward known as Evergreen Hall in Pennington, where for some years after Mr. Howe, assisted by two of his daughters, conducted a very popular Young Ladies school, which became widely known a few years later as one of the leading schools of its kind in the state.   After this school was purchased by Miss Mary L. Hale, about 1843, Mr. Howe taught several years in the old Academy at Pennington, when he removed to Trenton, and taught a school very similar to the Business Colleges of the present day.

Mr. Howe was a very accomplished gentleman of the old school, whom many of our readers will remember.   For some years before his death he was the Senior Warden of St. Michael's church in Trenton.   His death occurred on April 5, 1871, at the ripe age of nearly four score years, and the press of Trenton gave a glowing tribute to his memory, as a pious, patriotic, kind-hearted citizen, greatly beloved by a large circle of friends and acquaintances.

Referring again to the proprietors of the old mill at Glen Moore, the transfers have all been given from the earliest settlement of the country down to the period of the revolution.

Francis Blackwell, Jr., who purchased it May 31, 1771, was born July 20, 1746, and married Elizabeth, daughter of Ralph Hart. Mr. Blackwell resided many years on the farm just north of the borough of Hopewell, now owned by Prof. Edgerly, which he purchased of William Seaman of New Brunswick on June 26, 1786. The deed in the writer's possession, describes it as ''the premises on which Francis Blackwell now dwells,'' and as Mr. Seaman was a non-resident, Mr. Blackwell had doubtless occupied it several years prior to the purchase.

Francis Blackwell and Elizabeth Hart had at least one son, John, who is mentioned in the will of his uncle, Jacob Blackwell, as the ''son of my brother Francis.''   On April 22, 1791, he sold this farm of 133 acres to his brother-in-law, Moses Hart, and as nothing more is heard of any of the family, the presumption is that Francis joined the great migration of Hopewell families to Sussex County. Sussex included Warren County at that time, and we find the names of Francis, Robert, Elijah and John Blackwell, on the records of that county, a few years later.

Ralph Hart, alluded to above as the father-in-law of Francis Blackwell, Jr., was one of the leading citizens of Hopewell Township one hundred and fifty years ago. He was the son of Major Ralph, one of the pioneers of old Hopewell two hundred years ago. Major Ralph was a brother of Capt. Edward, father of Hon. John, the "signer," whose family record is found in number 23 of these articles.

Ralph Hart resided at Marshall's Corner, two miles west of Hopewell, the old house standing on the east side of the Trenton and Flemington road, a few rods north of the line of the old Mercer and Somerset railroad, now a part of the Doctor McCauley farm. Nothing remains to indicate the exact location of the house which sheltered this noted family of patriots during the revolution. Here his distinguished cousin, Hon. John, found refuge at different times, when his life was in imminent danger from scouting parties of the British army, who were unceasing in their efforts to capture him, that they might claim the large reward offered for his "body dead or alive."

When the army of Cornwallis was stationed at Pennington, in December, 1776, one of his outposts was near Rynear Vansyckel's old tavern, kept I think at that time by Jesse Christopher. This house stood on the east side of the Trenton road, about a half mile south of Mr. Hart's and nearly opposite the residence of Mr. G. B. Burd. When Mr. Hart learned that the enemy had made an encampment so near his residence, he at once drove nearly all his his stock over in the Woosamonsa mountain to a very secluded spot near Conrad Marshall's, now the residence of Mr. Azariah Phillips, leaving a trusty and faithful old slave, who was a genuine Guinea negro, in charge of the premises. That Mr. Hart was betrayed by some of his Tory neighbors, is evident from the fact that he lost all the stock that he had taken to the mountain, including some very valuable blooded horses, while some fat hogs ready for market, which he had left at the farm, were all the stock which remained after the British had resumed their march to New Brunswick.

On one occasion Mr. Hart discovered a detachment of British

cavalry approaching his house just in time to run out and throw himself in a ditch nearby, and nothing but the unswerving fidelity of the old slave prevented him from being captured. They questioned the old negro very closely about his master, but he resolutely denied all knowledge of his hiding place, and finally they held out a handful of gold, informing him that he could have a whole hat crown full if he would tell them where to find his master. Finding that he could not be bought they were obliged to give it up, thinking that probably Mr. Hart was many miles away, while in reality he was within the sound of their voices, trembling no doubt in every limb, lest the tempting offer should prove too great for his faithful old servant. The British entered the house and cut open all the feather beds, scattering their contents to the winds, their object being to ascertain whether they contained any silverware or other valuables.

Mr. Hart's old-fashioned high clock did not escape, and being too bulky to carry away, they beheaded it and took the time piece with them to headquarters. After they had left the neighborhood it was found in the hay mow in Jesse Christopher's barn on the farm of Gideon B. Burd. Here they had their headquarters, keeping their horses in the old barn while the hay loft furnished sleeping apartments for all that could crowd in.

The weather was extremely cold, and they visited every house in the neighborhood, robbing them of every blanket they could find, leaving some entirely destitute, in order to keep themselves as comfortable as possible. The old barn is still standing, and is one of the few relics which has withstood the ravages of time and it is an object of great interest to all who are familiar with its history.

May 11, 1904.

NUMBER XXVII.

Ralph Hart married first, Jemima, daughter of George Woolsey, one of old Hopewell's most prominent pioneers, who settled 204 years ago on the farm southwest of Pennington, now occupied by Charles M. Woolsey, who is a descendant of the sixth generation from the first owner, the farm having been in possession of the family continuously during this long period. Ralph Hart and Jemima Woolsey had one son and three daughters, viz : Noah, Jerusha, Hannah and Elizabeth.

Noah became one of the most distinguished physicians of his time, having had exceptional advantages, first as a student in Philadelphia and later in London and Edinburgh. He married in 1764, Rachel, daughter of Rev. Charles McKnight of Middletown Point, (now Matawan), Monmouth County, who, previous to the revolution, was one of the supplies for the New Side Presbyterian church of Pennington, which has been mentioned in a previous article. Mr. McKnight was a chaplain in the continental army, was taken prisoner, and his church burned in 1777. He died on one of the loathsome prison ships in New York harbor. On June 9, 1779, his son, Captain Richard, was captured at Tinton Falls, near Shrewsbury, and met the same fate as his father.

Dr. Noah Hart located in New York City soon after his marriage, and was very successful in his profession until his death, which occurred while he was still in the prime of life.

Jerusha, daughter of Ralph Hart, married Moses Hart, son of Nathaniel, and a cousin of her father. Nathaniel Hart died in 1742, while all his children were under age, his sons Moses and Ephraim under 16. A copy of his will is in the writer's possession, the original being on file in the office of the Secretary of State at Trenton.

In article number 22 of this series, we have given the genealogy of this Hart family back to John of Massachusetts, 1671, and John of Newtown, Long Island, 1712, giving documentary proof

that all the Hart families who settled in Hopewell Township about
1700, were of the same New England and Long Island family.

Moses and Jerusha Hart settled first on the small farm one mile
southwest of Hopewell now owned by Mr. Montag, where I think
Moses followed his trade of blacksmith for many years.   On April
22, 1791, he purchased the farm north of Hopewell as stated in our
last, where he died on June 3, 1812.   They had daughters Jemima,
Catharine, and perhaps others.   Mrs. Hart survived her husband
many years, residing on the farm where she died April 12, 1835.
They are buried at Pennington.

Hannah, daughter of Ralph Hart, married Lott Phillips, a revolutionary soldier in Capt. Henry Phillips' company, First Regiment, Hunterdon County.   His death probably occurred previous to
1782, as on September 18 of that year Mrs. Phillips presented a bill
for damages sustained, which were awarded in accordance with the
provisions of an act of the General Assembly of New Jersey, approved October 23, 1781.

"No 25.   Inventory of the loss and damage Hannah Phillips
sustained by the American troops in the year 1777.

	£—S—D	£– S—D
1 Pair Stays	0 35 0	
10 lb Wool and bag	0 23 0	
	— — —	2 18 0
1 Pr Steelyards	0 10 0	
15 Bottles	0 5 0	
1 Flannel Blanket	0 15 0	
	— — —	1 10 0
1 Pr Buckskin Breeches	0 20 0	
1 Pr Boots	0 15 0	
	— — —	1 15 0
		6 03 0

"Ralph Hart being duly sworn doth depose & say that he verily believes that Hannah Phillips was plundered of the articles
charg'd in the above inventory.   Signed Ralph Hart."

Elizabeth, daughter of Ralph Hart, married Francis Blackwell,
Jr., whose history is given in our last.

We have no record of the death of the first Mrs. Hart, but we
have the record that on September 5, 1770, he married Penelope,

daughter of Thomas Anderson, and granddaughter of Cornelius, another of the earliest pioneers of old Hopewell. They had one child, Mary, who became the wife of Esq. George Smith, son of Timothy, a short sketch of whose ancestry is given in article number 21. He was known as "Big George" to distinguish him from his nephew George, son of his brother Andrew, who was also a justice, and prominent in the affairs of old Hunterdon County.

"Big George" was the father of Capt. Ralph Hart Smith, and the grandfather of Stephen B. Smith of Pennington, whom many will remember as one of our leading citizens forty or fifty years ago, large hearted and liberal, as well as almost a giant in stature. George Smith and Mary Hart had also two daughters, viz : Ellen, wife of Morgan Scudder of Ewing, and Abigail wife of Dr. John S. Mershon of Lawrence.

Miss Ellen Scudder Mershon, a daughter of Dr. John and a granddaughter of Esq. George Smith, is still living and resides at Zanesville, Ohio, to whom the writer is indebted for some of the incidents given in our last. She states that she remembers hearing her grandmother Smith say that her mother, Mrs. Ralph Hart, was accustomed to dress in disguise, whenever the British were in the neighborhood, and that she never walked in the public road, nor remained two nights in succession in the same house. The British were especially anxious to capture Ralph Hart, or some of his family, for the purpose of compelling them to divulge the hiding places of John, the signer.

The will of Ralph Hart is dated December 3, 1782, and his first bequest is to Dr. Noah, to whom he leaves five pounds as his "birthright." To his youngest daughter Mary, then about ten years of age, he leaves "twenty pounds extra," besides bedding, etc. The balance of his estate is to be divided between his wife, Penelope, and four daughters, Jerusha, Hannah, Elizabeth and Mary, share and share alike. His executors are his son-in-law, Moses Hart, and Jared Sexton. The witnesses are his neighbors, John P. Hunt, Roger and William Larison.

On January 3, 1774, Penelope Hart was granted letters of administration on the estate of her father, Thomas Anderson. Her three brothers, Andrew, Reuben and Amos, who were evidently under age at that time, subsequently went to Kentucky about the same time as their neighbors, Jesse Hunt, Benjamin Guild and others.

On September 25, 1785, Moses Hart advertised the Ralph Hart

farm for sale in the Trenton Gazette, describing it as a very pleasantly situated farm of 122 acres, "whereon Ralph Hart deceased dwelt," lying three miles above Pennington, on the great road to Amwell, having thereon a large convenient stone dwelling house, with frame barn, and outbuildings.

In our last article the fact was mentioned that Francis Blackwell, Jr., son-in-law of Ralph Hart, resided on the farm north of Hopewell now owned by Prof. Edgerly.   On June 23 to 25, 1778, when the army under Washington was encamped on this, and the adjoining farms of Hon. John Hart and Joseph Golden, now owned by Messrs. A. L. Holcombe and the late Wm. B. Van Pelt, they had access to the public road through the lane by Mr. Blackwell's house.

Some of the officers were doubtless quartered there, and as Mr. Blackwell's furniture was damaged, and other property appropriated to public use, damages were awarded under the act given above in the case of Mrs. Phillips.

"No. 42.   Inventory of the loss and damage Francis Blackwell sustained by the American army in June, 1778.

	£—S—D	£—S—D
1 Clock	15 0 0	
1 Pr Tongs,	7 6	
2 Bu Salt,	15 0	
	— — —	16 02 06
1 Ax,	7 6	
1 Womans Saddle,	30 00	
1 Fat Calf,	20 00	
	— — —	2 17 06
1 Warming Pan	15 00	
1 Whitening Pott,	5 00	
	— — —	1 00 00
9 Geese,	18 00	
Half Hogshead Tobacco,	100 00	
	— — —	5 18 00
	— — —	25 18 00"

Many farmers brought in bills for damages done to fences at different times during the war, but the probability is that they did not destroy Mr. Blackwell's fences, as General Washington had given strict orders on June 22, before leaving New Hope, that no fences should be destroyed on the march.

In taking a retrospection of army life during the revolution, we love to think of the grand old patriots as staid, dignified old soldiers, whose only thought and purpose was to rescue their beloved land from the tyranny and oppression of the British crown. While that noble purpose was doubtless ever uppermost in their minds, we must remember that a very large proportion of the officers were very young men, and large numbers of the men serving under them were under twenty years of age, full of life and vivacity, who, when off duty, were intent on having all the excitement that their superiors would permit.

The old Blackwell mansion, we may imagine was frequently, if not constantly crowded with soldiers during their brief sojourn at Hopewell, and was the scene of many playful romps and scuffles. It was during one of these, no doubt, that his old-fashioned high clock was upset, and before order could be restored the machinery of the faithful old time piece was damaged beyond repair. To believe that the boys killed the fatted calf, and had music and dancing, will require no great stretch of the imagination ; and that they feasted on roast goose, costing "Uncle Sam" two shillings per head, and used a half hogshead of tobacco in an evening smoker, is evident from the items in the above bill.

Their merry making was of short duration, however, as the following order will show.

"Headquarters, Hunt's House, June 23, 1778. The troops will cook their provisions, and in every respect be in the greatest readiness possible for a march or action very early in the morning."

(Signed)

"GEO. WASHINGTON."

In Gen. Washington's report to Congress, dated Englishtown, July 1, 1778, he states that he sent a detachment of 1,500 well chosen troops on the 24th, to harass the enemy and impede their march, and the next day the main body of the army moved on to Kingston.

Hunt's House stood on the site of the present residence of Mr. George E. Weart, on the hill two miles northeast of Hopewell, and has been known as the Weart homestead since 1799, when it was conveyed by Wilson Stout to John Weart, the great grandfather of the present occupant.

The first pioneer of northern Hopewell, Jonathan Stout of Monmouth, settled there about 1704, and at his death in 1722, the farm passed to his son, Col. Joseph, who died in 1767, bequeathing it to his son Joseph, Jr. Jonathan Stout, a brother of Col. Joseph, married Elizabeth, daughter of Wilson Hunt, and it was her brother, John Price Hunt, who resided on the Col. Stout farm during the revolution. This fact gave it the title of Hunt's House on the military orders issued from Washington's headquarters at that time.

The great council of war held in this house was the turning point in the history of the great struggle of the colonies for independence. This scene is beautifully and grandly immortalized by one of the bronze tablets on the Battle Monument at Freehold, and is thus described.

"This tablet represents Generals Washington, Lee, Greene, Sterling, Lafayette, Steuben, Knox, Poor, Wayne, Woodford, Patterson, Scott and Duportail, as they appeared in the important council of war held at Hopewell, in old Hunterdon County, June 24, 1778.

"General Washington is listening attentively, as General Lafayette standing by the table is urging upon the council to decide on making a strong demonstration against the British column, even if it brought on a battle. The position and general expression of the other officers clearly indicates their opinion of Lafayette's appeal.

"General Lee, who preferred to let the British force parade across the state unmolested, looks anxious and indignant that his military experience does not entirely control the board. It is also easy to see that the foreign officers, Steuben and Duportail, want to make a strong attack, and not merely feel the enemy. General Patterson agrees with them, and so does the true-hearted Greene.

"General Wayne, always ready for fight, can hardly wait until Lafayette has finished that he may speak a few words of ardent patriotism.

"Colonel Scammell, Washington's adjutant general, who afterward gave his life for liberty on Yorktown's ramparts, is here engaged in noting the opinions of the general officers for the guidance of his chief."

The decision of this famous council was so important and far reaching in its results that a suitable memorial should be placed on the spot to perpetuate the memory of an event which was, in the opinion of many, the beginning of the end of the great struggle.

What a distinguished honor for old Hopewell to entertain such illustrious guests, and that this conspicuous event in the "great drama of war" should have been enacted within her boundaries. The decision reached at that time and the valor and courage of the troops on the plains of Monmouth, drove the haughty and cruel invaders from our noble little state which had suffered so much from the horrors of war.

On this historic spot the First Baptist church of Hopewell was organized on April 23, 1715, and when the first meeting house was erected in 1747, Col. Joseph Stout had his heart set on having it built on the site where the church was organized, but as it was not centrally located, and would be very inconvenient for the great majority of the congregation to reach, his proposition was overwhelmingly defeated.

The old Colonel felt so humiliated at his defeat, and so indignant and disappointed that he resolved to build a house larger than the whole congregation could build.

In 1752 he carried out his resolution, and built a stone mansion five feet larger each way than the meeting house, making it thirty-five by forty-five, with two stories and a basement, giving it a very imposing appearance from the south. In 1782, Col. Stout's son, Joseph, offered this fine property for sale and we give below the leading features of the advertisement as it appeared in the Trenton Gazette.

"TO BE SOLD, at public vendue, on Wednesday the 27th day of March 1782, on the premises, a very valuable plantation on which Col. Joseph Stout deceased, dwelt, now in tenure of Mr. John P. Hunt, situated in Hopewell Township, Hunterdon County, containing by estimation 296 acres of good land, 200 or more of which are cleared, the rest well timbered and watered with a number of good springs, has a quantity of good mowing ground, and more could be made with a little expense.

"On the premises are a large stone house two stories with nine rooms, well finished, six fireplaces and a large entry through the centre.

"A cellar and a cellar kitchen, a well of excellent water at the door, a stone barn, and other outbuildings, an orchard of grafted fruit, apples, peaches, pears, cherries of the best kind, and a variety of other fruits.

"The situation is very healthy and pleasant and would suit a gentleman or farmer.

"The vendue will begin at twelve of the clock on said day, when attendance will be given and conditions made known by Joseph Stout."

This is the picture of an old colonial house built one hundred and fifty-two years ago, and a description of one of old Hopewell's best farms about 80 years after it was reclaimed from the wilderness. Although advertised for sale at that time, the records show that in 1789 it was still in the possession of Joseph Stout, when he sold it to his cousin, Wilson Stout, who owned it ten years, when he sold it to Mr. John Weart as stated above.

Mr. John Price Hunt, who occupied it at the time it was honored by the presence of the Father of his Country, returned to the old homestead of the family at Marshall's Corner, after the death of his father, which occurred on February 26, 1782. The old house in which Wilson Hunt lived is still standing and is now occupied by Wm. D. Hill.

July 13, 1904.

NUMBER XXVIII.

In article 24 of this series note is made of the fact that Francis Blackwell of Hopewell sold the Glen Moore Mills to Rev. John Blackwell of the same place, on August 6, 1779. Mr. Blackwell was called to the pastorate of the Upper Freehold Baptist Church at Imlaystown in 1782 and doubtless disposed of the mills at that time, but we have been unable to find any record of the sale, nor when it passed to the possession of John Runyan of Amwell, who sold it to Moses Quick of Hopewell, on October 6, 1792.

John Runyan was the son of Thomas Runyan, who, in 1708, purchased of Daniel Coxe of Burlington, for thirty pounds, the tract now owned by Mr. Enoch A. Titus, adjoining the E. S. Wells farm on the south.

At that time William Hixson owned the Wells farm, and Captain Hunt the lands on the west.* A copy of the last will of Thomas Runyan, dated October 30, 1738, is on file in the office of the Secretary of State, at Trenton. He left the farm to his wife, Martha, and appointed his two eldest sons, Vincent and Thomas,† executors. The witnesses to the will were his neighbors, Josiah and Elizabeth Furman and Roger Wolverton.

John Runyan married, first, about 1769, Rachel, daughter of James Hyde of Hopewell, who owned the farm east of the borough now known as the Johnson farm, when the road from the Province line at Stoutsburg to Marshall's Corner was surveyed on March 18, 1723. (See article 21.) John Runyan and Rachel Hyde had nine children, viz: Anna Elizabeth, who died in infancy, Sarah, Vincent, Orminer, Rachel, John Hyde, Joseph, Francis and Anna

---

*The Capt. Hunt here mentioned was doubtless Captain Ralph, who was one of the pioneers of Lawrence township, and owned large tracts of land there and in Hopewell.

†The wife of Adam Conrad of Kingwood, and mother of Judge Conrad, deceased, of Pennington, was Sarah, daughter of Thomas Runyan, Jr., and she was left a legacy by the will of her father, dated January 23, 1770.

Elizabeth. John Runyan married, second, Rebecca Landis, and had five children, viz : Henry, Isaac, Catharine, David and Amos.

Rebecca Landis Runyan was one of the twenty-four children of Henry Landis of Ringoes, nearly all of whom intermarried with the leading families of old Hunterdon County, and reared large families. She was born May 6, 1761, and died in 1851, aged 90.

Catherine, daughter of John Runyan and Rebecca Landis, married George Lanning of Pennington, and became the mother of Aaron S. Lanning and John Lanning, two of the oldest and most respected citizens of Pennington. To Aaron S. Lanning, Esq., the writer is indebted for the record of the Landis and Runyan families, as well as many other items of local history, gleaned from his very interesting collection of old colonial documents.

Several months ago the writer visited the old burial plot of the Landis and Runyan families, which is located at Ringoes, about forty rods west of the Presbyterian Church. The plot is now an almost impenetrable tangle of briars and bushes interwoven with grapevine and woodbine, and the tombstones so displaced and disfigured by the lapse of time, that but few of the inscriptions were decipherable. It is a sad reflection that so many of the last resting places of our ancestors have been so utterly neglected and forsaken, and more especially, when we know that very many revolutionary heroes, whose memory we would delight to honor, rest in the unknown graves of those neglected spots.

On the occasion of this visit the writer was very forcibly reminded of some lines penned many years ago by an unknown author describing the neglected condition of hundreds of old burial places scattered over the country. We will not vouch that the lines are quoted correctly :

"Overgrown and neglected, deserted forlorn,
　A thicket of woodbine, of briar and thorn,
Is that home of the dead, that last place of rest
　For the mouldering clay of the good and the blest.

The stones which affection once placed o'er the dead,
　Their names to preserve and their virtues to spread,
Father time has so ruthlessly marred and defaced,
　That the loving inscriptions can scarcely be traced:

Soon the plow will o'erturn the root and the blade
　Of the sod once upheaved by the mattock and spade,
And the place, once so sacred, will then be forgot
　With the beings who wept o'er their dead on this spot."

Moses Quick* owned the old mills purchased of John Runyan less than four years, and sold them on August 3, 1796, to Richard French, a millwright of Chesterfield, Burlington County, the boundaries of the mill tract being the same as described in former articles.

The abutting property owners had changed, however, the farms of James Larison being owned by his sons, Elijah and David, and the lot of Jonas Wood being owned by Ralph Hunt, son of Azariah, (who in 1753 was the assessor of Hopewell Township).

Richard French owned the mills less than two years, and on April 2, 1798, sold them to Captain Ely Moore of Pennington, and for the period of one hundred and six years they have been in possession of the Moore family, descending from father to son. Joseph H. Moore, the present owner, is the great-grandson of Captain Ely, who was a revolutionary soldier and ensign in Captain John Hunt's company—First Regiment, Hunterdon County -- enrolled June 17, 1776.

The farm on the west side of the brook, now the homestead farm of E. S. Wells, first came into possession of the Moore family May 1, 1806. On that date Wilson Hunt† and Mary, his wife, conveyed it to Joseph and Charles Moore‡ brothers and co-partners, for $6,140.08, the farm containing one hundred and sixty-four acres.

The co-partnership was of short duration, being terminated by the sudden death of Mr. Charles Moore, and on October 30, 1807, Capt. Ely and Elizabeth, his wife, gave Joseph Moore, the surviving partner, a quit claim deed for the one half share of the farm for the sum of three thousand and seventy dollars. The deed contained the following clause, viz : "Know ye therefore, that the said Charles Moore died intestate, leaving no widow or lineal descendants, and by the law of descent, Ely Moore, father of the said Charles Moore, deceased, is the heir at law, and therefore seized of

---

*The father of Moses was John Quick, son of Francis, and his mother was Elizabeth, daughter of Benjamin Stout and Ruth Bogart. He married Sarah, daughter of Jared Sexton of Hopewell, and during the period between 1795 and 1840, he was a very extensive dealer in real estate, his name appearing very frequently in the old records of Hunterdon County.

He died December 3, 1847, aged 81, and his widow died June 27, 1853, aged 88.

†Wilson Hunt was the son of Deacon James of Hopewell, and at the time of the transfer was a resident of Lamberton, now a part of the city of Trenton. Later, he removed to Hightstown.

Among the children of Wilson, were Thomas, born at Glen Moore in 1799, who became a wealthy merchant and importer of Brooklyn, N. Y.; and Wilson G., of New York City, who was born at Glen Moore, in 1805, and died about 1892, leaving a fortune valued at five millions

He left a will and among other bequests was one of ten thousand dollars to the Baptist Church of Hightstown, of which his father was a deacon about 1820.

‡This clause from the old deed is quoted in order to establish beyond question the identity of Charles Moore, as by some strange oversight his name is omitted in the previous sketches published of the Moore family,

of an indefensible estate of inheritance to one equal, undivided one half part, of the before described tracts of land,'' etc.

Soon after Joseph Moore became the sole possessor of the old mills, his energy and enterprise placed them on a paying basis, and they became widely known as a grain market for the farmers of the surrounding country.   In 1820, Mr. Moore built the large brick mansion which is now the country residence of Mr. E. S. Wells, and in 1828 he built the large flouring mills, which are still standing, adding a linseed oil mill, which for many years made a market for an important product of the farms of Hunterdon County.

Joseph Moore was born July 20, 1780, and on March 1, 1806, married Sarah, daughter of Thomas Phillips of Hopewell.   Their children were as follows, viz : (1) Mary M., born January 14, 1807, married John, oldest son of Isaac Golden of Hopewell, whose history is given in number 13 of these articles.   Mrs. Golden died February 12, 1828, at the age of 21 years, and is buried in the family plot of the Golden family, on the farm of Mr. A. L. Holcombe.

(2) Charles, born December 17, 1808, died in infancy.

(3) Imlah, born April 13, 1810, married Amanda, daughter of Joseph Howell, and resided in Trenton.

(4) Charles, born April 11, 1812, married Lydia Howell, sister of the above, and also resided in Trenton, where for many years he and his brother, Imlah, were the proprietors of the large flouring mills on South Warren Street, well remembered by many of our readers.

(5) Ely, born March 19, 1814, married Juliet Ann, daughter of Benjamin Stout Hill, who resided on the farm now in possession of Dr. Macauley, at Marshall's Corner.   Mr. Hill was the pioneer of peach culture in this region, planting his orchard about 1840.   His venture was considered very visionary by his more conservative neighbors at that time, but it resulted in the development of one of the most successful and profitable branches of horticulture ever introduced into Hopewell township.   Mr. Hill did not live to see the success of his enterprise in producing peaches for the New York market, but his family realized a profit of several thousand dollars from the orchard first planted, and as a consequence, peach culture developed into the leading industry of the farmers of Mercer, Hunterdon and adjoining counties.

Ely Moore and Juliet A. Hill had four children who lived to maturity, viz : Elizabeth, first wife of Charles H. Blackwell, of our

borough ; Mary J., who married Garret W. Voorhees of Blawenburg, Somerset County ; Joseph H. (the present proprietor of the
Glen Moore mills) who married Anna D., daughter of David L.
Blackwell, and Frank V., who married Adelaide Cubberly of Hamilton Square. Ely Moore died September 25, 1863, aged 49 years.

(6) Thomas P. Moore, born February 16, 1817, remained a
bachelor until nearly fifty years of age, when he married the widow
of his brother Ely, and continued to reside on the homestead farm
until his death, which occurred August 2, 1880, at the age of 63
years. After his death his widow removed to Hopewell and resided there until her death, which occurred February 13, 1895, at
the age of 74 years.

Ely and Thomas P. Moore succeeded their father in the ownership of the Glen Moore mills and farm, and their warm-hearted and
generous hospitality will long be remembered by all who were so
fortunate as to enjoy their acquaintance and friendship. Their
"latch string" was always on the outside to rich and poor alike,
and the unfortunate always knew where to find sympathy and substantial aid in their extremity. Thomas P. Moore was a public
speaker and debater of unusual force and eloquence, and some forty
or fifty years ago, when "debating societies" were popular, he was
in great demand and never failed to draw a crowd.

(7) Catherine, born March 18, 1820, married William A., son
of Samuel Green of Ewing Township, and they resided many years
on a farm adjoining his father. Mrs. Green died November 1, 1873,
leaving two sons and one daughter, viz : Maxwell, who married
Harriet Van Cleve; Joseph, who married Helen Foraker, and
Mary, who married Col. B. Ridgway, and resides at Jenkintown,
Pa.

(8) Elizabeth, born April 1, 1823, is well remembered by the
writer as a faithful and devoted teacher in the Sunday School of
which he was a member more than fifty years ago. She married
June 1, 1853, Rev. Joseph W. Blythe, a Presbyterian minister of
Cranbury, N. J., and soon after their marriage they removed to Indiana.

Sarah, wife of Joseph Moore, died November 25, 1823, and he
married, second, Leah Wilson, who died July 2, 1841.

The death of Joseph Moore occurred May 9, 1852, at the age of
72 years.

November 23, 1904.

NUMBER XXIX.

Two English families of distinction, the Earls of Mount Cashill and Droheda, claim their descent from Sir Thomas DeMoore, who came over from Normandy with William the Conqueror, and was a commander under him in the great battle of Hastings, which was fought with Harold, king of the Anglo-Saxons, on October 14, 1066. The name of Sir Thomas was found in a list of the survivors after the great conflict. The family of Moore dispersed throughout the British Isles and became distinguished in every department of human effort.

The Moore family in Hopewell Township, trace their ancestry to Rev. John Moore who emigrated to this country from England about 1739-40, and became a Presbyterian clergyman of considerable prominence.

Rev. John Moore's name appears in the records of Southampton, Long Island, in 1641, and in October 1644, he was one of the deputies appointed to negotiate terms of union with the New England Colonies. In the same month, he received an appointment to collect subscriptions for scholars at Harvard College. He was licensed to preach previous to 1649, as he preached at Southampton, and, in the same year, became the second pastor of the church at Hempstead, L. I. The records show that he was the first pastor of the Presbyterian church of Newtown, L. I., in 1652, and that his death occurred on September 17, 1657, while he was still in the pastorate. He had married, either before or very soon after the emigration, Margaret, daughter of Edward Howell of Wedon, County of Bucks, England. She was of the same noted English family of Howell from whom all the Howells in America are descended, and can trace their ancestry back one thousand years.

The first recorded trace of the name is of "Howel Dda, or Howel the Good," who flourished A. D. 900 to 950. We have neither time nor space to quote the history of this noted Welch King of the Middle Ages, but will only quote the Welch tradition which descended through many generations, that "Howel the Good, was the chief and glory of Britons;" that he loved peace, feared God and governed conscientiously. We would refer the reader to a very interesting genealogical and biographical memorial of the Reading, Howell and other families, published in 1898, by Prof. J. G. Leach, LL.B. Prof. Leach is descended from this family through one of its collateral branches, and has published a large volume which embraces many of the old Hunterdon County families.

The Howells of Westbury, in Marsh Gibbon, County of Bucks, England, descended from Howel, Prince of Caerleon-upon-Uske, in Monmouthshire, whose coat of arms they bore.

William Howell of Wedon, in the parish of Waygate, made his will November 20, 1557, and gave legacies to his wife Anne and children : John, Henry, Jacob, Isabell, Jane, Cecil, Agnes, Anne, Joanne and Alice. He also gave legacies for the relief of the poor of six of the neighboring parishes, and also to the church of Hardwick, directing that his body be interred in the chancel before the high altar of the church. Henry, son of William, resided on the Manor of Westbury, which his father purchased in 1536, and at his death, July 7, 1625, his son Edward became possessed of the estate, which he sold on June 8, 1639, and in the deed is styled Edward Howell, gent, of Greevelltorpe, County of York.

Edward emigrated to America about this time, locating at Lynn, Mass., where he held 500 acres. He removed to Southampton, Long Island, in 1640, and was one of its founders and a member of the Governor's Council of Connecticut, 1647 to 1653. His death occurred about 1655. He had a son, John, who was also prominent in the civil and military affairs of Southampton.

Margaret, mentioned above as the ,wife of Rev. John Moore, was born at Marsh Gibbon, and was baptized there November 24, 1622, which is supposed to have been near the date of her birth. Her brother John, mentioned above, was baptized at Marsh Gibbon, November 20, 1624, and died November 3, 1696, aged 71, and the Howell coat of arms is engraven on his tombstone at Southampton, L. I.

Rev. John Moore and Margaret Howell had at least five children, as follows : John, Gershom, Joseph, Samuel and Elizabeth. Elizabeth married Captain Content Titus, of Newtown, Long Island, and through this line the writer traces his ancestry to Rev.

John Moore and the Howell family. (See Titus family in No. 14 of these articles).

We shall not at this time trace the descendants of any of this family except in the line of the Moore family given in our last, who are descended from Samuel, (known as Captain Moore), fourth son of Rev. John. He was commissioned captain of the Newtown militia, February 19, 1690. Previous to this time he had served as Lieutenant, Gershom, his brother being the Captain.

In 1662, Captain Samuel received a grant of land at Newtown. On December 4, 1666, was elected Freeholder, and during the next thirty years he was constantly in the public service, holding many offices of trust and responsibility. He married Mary, daughter of Thomas Reed, who, about 1655, erected the building which served as church and residence for Rev. John Moore. On October 3, 1662, he, with others, purchased of the Indian chiefs Womatupa, Wonoxe and Powatahuman, the tract of land on the south side of Long Island near Jamaica, known as "Plunders Neck."

The children of Captain Samuel Moore and Mary Reed were: Samuel, Joseph, Benjamin, Nathaniel, Margaret, Mary, Elizabeth and Sarah, and their descendants were very numerous and widely scattered, and for the past two centuries have been among the most distinguished families in the country.

The fourth son, Nathaniel, was the pioneer of the family in old Hopewell Township, and was born at Newtown, L. I., March 14, 1687, and on November 11, 1708, when but little over twenty-one years of age, he, with John Cornwell, John Mott and Thomas Reed, purchased 1350 acres of land in Hopewell Township, on a part of which the village of Queenstown, now the Borough of Pennington, was afterward located.

He married about the same time Joanna, daughter of Rev. John Prudden, of Newark, N. J. She was born December 16, 1692.

Her father was born at Milford, Ct., November 9, 1645, graduated at Harvard College, 1668, and was the principal of a grammar school at Roxbury until 1670, when he was called to the pastorate of the Presbyterian church of Jamaica, L. I. In 1674 he was the first pastor of the First Presbyterian church of Newark, N. J., and in 1676 returned to Jamaica and was their pastor until 1692, when he again went to Newark, and for the second time became the pastor of the First Presbyterian church, where he remained until 1699. He spent the closing years of his life in teaching and died December 11, 1725.

Rev. Peter Prudden, his father, had an eventful career, preaching in Hertfordshire, England, until 1637, when he was driven out by persecution. He emigrated to America, arriving in Boston, June 26, 1637 ; proceeded to New Haven, Conn., and became one of the founders of the New Haven Colony. On August 22, 1639, he founded the church of Milford, Conn., and was the pastor there until 1656. On August 25, 1889, a tablet to the memory of Rev. Peter Prudden was unveiled at the commemoration of the two hundred and fiftieth anniversary of the First Church of Christ, at Milford.

Nathaniel Moore and Joanna Prudden settled on a part of the tract purchased in 1708, erecting their cabin at the intersection of the road (or path) leading from the little settlement at Maidenhead (now Lawrence), to the settlements on the Neshaminy, now Hartsville, Pa., and the Indian path leading from their wigwams at the falls of the Delaware, now Trenton, to those among the then far off hills on the banks of the Raritan and Musconetcong.

The first Moore house stood one mile south of Pennington, on or near the site of the residence of Mr. H. W. Baldwin, who is a descendant of the pioneer, Elnathan Baldwin, who married Keziah, daughter of Rev. John Prudden and sister of Mrs. Nathaniel Moore. The two sisters were located very near each other, Mr. Baldwin's house standing about half way between Mr. Moore's and the present site of Pennington. It occurs to the writer just here, that seldom has any community been blessed with such a strong, sturdy and eminently religious class of pioneers as those by which Nathaniel Moore was surrounded at the time of his settlement, many of whom were related to him or to each other, either by blood or marriage.

Nearly all the earliest pioneers of old Hopewell of 1700 to 1720, came from Long Island and at about the same time ; and the friends whom they left behind, said that they had gone "away over in the Jarseys." Of these first settlers who built their cabins in the wilds within a radius of two miles from the crossing of the paths at Nathaniel Moore's, we might mention Sheriff John Muirheid, his nearest neighbor on the west, and Elnathan Baldwin, at about the same distance on the north ; also George Woolsey, John Welling, Enoch Armitage, John Titus, Robert Blackwell, Thomas Burroughs, William Cornell, John Carpenter, Thomas Reed, John Ketcham, Capt. Ralph and Edward Hunt, Robert Lanning, Abraham Temple; also the five Hart brothers, Capt. Edward, John, Joseph, Ralph and Nathaniel and others, whose names are not intentionally omitted but do not occur to the writer.

We might mention at least fifty more families who settled at the same time just outside the limits of this little circle, of whom we have given sketches in previous articles or hope to give as we proceed.

These were men of noble characters and sterling worth, who, with those mentioned above, did their part in laying the foundation of a model community, which, after the lapse of two centuries, has but few equals in all those characteristics which constitute an enlightened Christian civilization.

The above named pioneers and the others to whom reference is given, were the children of the pioneers of Long Island and the grandchildren of the pioneers of New England, those noble men and women who braved the dangers and perils of the wilderness that they might here enjoy the religious liberty which had been denied them in the Fatherland.

Nathaniel Moore was a public spirited citizen, and was one of the trustees of the Presbyterian church of Pennington in 1725, and in 1731 was a trustee of the parsonage and Latin school fund. He was also elected a Justice in 1725 and one of the Board of Freeholders in 1739.

The children of Nathaniel Moore and Joanna Prudden were: (1) John, known as "Capt. John," who settled on a part of the original tract; (2) Samuel, who also settled on a part of the above tract, now owned by Mrs. Anna Curlis, of Pennington; (3) Joseph, who owned the part of the tract lying on the west side of the road at Pennington; and (4) Benjamin, who succeeded his father on the homestead.

The three daughters of Nathaniel Moore, viz: Phebe, Abigail and Sarah, married into the families of Green, Smith and Temple, all sons of worthy pioneers of old Hopewell Township, of whose history of short sketches will be found in Rev. Dr. Cooley's "Early Settlers of Trenton and Ewing."

Nathaniel Moore died September 6, 1759, aged 72 and is buried at Pennington. His will is on file in the office of the Secretary of

State at Trenton, and is dated July 1, 1758.   As an item of historical interest we will give a synopsis :

The first item is a bequest to his wife Joanna, of a lot of land
estimated at 10 acres situated in the town of Newark, "that she had
from her father."   He also left his wife a share of his personal
property and a one-third share of the proceeds of the plantation
while she remained his widow.   He also makes a bequest to his son
John, who, he states, is already invested with a part of his said
lands.   To his son Benjamin, he leaves the homestead farm, and also a tract estimated at 50 acres, which he purchased of Ralph Hunt.
To Samuel, he leaves the land purchased of Philip Phillips, "situated in Queenstown (otherwise Pennington), adjoining lands of
Benjamin Ketcham."   He gives daughters Abigail and Phebe "60
acres of land adjoining the aforesaid John Moore," also two lots of
land purchased of Philip Phillips, being the sixth and seventh lots,
from Benjamin Ketcham's, also two other lots, one of which he purchased of Samuel Tucker, and the other of the executors of William
Cornell, dec'd.   He gives to his four sons, John, Samuel, Joseph
and Benjamin, all his wearing apparel and also one undivided right
in the schoolhouse lot in Pennington and one right in the Trenton
library.*   To his granddaughters, Joanna and Sarah, ("daughters
of Benjamin Temple and Sarah, his wife,") each fifty pounds proclamation money.

He appointed his wife Joanna and his sons John and Samuel,
his executors.   The witnesses to the will are Rev. William Kirk-
patrick, Elnathan Baldwin and Josiah Ellis.

January 4, 1905.

---

*The schoolhouse lot was conveyed by John Smith, merchant, to Nathaniel Moore,
William Cornwell, John Everitt, Ralph Hunt, Jonathan Furman, Reuben Armitage and
Stephen Baldwin, for the sum of ten pounds.

So far as known, this schoolhouse was the first public building in which religious services were held within the present limits of Hopewell Township.   It was called the
"new meeting house by John Smith's," and was built before the village of Queenstown (now
Pennington) had received its name.

NUMBER XXX.

Joseph Moore, the third son of Nathaniel, who, as stated in our last, owned the tract on the west side of the road at Pennington, resided in a house which stood on the site of the late residence of John E. Burd, deceased. He was born in 1721 and married about 1744, Christian, daughter of Richard Green, and granddaughter of Judge William Green, a pioneer of Old Hopewell (now in Ewing) Township. Her mother was Mary, daughter of George Ely of Trenton, who was a member of the first common council of the Borough of Trenton in 1746, and Col. George Ely of the Third Regiment, Hunterdon County, June 21, 1781, was doubtless her brother. From this time the name "Ely" was adopted as a Christian name in the Moore family.

The children of Joseph Moore and Christian Green were Ely, Moses, Ephraim and Elizabeth, wife of Col. John Van Cleve of Hopewell.

Joseph Moore married second, Mary, daughter of Reuben Armitage. The will of Mr. Moore is on file in the office of the Secretary of State at Trenton. It is dated January 1, 1773, and proved December 1791. As matters of historical value we give some of its provisions.

He makes bequests to his wife Mary, and second, leaves to his eldest son, Ely, all his homestead plantation with the improvements, lying on the west side of the road at Pennington, and also all the land on the east side of the road that formerly belonged to said plantation, bounded north by lands of Henry Woolsey, east by Samuel Moore, and south by Benjamin Moore. To his second son, Moses, he bequeaths all the plantation which he purchased of Cornelius Ringo, and to his son, Ephraim, two tracts of land, one of which he purchased of Nehemiah Howell, and the other of Peter Covenhoven. To his daughter, Elizabeth, he leaves 300 pounds, to be paid to her when she arrives at the age of eighteen years, his sons, Ely, Moses and Ephraim, to have an equal amount divided between them at the same time.

It is his will that his sons, Moses and Ephraim, shall remain on the homestead and assist their brother, Ely, in working it until they shall arrive at the age of 21 years, and that their sister, Elizabeth, shall have her home there with them so long as she remains unmarried. He appoints his wife Mary, executrix, with his son Ely, executor, and the witnesses are Samuel Moore, Alexander Biles, Jr., and Josiah Ellis.*

Capt. Ely Moore, son of Joseph, was born in 1745 and married Elizabeth, daughter of Cornelius Hoff of Hopewell, and their children were Joseph, of whose family a sketch is given in our last; Sarah, the third wife of Benjamin Stout Hill; Fanny, wife of Col. Ira Jewell of Hopewell†; Charles, the partner of Joseph in the Glen Moore mills; and Elizabeth, who married John Maxwell, a gentleman of wealth and distinction who resided at Savannah, Ga.

Capt. Ely Moore was a revolutionary soldier, and an ensign in Capt. John Hunt's company, First Regiment, Hunterdon County, June 17, 1776; and after the war served as Captain of a company of militia, and was one of the leading citizens of Pennington, residing on the homestead until a few years after the death of his father.

On April 2, 1798, he purchased of Richard French the Glen Moore mills, together with the mill tract on the east side of the brook, and resided in the old house which stood near the site of the the residence of his great grandson, Joseph H. Moore, Esq.

He died October 1, 1812, aged 67, and his widow resided there

---

*Josiah Ellis was a school teacher at Pennington and the following is a copy of an old receipt in the possession of Aaron S. Lanning, Esq., of Pennington.

"Received this 25th day of November 1778, of Mr. Edward Cornell the sum of twelve shillings in full for schooling his children and his demand to the day of the date hereof."

by me, "Josiah Ellis."

†Col. Ira Jewell resided on the hill one mile west of the Borough of Hopewell, his house occupying the present site of the mansion now owned by M. Montag. He was by trade a blacksmith, his shop standing against the high bank on the east side of the road. He was one of the leading citizens of the township, always at the front in all the public meetings of his time. On the occasions of general training he was the most conspicuous officer on the field. Dressed in full uniform with cocked hat, red sash and belt, large gilt epaulettes and glittering sword, and sitting erect on his large bald faced horse he was much admired. The old soldiers who had served in the war of the revolution said that he bore a striking resemblance to General Washington, being tall, straight and very dignified in appearance and manner.

By his marriage with Fanny, daughter of Capt. Ely Moore, he had two children, Charles M. and Sarah, who married William Burroughs Blackwell of Titusville. We hope to give the history of the descendants of Col. Jewell in a subsequent article.

until her death, which occurred February 17, 1839, at the age of 86 years.

The inventory and appraisement of the personal property was made by Isaac Golden and David Hunt of Hopewell, on November 4, 1813, and was filed by Joseph Moore, administrator, September 3, 1814, at Flemington.

We have in our possession the copy of an old revolutionary document which we will publish here as an item of history.

No. 27. Inventory of the loss and damages Ely Moore sustained by the Continental army in December, 1776.

	L.	S.	D.
1 Mare	15	0	0
500 lbs Hay	0	20	0
1 Knapsack & 2 Shirts	0	30	0
2 Pair Stockings	0	10	0
1 " Corduroy Breeches	0	30	0
1 Blanket	0	15	0
1 Silk Hankerchief	0	6	0
1 Great Coat (new)	2	5	0
1 Glass, 1 Silver Teaspoon & 1 Butcher Knife	0	7	0
	23	05	06

Sworn to by Ely Moore.

Cornelius Hoff, the father-in-law of Ely Moore, also brought in a bill at the same time, in accordance with an act of the General Assembly of New Jersey approved October 23, 1781.

No. 26. Inventory of the damage and loss Cornelius Hoff sustained by the Continental army in December, 1776:

	L.	S.	D.
1 New Br'd cloth vest & 1 Silk and Cotton do	2	05	0
1 Pair Corduroy Breeches	0	30	0
4 Pair Stockings	0	16	0
2 Basons	0	07	0
	4	18	06

Joseph Hoff being duly sworn doth Depose and Say that a number of the Cont'l troops staid one night at the claimants house and the above mentioned articles were missing in the morning & he Verily believes they took them.

Sworn, September 17, 1782. Signed, Jos. Hoff, P. Gordon.

Capt. Moses Moore, brother of Capt. Ely, was born at Pennington, and was one of the patriots of Old Hopewell. He was First Lieutenant in Capt. John Hunt's Co., First Regiment, Hunterdon County, May 10, 1777, and later was enrolled in Capt. John Phillips' Co. Third Regiment. He was in the battles of Trenton, Princeton, Monmouth and perhaps others, and at one time was in command of a company of "Jersey Blues." He married Elizabeth, daughter of Chreinyonce Van Cleve, and sister of Col. John, of Hopewell. They removed to Sussex County, N. J., and among their children were John Van Cleve, sheriff of Sussex, and Hon. Ely Moore, who was elected a member of Congress from New York City in 1834, served two terms and held important government positions under successive administrations until his death in 1860.

Dr. Ephraim, son of Joseph, never married.

Elizabeth, daughter of Joseph Moore, married Col. John Van Cleve, another revolutionary patriot of Old Hopewell. They resided on the farm near Harbourton, known as the "Hopewell Poor Farm," located in one of the loveliest and most picturesque little valleys to be found in the state.

The writer has a distinct recollection of having the little one-story stone house pointed out to him some forty years ago, by Rev. Dr. Hale of Pennington, with the remark, "All the children of Col. John Van Cleve were born and reared in that little house, and all his daughters were married there. People of their standing and prominence would not think they could rear such a large family in so small a house in our day." The little house still stands and for many years has been used as a home for the homeless and friendless of our township. As such it has served a noble purpose and should be preserved as a relic of colonial times being the home of a noble and patriotic old family of the revolutionary period, when it cost something to be a patriot.

The Holland ancestor of Col. John Van Cleve was Jan, Johan, or Johannes, (pronounced in English, John, but in Dutch, Yon, Yohan, or Yohannes) Van Cleef. He married Engeltie, (Agnes) daughter of Lawrens Pietersen, and emigrated from the Netherlands in 1653, settling at New Utrecht, Long Island, of which he was one of the founders.

In 1686, when Governor Dongan granted his patent for a large tract of land there, the name of Jan Van Cleef is found among them.

Col. John of Hopewell was a great great grandson of the emigrant, through the line of Benjamin, John, and Chreinyonce, who married Penelope, daughter of Philip Phillips, of Lawrence. They had nine children all of whom (except Samuel) married, and were among the leading families of the township at the time of the revolution.

The old family bible of Col. John Van Cleve was found a few years ago by the writer in possession of a gentleman in Burlington County, who knew nothing of the Van Cleve family nor how it came into the possession of his father, unless it had been purchased with a lot of old books at a sale. As its historical value was not appreciated by its owner it was purchased by the writer as a relic.

On a tablet inside the front cover is found this inscription. "The Property of John Van Cleve and Elizabeth Van Cleve."

We give below a copy of the family record.

"John Van Cleve, born February 6, 1757. Elizabeth Moore, wife of John Van Cleve, born September 5, 1758. John Van Cleve and Elizabeth were married March 20, 1777."

Then follows the record of their children.

"Chryonce Van Cleve, born December 8, 1778; Christiana Van Cleve, born October 20, 1780; Elizabeth Van Cleve, born September 8, 1782; Joseph Moore Van Cleve, born November 2, 1784; Penelope Van Cleve, born January 8, 1786; Samuel Van Cleve, born May 2, 1788; Ann Van Cleve, born December 13, 1793; Charles Van Cleve, born January 2, 1797; Patty Van Cleve, born September 9, 1800."

These nine children all married as follows :

Chryonce married Sarah, daughter of John Smith.

Christiana married Cornelius Hoff, Jr.

Elizabeth married Daniel Blackwell of Hopewell, the grandfather of our townsmen, R. M. J. and John V. Blackwell and also of David L. and Nelson D. Blackwell, whose mother was a daughter of Daniel.

Joseph M. Van Cleve married first Charity, daughter of John Stillwell, and second, Sarah, her sister, and a sketch of their family is found in No. 24 of these articles.

Penelope married Daniel J. Blackwell of Stony Brook, east of Pennington, his son, Henry J. Blackwell, now occupying the homestead.

Ann, (or Nancy) married Nathaniel R. Titus, and resided near Pennington.

Samuel married Phebe, daughter of John Stillwell, and had one son, Rev. Crook Stevenson Van Cleve, mentioned in number 24.

Charles married Sarah, daughter of John Waters, and among their children were John the grandfather of Mrs. E. V. Savidge, the wife of one of the proprietors of the Hopewell Herald, Samuel Ege, and Charles, who when a boy twelve years of age was accidentally drowned by breaking through the ice near the mill at Glen Moore. Charles Van Cleve had also three daughters, Charity, Mary and Eliza.

Patty, (or Martha) youngest daughter of Col. John Van Cleve, married William T. Phillips of Hopewell, the grandfather of our townsman William I. Phillips.

Col. John Van Cleve was enrolled in Capt. Henry Phillips' company, First Regiment, Hunterdon County, May 10, 1777, and was Lieutenant colonel of Militia in 1805. The following order signed by him giving his rank at that time is still in existance.

Mr. Israel Howell collector.

Trenton, N. J.

You will please remit the fine of John Osborne.

Signed, John Van Cleve, Leut. Col.

James Stevenson, captain.

Henry Wickham Blachley, Surgeon.

Dated November 11, 1805.

Col. Van Cleve died in 1814 and the inventory and appraisement of his personal estate was made by his neighbors, John P. Hunt and Daniel G. Howell, on November 21, 1814. The administrators of the estate were his son, Joseph M. Van Cleve, and John Carpenter.

February 15, 1905.

Editor's Note—At the time this book is being published in 1908, the bible which belonged to Col. John Van Cleve is the property of Col. Jas. R. B. Van Cleave of Springfield, Illinois.

NUMBER XXXI.

In previous articles of this series are given a list of the owners of the old Moore homestead, and also of the mill at Glen Moore from William Hixson, Joshua Ward, Philip Ringo and Johannes Hendrickson 1708 to 1735, and through the successive owners down to Joseph H. Moore the present owner.

From 1751 to 1766, the mills and farms were owned by Hon. John Hart and his brother Daniel ; and in article number 22 is given the family record of Hon. John Hart, and reference to his father, Captain Edward, who organized the first corps of volunteers, known as Jersey Blues, in this state.

In Sanderson's "Biography of the Signers," reference is made to the military service of Capt. Edward Hart, which, although often quoted is incorrect. He states that Capt. Edward participated in the battle of Quebec on June 13, 1759, while it is a matter of record that he had been deceased several years previous.

Several months ago, as the writer was delving among some of the musty old records in the office of the Secretary of State at Trenton, he found in a book containing the records of civil commissions of various kinds, the original warrant issued to Edward Hart in 1746, which establishes the date beyond question.

It is signed by ex-Governor Hamilton, who was governor of the Provinces 1736 to 1738. As it is a fragment of colonial history concerning one of old Hopewell's pioneers, who owned the tract of land now included in the farms of William I. Phillips, Prof. Edgerly and William B. Van Pelt, deceased, we will publish the warrant in full, which is as follows:

WARRANT TO EDWARD HART TO RAISE MEN.
By the Honorable John Hamilton, Esq., President of His Majesties Council and Commander-in-chief of the Province of New Jersey :

Whereas, His Majesty out of tender regard for the welfare of the subjects of his Dominion on the Continent of America, has been pleased to undertake an expedition against the subjects of the

French King at Canada, and has directed that as many men as time will permit shall be enlisted into his service to joyn the forces from the other colonies to Rendezvous at Albany, from thence to proceed to Canada under the command of General Gooch. And Whereas, it is the intention of the Legislature of this Province that Five hundred able bodied freemen, and well affected Indians should be enlisted in this Province for the same service. I do hereby Authorize and Impower Edward Hart, of Hopewell, in the County of Hunterdon, to Enlist one hundred able bodied freemen and native Indians, to serve in a company under him, the said Edward Hart as Captain, in the Aforesaid Expedition, and also to nominate and appoint Subaltern officers in the said Company. Hereby Promising if the said Edward Hart shall enlist one hundred able bodied freemen and native Indians, and Produce them to be reviewed at Perth Amboy, by the Commissioners to be appointed for that purpose before the number of Five hundred men, shall be otherwise completed within this Province.

That the said Edward Hart shall be Commissioned as Captain of said Company and the other officers shall also be Commissioned to serve in the Rank he has placed them and that every soldier in said company so enlisted and reviewed, shall be entitled to the Bounty money, subsistence and other encouragement, to be settled by an act of the General Assembly of the Province.

Given under my hand and Seal at Arms at Perth Amboy, the twenty-fifth day of June in the twentieth year of His Majesty's Reign, Anno Domini, 1746.

JOHN HAMILTON.

By His Honors Command,

Chas. Read, Secretary.

These officers were sworn on the 3d day of September, 1746, and certificate thereof endorsed.

On December 24, 1746, ex-Gov. Hamilton, being ill, requested James Hamilton and Hunter Morris to report for him that the 500 men had been raised and sent to Albany, and that 10,000 pounds had been "lent" for their uniforms and equipments. A large amount of correspondence in reference to this expedition is to be found on file among the State papers, but very little history has ever been published concerning it.

In article number 23, we gave a traditional account of the tragic death of Daniel Hart which occurred on the farm now occupied by

Mr. E. S. Wells, and was supposed to have taken place about the close of the Revolution. Since the publication of that article, the writer found in the Library of the Salem County Historical Society at Salem, N. J., a copy of the Pennsylvania Chronicle published October 19, 1767, in which an account of the tragedy is given. With the exception of the date the historical account will be found to be substantially the same as the tradition, but as history is better than tradition we copy the article in full which is as follows:

"On the twelfth of October, in the morning, a negro fellow, Cuff by name, belonging to Daniel Hart in the County of Hunterdon, and Township of Hopewell, attacked his master with a knife and axe, with which he gave him many wounds on his head, arms and back, of which he expired on the same day about five o'clock in the afternoon. The son going to assist his father, the negro made a pass at him with the knife, wounding him in the face and then made his escape immediately taking his weapons with him. He had on him when he went away a tow shirt and trousers, and is of middle stature and of good countenance.

"He ran away from his master three times before and was seen near Cranbury, and at the North river, and the last time was taken up at the Blue Mountains. It is requested that all officers and others will use their utmost endeavors to detect him, that he may be brought to justice."

During the succession of owners of the old mill and farm, from 1735 to 1760, the period was known as the "Golden Age," and was remembered and spoken of by the old settlers as the most prosperous and happy period since the settlement of the country. This was the transition period, as farms were being reclaimed from the primeval forest, and the virgin soil possessed in abundance all the elements necessary to the perfect development of all the farm products congenial to this latitude. This, together with very favorable seasons, such as have seldom, if ever, been equalled for so long a period in the history of the country, combined to reward the husbandman with very abundant harvests.

During this prosperous era, good dwellings and large, substantial barns were substituted for the log cabins and stables of the emigrants, and in some portions of the State these old houses and farm buildings are still to be found in good repair, reminding us of an age when our colonial ancestors built for durability rather than for display. The immense oak beams of the old barns, strongly framed, and in many instances dovetailed together, defied alike the summer cyclone and the winter tempest, and the skill displayed in their construction is a monument to the skill of the old colonial mechanics. The framework of their dwellings was nearly as heavy and substantial as the barns, the joists in the ceiling being eight by fourteen inches, and placed at a distance of thirty inches apart, being framed with the express purpose of sustaining the weight of all the wheat that the upstairs rooms would hold without the slightest danger of collapse.

The manner of living among the well-to-do farmers of the Golden Age, was in marked contrast with that of the same class at the present day, for while the comforts and conveniences known to that period were multiplied, their dress, furniture and habits, remained the same as that of the emigrants of a half century earlier. The wooden plate, (or trencher) and the pewter spoons and platters, graced the tables of the most wealthy, the dishes in daily use being almost exclusively of pewter, and the knives and forks being all home made. When not in use the plates and platters were used as decorations, being placed on edge in the "dresser," which occupied a place on the side of the kitchen, comparing in size with the number comprising the household.

Heavy penalties were imposed by the English government to prevent the colonists from establishing manufactories, and they were compelled to manufacture all their woolen, linen and other fabrics in their own families ; all their clothing, even to hats and shoes being home made, and from materials produced on their own farms. Their houses were veritable workshops, being well supplied with looms and spinning wheels, which like the fabrics manufactured on them, were all home made.

The daughters of the family were all instructed in the art and mysteries of spinning and weaving all the linen and woolen goods, and making them into garments for all the family. They also spun all the thread used, not only to manufacture the garments, but also that used by the farmer in making his shoes and harness. The farmer's daughter of colonial times could preside at the loom and spinning wheel with as much dignity and grace as her great-great-granddaughters of the present day can at the piano.

To acquire the art of spinning and weaving the finest linen was a great accomplishment, and no young women was considered a suitable candidate for matrimony until she had completed her education in that line, and had cupboards and bureaus well filled with sheetings, blankets, rolls of linen and woolen textiles in variety, all spun and woven by her own hands, for use when she should become the mistress of her own home. These old fabrics have been handed down to us as priceless treasures and heirlooms, and what tender emotions thrill our hearts as we gaze almost reverently at them, feeling that they are something too sacred to be put to a common use. How vividly they recall the patient industry of loving hands which years long agone have forgotten their cunning, and have rested from their labors, leaving behind them these mementoes of their tender solicitude in providing for the generations which were to come after them.

The sons of the family were all required to learn trades, and were often indentured to a neighboring mechanic while in their early teens. They married early in life as a rule, and when ready to establish homes for themselves, they were in most instances provided with farms, which they cultivated, working at their trades for themselves, and also for their neighbors as they had opportunity. It was not unusual to find the grown sons of a family competent to build their own houses and barns, and fill them with neat and substantial furniture and implements in their variety, without expending a dollar for outside help.

Carpets were unknown in colonial times, even in the houses of the wealthy. The floors were scoured with a great deal of care every day, where they were in daily use, and were as white as the tables from which they ate their meals—no cloth being ever used on their tables—and after the housewife had finished scrubbing, woe to the heedless urchin who ventured to step his foot over the doorsill without first taking off his shoes. The floor of the spare room (if they were so fortunate as to have one) was scoured and and then covered with white sand brought from the seashore where it was possible, and a sanded floor was considered a great luxury to be found only in the houses of the thrifty and well-to-do.

Stoves were unknown before the beginning of the last century, the houses being heated by large fireplaces, in which all the cooking and much of the baking was done. The old crane, trammels and cooking utensils, have long since been exiled or used to decorate the lawn, where the rising generations view them with wonder.

The old pioneers built their bake ovens at some distance from the house, without so much as a shed of any kind to cover them ;

but the next generation built a small kitchen over them, which was called the ovenshed. Since the writer's memory, these old over-sheds were veritable curiosity shops, and if any farm tool or imple-ment was missing, the first place to be searched was the ovenshed. These old ovens were often erected on four short posts set in the ground, and on them a frame, on which a level brick or stone bot-tom was laid, which was generally four feet in width by six or eight in length, and was arched over with brick.

The writer remembers one of these old ovens in his early boy-hood, and when bake day arrived he was sent out in the morning before school time to hunt up a lot of old fence rails, which were considered indispensable on such occasions. These were cut the proper length, split up small, and the old oven filled up and fired by throwing in a shovelful of live coals, and fanning them to a blaze. After the wood was consumed and the oven thoroughly heated, the coals were removed, the ashes carefully cleaned out, and the oven was ready for business. An old iron shovel with a long wooden handle was then brought into requisition, with which the loaves of bread, dishes of pie, &c., were placed in position, the door closed, and the "goodies" baked to a finish.

Many of the older people will, with me, feel their mouths water as they recall the delightful flavor of the cake and pumpkin pies that our grandmothers used to bake in the old ovens, many of which had been doing duty for several generations. There are many who doubtless think that the ranges and the cooking stoves of the pres-ent day, with all their modern appliances and improvements, are far superior and do the work better than the rudely constructed old ovens of our colonial ancestors ; but we must confess that there is a sweet smelling savor lingering in our memory, which time cannot wholly efface.

March 15, 1905.

NUMBER XXXII.

In several of our previous articles, reference has been made to Doctor Roger Parke, who, so far as known, was the first white settler within the present limits of Hopewell Township.

There is a singular fascination about every scrap of tradition concerning this old pioneer, who settled on the farm now occupied by Mr. C. E. Voorhees, two miles west of Hopewell Borough, his farm two hundred years ago including several of those now adjoining Mr. Voorhees.

It is an old tradition that when he first settled there, the Red men of the forest still had their wigwams, and held their Powwows, on the banks of Stony Brook at that point ; and that the dusky maidens admired their beauty as reflected in the crystal waters of the stream, while the young braves reclined on its green banks, under the grand old trees which were still standing within the memory of the writer, and were the beauty and glory of the romantic old homestead.

This spot was the birthplace of the writer, and in his boyhood it was one of the traditions of the place that the old Indian medicine men had taught Doctor Parke their mysterious arts of healing, and that the herbs and plants which flourished in such great variety all about the place, had, many of them, been planted by him and their leaves, blossoms, barks and roots, used in his practice.

Occasional reference to Doctor Parke, made by the old people of the neighborhood, awakened an intense desire to know more of this traditional old doctor, of whom the "oldest inhabitant" seemed to know so little, and who had his residence there, years before the birth of the writer's great great grandfather.

To my youthful imagination, the man who had the courage to live among a barbarous and savage race, whose cruelty and treachery were proverbial, was an immortal hero, and deserved a more imposing monument than the rough sand stone in the old family graveyard, which bore the simple and very vague inscription, "R. P. 1755, A. 91."

One of my earliest recollections was of the old garden, which occupied a part of the same spot as at the present, a considerable space of which was, at that time, devoted to beds of herbs, both annual and perennial, some of which bore large showy flowers, while others were very insignificant, proving that they had been planted for use, rather than beauty. The dilapidated old fences were overgrown with a thicket of vines and shrubbery, which also had their uses in the old doctor's time ; but in the writer's boyhood, was a favorite summer resort for the robins and catbirds, whose happy voices blended very harmoniously in the early morning, but created a frightful discord later in the day, as they spitefully snarled and scolded over the right of possession to the old garden.

Some of the herbs in this garden were not native to this locality, but had been brought from other states and transplanted, on account of their valuable medicinal properties ; and the old Larison family, who were descended from Dr. Parke, and succeeded him on the homestead, were familiar with their uses, and had carefully guarded them while they remained on the farm.

A few years after the old farm came into the possession of the father of the writer, the old house which had sheltered Doctor Parke and at least three generations of his descendants in the Parke —Larison line, was taken down, and a new house erected near the site. The old garden was not spared in the march of improvement, for while it was in keeping with the old house and its surroundings, it was strangely out of harmony with the new order of things, and was "cleared up."

While some of the herbs were transplanted to the new garden, most of them (which were called by the old people, "Old Doctor Park's Yarbs,") were consigned to the brush pile, but not to oblivion, as many of the same varieties are still found on the shelves of every up-to-date drug store in the country. After the lapse of two centuries a few still survive on the farm, to recall the memory of the famous old doctor, who had here stewed and brewed the bitter concoctions, which won for him the distinction of being the pioneer physician of old Hopewell.

So far as known he was the only physician in this region for many years, and rode on horseback over these hills and mountains, when very few houses stood between the Delaware and the Millstone, and all the country to the north was still the home of the Lenni Lenape. On these long lonely rides his saddle bags were well supplied with an assortment of remedies for both external and internal treatment.

It was not a prescription age, and as no drug store existed nearer than New York or Philadelphia, he carried an apothecary shop with him.   He had his cere-cloth, salves, ointments, washes (or liniments), plasters and poultices, for external application ; and besides these, his pills and powders, which were used on all occasions. These latter, the old doctors called their "pukes and purges," but in the more polite usage of our times, would be termed emetics and cathartics.   His constant companions were the lancet and horn cup for bleeding and cupping, which were considered indispensable to the outfit of every doctor and chirurgeon of "ye olden time."

It is not known whether Dr. Parke had received any medical education before emigrating to this country, but the fact that his name is not found in any of the biographies of early physicians in this state, is no proof.   It is a well known fact that some of the pioneer physicians, who had a very extensive practice before the revolution, and served as surgeons in the army for a time, are not mentioned in any of the histories heretofore published.   His home was a Mecca for the afflicted, who made long pilgrimages to be treated for cancers, ulcers, catarrh, rheumatism and other diseases, not too severe to admit of the patient making the journey on foot or on horseback, as we must not lose sight of the fact that in Dr. Parke's day there were no wagon roads.

One of the popular modes of treatment practiced by the Indian "medicine men," and doubtless by Dr. Parke also, was the "sweating and plunging" remedy, which was invariably resorted to in obstinate cases which refused to yield to ordinary treatment.   It was heroic treatment and in some instances, where the patient was low in vitality or the diagnosis of the "medicine man" was at fault, it was attended with fatal results.   Yet it was said that they performed some wonderful cures, which seemed little less than miraculous.

The mode of treatment was to heat a large stone red hot, and then cover it with a heavy tent of skins, tightly sewed together (such as were used by them in winter) then place the patient inside in a perfectly nude condition.   The stone was then frequently wet with water until it caused the perspiration to "stand out like beads," and in this condition the patient would be hurried to the near-by brook and plunged in, only for a moment, when he was taken back in the tent or hut, and covered with skins or blankets, until the perspiration was more profuse than before, if possible.

Hon. Ralph Voorhees, who wrote several articles on the early settlers of the Raritan valley, which were published in the magazine "Our Home," tells the story of Cornelius Wyckoff, of Middlebush, Somerset County, who was affected with a severe attack of rheumatism. A friendly Indian living in a hut nearby told him that if he would submit to the above described treatment he could cure him. Mr. Wyckoff finally consented and was taken to a little sod structure built in the side of the hill, where the means were applied to produce an extraordinary perspiration. A hole had been previously cut in the ice of the brook sufficiently large to admit the patient, and into this he was plunged.

The Indian then took him out, wrapped him in a blanket, carried him to the house, put him to bed and then heaped blankets over him until, as it was told, "the perspiration ran down the bed posts." "That will do," said the doctor, "remain there until you and everything become dry, then be careful for some days, and you will be well." The patient followed the doctor's advice, and in a few days all stiffness and pain left him, and the result was so marvelous that he "felt as if he had neither limbs nor body—so comfortable. He became entirely well and lived many years afterward."

On the farm of Mr. C. E. Voorhees on Stony Brook are two anvil shaped stones, now in use as stepping stones in his driveway. These Dr. Charles Abbott of Trenton (who is beyond question the best authority in the state on the manners and customs of the Aborigines) thinks from the description given him, may have been used as "sweating stones," as others very similar in appearance have been found elsewhere, which had doubtless been used for that purpose. These were found on the farm now owned by Joshua J. Hunt, on the opposite side of the brook from Mr. Voorhees, one of them being taken out of the brook by the writer, where it had been thrown by a former owner of the farm to get it out of the way.

It is very evident that they have been dressed to their present shape, and were designed for some especial purpose, but the oldest persons in the neighborhood could give no account of their history. They were placed in their present position by the writer over twenty years ago and have been objects of peculiar interest, as well as subjects of much speculation as to their history and design. Some have pronounced them prehistoric as they differ from any rocks in that immediate locality, and the race of Indians, who inhabited this region at the time of its occupation by the whites, were too indolent to have dressed them to their present shape, or to have brought them to the place where they were found.

The spring on the farm of Mr. Hunt near which they stood for generations is now at a considerable distance from the brook, but in the boyhood of my father, some eighty years ago, it was on the edge of the brook, and of a beautiful clear pond. As the spring had a flow of about one hundred gallons per minute and a uniform temperature of fifty-two degrees throughout the year, the pond seldom froze over in the most severe weather, and in summer was too cool for comfortable bathing. This was an ideal spot for an "Indian sweat house," and as the stones were only a few yards distant when first remembered by the old people of the neighborhood, it is quite probable that it had been used for that purpose. It is a matter of history that one of these "sweat houses" still existed near the village of Crosswicks after its settlement by the English.

That Dr. Parke was a man of considerable prominence two hundred years ago, is obvious from the fact that soon after the year 1700, the old "Indian path to Wissomency," (as it was called in the earliest deeds) began to be designated in the deeds from Trenton to Stony Brook as "Rogers Road," instances of which are given in previous articles.

The origin of the name was a puzzle to the writer, until in an old book of court records in Flemington, he found the record of the original survey of the road from Ringoes to Marshall's Corner, dated March 30, 1722, a copy of which will be found in article number 21 of this series. We will republish the last course given in said survey, retaining the capitalization and spelling. "Thence along a line of Marked trees as aforesaid to a Hickory tree standing near Samuel furmans Corner, by the side of Roger Parks his road."

"Furman's Corner" is now known as Marshall's Corner, and this settled the vexed question as to who the road had been named for, and now the question arose, why should it have been named for Roger Parke? There seems to be but one plausible solution, and that is, that he was the pioneer who opened up this road to the white settlers and caused the name to be changed from the "path" of the red man, to the "road" of the pioneer.

Roger Parke resided near "Crosswicks' Creek," a few miles east of Trenton in 1690, and about that time commenced his study of the

Indian practice of medicine with the Indians at Wissamenson. To do this, he probably made frequent pilgrimages over this path until it began to be known as "Rogers Road."

A few years later when Doctor Parke made his home at Wissamenson, many of his Quaker neighbors of Crosswicks and the "Falls" (now Trenton) doubtless followed him for treatment, as they had been associated with him in the Friends meeting at Crosswicks and Chesterfield, before he settled" away up in the woods," on the banks of Stony Brook. It is a well known custom of the Friends to which they still religiously adhere, to call people by their Christian names, consequently it was not "Mr. Parkes road," but in speaking of it they would say, "this is Roger's road," or "the road to Roger's."

Doctor Parke was an influential member of the Society of Friends, and may have been a relative of the noted author and zealous Quaker preacher, Jas. Parke, who was born on the border of Wales in 1636, and was cotemporary with George Fox, the distinguished founder of the Society. The following record copied by the writer from an old record book of the "Friends meeting," is in proof of his prominence in the church.

"2d 8th mo. 1684. Thos. Gilderthorpe, Roger Parke and Robert Wilson agreed that a week day meeting be held at the ffalls upon a fifth day of every week, (except that week the monthly meeting is at Francis Davenports) one day at Mahlon Stacy's, one day at Thomas Lamberts and one day at Thos. Sykes."

April 12, 1905.

NUMBER XXXIII.

In Liber B., Part 1, Book of Deeds, on file in the office of the Secretary of State at Trenton, is found the record of a deed dated May 24-25, 1682, from Edward Bylinge to "Roger Parke of Hexham, county of Northumberland, England, yeoman," for 200 acres of land, to be laid out in "West Jersey." On November 11, 1686, "Roger Parke, late of Hexham, now of Crosswicks Creek," sold the above tract to John Watkins, of Middlehook.

In 1875, the writer found in the possession of Misses Susan and Sarah Sexton, who were descendants of Doctor Parke, the original parchment deed from Anthony Woodhouse to Roger Parke of Crosswicks, dated the thirteenth day of the eleventh month, called January (old style) 1685, for "one two thirtieth of a Proprietary in the first ten Proprietaries," the consideration being the sum of six pounds, sixteen shillings, current money of said Province. If this deed is still in possession of either of the above named sisters, it is the oldest known document of the kind in existence. The writer had a synopsis of this deed published in the Trenton State Gazette, in July, 1875.

In 1687, Roger Parke owned 200 acres near Crosswicks Creek, and served on the grand jury from that locality in 1688, and again in 1690, and was foreman of the grand jury in 1692, and in 1698 was one of the Judges of the Court of Common Pleas.

In Revell's Book of Surveys, Liber A., Page 14, "Reversed side," is found a record of the original survey of the Parke tract on Stony Brook, at Hopewell. It is dated April, 1697, and commences as follows, "Surveyed then for Roger Parke 400 acres on the north side of Stony Brook at Wissamenson." This survey began at a white oak tree at the bend of the brook, a half mile north of the ford (now Moore's mill at Glen Moore), from thence it ran west through the swamp, to a point north of the present location of the iron bridge, near C. E. Voorhees'. From this point the brook had a well defined channel, which was followed "up ye several courses thereof," to an elm tree standing on the north side of the brook above the slate quarry, on the farm of W. W. Kirkendall. Thence north to a point near the late residence of Wm. S. Stout, deceased, thence east to the northeast corner of the farm now owned by Amos Sked, thence south following his line and that of the E. S. Wells farm (formerly Samuel Ege's) to the Stony Brook road near the old baryta mines, and thence to the place of beginning, "containing 400 acres, besides allowance for ways."

In May, 1697, Roger Parke had 100 acres surveyed for his daughter, Anne Parke, adjoining his tract on the east, which is fully described with a history of its subsequent owners, in number 17, and several of the succeeding articles of this series. On June 12, 1698, Roger Parke received his deed, and on August 9, 1698, Anne Parke hers, for the above tracts, and by subsequent and more accurate surveys, they were found to contain about 650 acres. On June 16, 1699, "John Parke of Parkesberry," in the County of Burlington, purchased of Thomas Revell, agent for the West Jersey Society, 300 acres adjoining his father on the north. If his tract exceeded the number of acres specified in his deed as much in proportion as the tracts surveyed for his father and sister, the Parke family had fully 1000 acres lying in one body, between Stony Brook and the mountain (or "Rocks," as the mountain was then known) bounded on the east by the road leading from the Stony Brook road at the mines, by way of Mr. Montag's north to the old 30,000 acre line, near the southern boundary of the farm now owned by Zephaniah Hixson, and thence west to the road leading from Stony Brook to Runyan's saw mill.

This north line of the 30,000 acre tract of Col. Daniel Coxe was subsequently changed, and all the deeds conformed to it, calling it Doctor Coxes's "true line," and on and near this line was located the old driftway known for many years as the old "Bungtown road" leading to Coryell's ferry—now Lambertville—which was in use until the old turnpike was opened up in 1820-21.

After the Parke family had located their lands, their next thought was to provide homes for their families, and in this it was the custom for the pioneers to assist each other. It seldom required more than two or three days to get a log cabin enclosed. As there were no saw mills, they selected a straight grained red, or black oak tree, from which they split boards and plank for roof, door and floor. The hinges and latches were all made of wood and the doors pinned together with wooden pins, not a handful of nails being used in building a house in those days. The windows were made of oiled paper or deer skin, dressed thin enough to admit the light. The fire-places were without jambs and stretched all the way across one side of the cabin and were made deep enough so that large logs could be piled in, and the family could all be accommodated with a seat at the fire.

Having built their houses and made a table, a bedstead and some benches for each, the pioneers next turned their attention to clearing a field large enough to raise some buckwheat, beans and potatoes. The largest trees were left standing and girdled by cutting a deep notch all around them, which stopped the flow of sap and killed them the first year, after which crops could be raised without the trouble and expense of removing them. Where the trees were very large and scattering the land could soon be made tillable in this manner, as there were no small trees or bushes near them, and in clearing the land of the smaller trees, they were cut down, dragged together and burned.

A portion of this land was devoted to raising flax, which the pioneer would need for garments by the time it could be grown and manufactured, as it all had to be spun, woven and made up on the farm. No wool could be produced by the pioneers for many years after their settlement, on account of the depredations of wolves, which were very numerous and troublesome. Wool for underwear, stockings and blankets was brought on horseback from the older settled portion of the country, where wolves were less numerous or had been exterminated. The outer garments of the pioneer were principally from the flax grown on his farm, first spun and then dyed, with the barks of the trees grown on the farm, to any color desired, after which it was woven and made up by the mother and daughters of the household.

Next to flax, the most important crop the first year was buckwheat, as it could be quickly and easily grown and served as a substitute for bread, as well as feed for the few animals kept on the farm. The pioneer scratched over the ground the best he could with a knotty log, and harrowed in his buckwheat with a heavy brush, as the wooden tooth harrow could not be used until the roots and stumps had decayed.

His buckwheat was cut with the sickle as scythes were not in use until 1750, and when it was ready to thresh, a piece of ground was cleared off, a post placed in the centre, around which a team of horses were driven, until the ground was tramped very solid, when the grain was thrown on and repeatedly shaken up until the horses had threshed it. Fanning mills were not in use until about 1750 and the grain and chaff were heaped up and left until there was a good stiff beeeze, when it would be tossed up until cleaned, when it would be put in a bin built of rails and thatched over with straw. Here it would be left until needed, when it would be ready to be crushed with the "plumper" as described in Number 22, or loaded on the backs of his horses, and a trip made to mill, which in the case of the Parkes, was through the forest to the log mill of Mahlon Stacy, which stood on the bank of the Assanpink where it is now crossed by Broad Street, Trenton.

To scores of others, "going to mill" involved a journey of from fifty to one hundred miles or more and then the grain was only ground, not bolted, and the good wife was obliged to bolt it through a cloth of homespun before it was ready for the griddle. The first mills were erected on the small streams, on which dams could be built with small expense, and they were a great curiosity, being constructed by the pioneer. The wheels were all of wood, pinned together with wooden pins and some of these mills ground only five to ten bushels per day and were often unable to run on account of ice in winter and droughts in summer.

Very little corn was planted the first few years, as it could not be cultivated with the wooden plows then in use, on account of the stumps and roots, and cultivation with the hoe was very tedious and laborious work. Very little grain was grown for market for many years after the first settlement of the country, as the demand was very limited, the price very low and transporting it to a navigable stream, on the backs of pack horses, attended with great difficulty.

In later years, when corn became one of the staple products it was often all shelled by hand, before the big fireplace in the kitchen on the long winter evenings, with no other light than that from the blazing logs. The contrivance used for shelling was not patented and consisted of a wash tub with the long handled frying pan run through the handles of the tub and held firmly in place with corn cobs. Two good men, one on each side of this "machine," would keep a third man hustling to carry the corn in from the crib as fast as they could shell it. Thousands of bushels of corn were shelled in this manner, not only by the pioneers, but by the three or four generations succeeding them, for one hundred and forty years after the settlement of the country.

Within the writer's memory a favorite method was to run the bayonet of an old musket through the top of a box, and it seems almost incredible that they were used in this manner until the middle of the steel bayonet was nearly or quite worn away in the service. The scriptural injunction of ancient times "beat your swords into plow shares and your spears into pruning hooks," was exemplified in the peaceful triumph of the bayonet of modern times. Corn was also shelled off with horses or flails, within the memory of the writer, before the pigeon hole shellers came into general use or the larger shellers were invented.

The scriptural injunction to "beat the swords into plowshares" was not obeyed literally by our forefathers of colonial days, as their plows were very rude affairs constructed wholly of wood, the mold board being cut from a tough cross-grained white oak knot and often not a pound of iron used in its construction. In later years a small plate of iron was nailed to the point, to be used especially in stony land.

It must be remembered that no farmer at that time sowed a pint of grass seed, and never plowed a field that was in sod, consequently the wooden plows served a fair purpose to stir up the loose soil. The first wrought iron plow share was introduced in 1776, and long after that time the mold boards were plated with strips of iron, made from old horse shoes, hammered out very thin and nailed on. The proper shape for the mold board of a plow was suggested by Thomas Jefferson and the first cast iron plows were invented by a New Jersey farmer named Newbold, but their use did not become general until about the beginning of the last century on account of a prejudice existing against them.

Harvesting until after the revolution, was all done with the sickle, and when the grain cradle came in use farmers were as much delighted, as their grandchildren were with the self binding harvester.

At the time of Doctor Parke's settlement on Stony Brook fruit growing was not yet in its infancy. Improved varieties of peaches, plums, pears and grapes were unknown, the only supply of grapes being those found growing wild in the woods and along fences and waste lands. Vegetables were abundant, but not in as great variety as at present. Tomatoes, sweet corn, lettuce, egg plant and celery were unknown, which in our day are considered almost in-pensable. Farmers' tables were bountifully supplied with ham, bacon and smoked meats, but fresh meats were rarely seen except during the winter season. Game was plentiful but the industrious farmer who had his farm to clear spent very little time in the chase.

While the Indians remained they were very serviceable in sup-plying the settlers with game, fish, skins and furs, which they dis-posed of in exchange for salt, tobacco, gunpowder and other articles, which all the first settlers kept on hand for barter. The skins and furs which were purchased for a trifle, often bringing them quite a revenue in the markets of New York or Philadelphia, a small bun-dle of furs that they could carry on horseback often bringing more ready cash than a crop of corn.

The first wagons of the settlers were constructed wholly of wood. The wheels were made with very heavy rims, all pinned to-gether with wooden pins, the wooden tires being fastened on in the same manner. To build a wagon of the rudest description required time and skill, and as sleds were very simple in their construction, they were used extensively about the farm in summer as well as winter, as they were loaded lightly and the hauls were short. All the crops were either hauled together on the sled or carried. They were made entirely of wood, not a pound of iron being used, the shoes being pinned on with wooden pins and as they were made from hickory saplings split in half, they were hard and smooth and a considerable load could be hauled on the bare ground.

Surrounded as we are with the comforts, luxuries and con-veniences of our twentieth century civilization, it is difficult to real-ize anything of the severe hardships and privations our colonial an-cestors endured to establish a home in a wilderness, which they by their fortitude and indomitable courage, conquered, and left as a precious legacy to their descendants, who now occupy this beautiful valley.

June 14, 1905.

NUMBER XXXIV.

In Revell's survey of the tract for Doctor Parke, described in our last, he locates it "at Wissamenson." In a deed recorded about the same time for a tract west of the road at Marshall's Corner, it is described as "near Wissa Menson," dividing the name, and also locating it "near," instead of "at," as in the Parke deed. In a deed to Thomas Hutchinson, dated May 13, 1689, for a tract in Southern Hopewell (now Ewing) Township, the road to Stony Brook is described as the "Indian path to Wisomoncy."

In the oldest work, describing the Indian race in New Albion (now New Jersey) published in pamphlet in 1648, the Wicomeses are described as a small band of about 250 men. This is doubtless the same tribe which, at the time of the settlement of the English at Burlington, was known in some localities as the Minsiminni and Minisinks.

Many of the old Indian names were too lengthly to suit the English, and the above names were abreviated and became Minsi, Mense, Munsey and Monsey. Many of the names were difficult of pronunciation, and as the Indians had no written language, the white settlers experienced great difficulty in writing them in English so that the original pronunciation would be retained. Many of the grand old Indian names, which sounded very romantic in their language, became so distorted that they could not be recognized by the "Original People," as the name Lenni Lenape signified in their language.

It is evident that the name "Wissamenson" had its origin with the Aborigines long before a white man set his foot on New Jersey soil, and it is also evident, that when Mr. Revell explored these hills and valleys, he had a struggle with some of the long words given him by his Indian guides, from the fact that he has given us several different spellings of the same word.

At the time of the landing of the Pilgrims, the great Algonguin Lenape had possession of the territory from the Alleghany range to the Hudson river. Their northern boundary was disputed by their powerful and warlike neighbors, the Iroquois, with whom there was a constant struggle for supremacy. This continued until about 1660-70, when the power of the Lenape was completely crushed, and the Iroquois remained their masters, so long as they continued to occupy the valley of the Delaware.

The Lenape (or Delawares) were nearly annihilated, and from a nation numbering some sixty thousand warriors, occupying the territory between the Hudson and the Delaware, they were reduced to about two thousand who were scattered all over the state in small bands, and had managed to escape from their cruel and relentless foes. These were sub-divided into about twenty bands or families, averaging about one hundred, although some of them could scarcely muster sixty men. These families were found settled in little villages on smaller streams, where they would be more secure from roving bands of Iroquois, who still roamed over the country, but generally followed the courses of the Delaware and Raritan.

When the white men came, the small bands of the Delawares welcomed them as their protectors and defenders from the cruel enemies of their own race, and were ready to make treaties, sell them lands, and induce them to settle. At the time of the European occupation, the Lenni Lenape were found divided into three tribes, or sub-divisions of the same tribe, again divided into small bands as above stated. The Monseys or Mensies (signifying wolf) occupied the hill and mountain ranges from the Hopewell hills north, while the Menamies, or Turtle, and the Unalachtgo, or Turkey, occupied their little villages between the Delaware and the ocean from Egg Harbor and Sandy Hook to the mountains.

A short time before New Jersey began to be settled by the white people, the Monseys relinquished their rights to nearly all the lands south of the Musconetcong and retired to the territory now known as Warren, Sussex, Morris and Passaic Counties. That the Minsi, Monsey, Mense, or Munsey tribe had their wigwams in every valley and ravine, among the hills of old Hopewell Township from the Province Line to the Delaware at different periods is altogether probable.

The hills and mountains from the Sourland range north, were known to coast tribes as the home of the Monseys, or Minsies, and the path leading to the hills from tide water at Trenton, was known as the "path" to the Monseys. This path became the great highway of the pioneers, through Ringoes, Quakertown and Pittstown, passing through the gap in the Musconetcong mountain at Glen Gardner, to Hampton, Belvidere and the Delaware Water Gap.

It is foreign to the scope of these articles to give a history of the Aboriginal inhabitants of this valley, or the surrounding hills, at the time of the occupation by the English, but in response to a request will give a brief sketch of some of their customs and manners prevailing at that time.

As stated above, the Indians had been quite numerous before the Iroquois had commenced their war of extermination, but when the pioneers came to settle the "goodly land," they found no enemy to molest, but rather friendly allies, who rendered very valuable service to the new comers. The small and peaceable bands were found located on the south side of the hills, in ravines or glades where they were sheltered on two or three sides, and surrounded by heavy forests, which afforded some protection from the fierce blasts of winter.

These villages were located with a view to winter occupation only, as in summer they were often entirely deserted, the whole population being away in temporary camps, the squaws cultivating the crop of corn and beans for succotash, (called by them sicquotash) and the braves seeking for the best places for fishing and hunting.

The Indians took no pains whatever to have their cultivated fields convenient to their villages, but they were frequently located miles away. They had their fields where the timber had been disstroyed by forest fires, and left a rich deposit of ashes to add to its fertility, or where the timber was scattering, and the land had good natural drainage. If the fields were too remote from the villages, a temporary camp would be made near them at planting and harvesting time, to be occupied by the squaws and papooses at night, the squaw working in the field all day, with the papoose strapped over her shoulders. Two or three old men also remained at the camp, to keep the squaws from quarrelling and fighting over the division of labor and the distribution of the spoils.

The able bodied men never came to the fields at the time of planting or gathering the crops, being at their fishing or hunting camps. They preferred to take the risk of starvation in winter rather than to assist the squaws with the work, that being too degrading for a warrior.

It is a tradition that when the corn fields were near the bays and rivers where fish were plenty, they would "plant" a fish with every hill of corn as a fertilizer. They taught the pioneers this custom, and it is still practiced by the farmers in the vicinity of the Delaware and the seashore.

The Indians of this region went to the seashore every autumn and gathered clams, which they dried for winter use. This afforded them a wholesome and palatable diet, assisting very materially in the bill of fare, when the snows were too deep to venture out on the chase. They also laid in a store of nuts, chesnuts especially, which, when roasted or boiled, added to the winter fare as a substitute for bread, if the supply of corn and beans should become exhausted.

Whenever the snow was crusted over sufficiently to bear their weight, they sallied forth and captured deer in great numbers, as they broke through the crust and soon became fatigued and helpless. After taking off the skin, the choice pieces of venison were hung up near the wigwams and after undergoing the freezing and thawing process for several moons, they became very tender, and were considered by the red man perfectly delicious.

When the streams were frozen over they caught a great many fish, by cutting a hole in the ice, covering their heads and shoulders with a blanket, which enabled them to see the bottom of the stream very distinctly. The fish were so plentiful that in a short time they could spear an abundant supply for several days. In summer they shot fish in great numbers with their bows and arrows, and before there were any milldams to obstruct the streams, shad came up the Millstone and Stony Brook to spawn, and were easily taken.

A great many stone arrow heads were found along the brook, and in the garden and fields near by, at the time of the writer's boyhood, and his father informed him that the long and narrow points were used by the Indian boys to shoot fish. This information made a great impression on the mind of the small boy and awakened an intense desire to have just such a bow and arrow, and play Indian.

To humor his whim his father fitted him out, and he started for the brook fully expecting to return with a well filled basket of suckers and pike, which were quite plentiful in the broad and shallow pond in front of the house at that time. If there had been sturgeon or even big shad in Stony Brook that bright summer day, he might have met with some success, but the small fry were very shy, and also very lively, as they darted from one big stone to the next, and back again with almost lightning like rapidity.   Not being an expert marksman, he missed the fish, and hit the stones every time, and after wading around a short time, he returned with an empty basket, a broken arrow, and almost a broken heart.

His one great ambition to play "Indian boy" had suffered a most distressing and humiliating defeat, and he returned a sadder and wiser lad, with the firm conviction that he had mistaken his vocation.   However, his father fixed him up again and in time he became quite an expert in that line.

The writer has visited the Indian wigwams in the West, which do not differ materially from those of the eastern tribes of two hundred years ago.   Like the birds of the air in building their nests, instinct is their architect, and although the savage is invested with intellect and reason, his style and habits admit of no changes.

In approaching an Indian village at the distance of a half mile, the huts have the appearance of huge hay stacks, blackened by exposure to the elements.   They are in no regular order, some standing quite near together, while others are a considerable distance apart.   They are constructed circular in form, and about twenty, and some thirty feet in diameter, the outer row of posts being about five feet in height, and quite near together.   At a distance of about six feet inside this row, there is another row of posts, set eight or ten feet apart, and about ten feet in height.

The outside row is tightly woven in basket work with small saplings, and the roof of the same material, the rafters being made of larger poles all running to the centre, or apex, and supported by poles running on top of the inner row of posts, which prevents their "sagging."   When the frame work is finished it is like a huge basket, and is so strongly woven together that it could be taken up by the wind and rolled across the prairie a considerable distance without going to pieces.   Outside this basket work a row of sods is laid as high as the outside posts, and the roof covered either with bark, skins, or a thin layer of sods.   An aperture is left at the apex, to give the smoke egress, also serving for ventilation, as when the wigwam is lined with skins tightly sewed together, it is impervious to wind.

Between the inner and outer row of posts are the beds, which are elevated at a proper height from the ground to be comfortable as seats, these being the only chairs a wigwam affords.   One either sits on the side of the bed or on the ground floor, the latter being preferable, as the squaws have not learned the use of insecticides, or disinfectants.

In the centre of the wigwam is a large basin-shaped cavity, at least six feet in diameter. This is the Indian's fireplace, and when the fire is first started the smoke is so dense that it is impossible to see across the room. The inmates are now compelled to call on their neighbors, or remain outside, leaving the door open to force the smoke out at the top. When the fire burns down they return to find a hot bed of coals all ready for cooking, and the wigwam thoroughly heated. The door is then closed and they are ready for the fireside meal and the social smoke, which invariably follows.

The inside row of posts supporting the beds, are decorated with matchcoats, leather breeches, moccasins, saddles, bridles, blankets, skins of various kinds, and every imaginable article known to Indian life. The beds are all around the wigwam, and at the distance of about the length of an ordinary bedstead, piles of skins or blankets are thrown across to separate each bed from its neighbor.

On entering an Indian wigwam, you neither ring the bell, knock at the door, nor send up your card. If the buffalo skin stretched across the door is fastened on the inside there is nothing to do but wait, or try some other hut. If the door is not fastened, you pull it aside, and you are in the mansion. In some of the winter huts there is a long dark passageway to be explored after the outside door has been opened.

The writer on his first visit felt a little delicacy about entering one of these wigwams unannounced, but was informed that when the Indian visits his white neighbor, he never knocks or rings, but tries the door and if it is not fastened, he opens it, looks in and gives the usual salution, which is simply a nod and "Howdy." Before going to the door however, he announces himself from the outside, if the curtain is not drawn. This he does by putting his face close to the window so that he can see all around the room.

The settler's wife on the frontier is frequently frightened nearly out of her wits, as her attention is attracted by a shadow falling across the floor, and she looks up to see the homely and very solemn face of a "big Indian" pressed close to the window pane. Like the tramp of our acquaintance, if a lunch or piece of pie is passed out to him, he will not attempt to enter, but goes away satisfied.

1905.

NUMBER XXXV.

Among the Archives of the Supreme Court of this State is found the record of the famous trial between Doctor Daniel Coxe and fifty of the early settlers of Hopewell Township, who had purchased their lands of Thomas Revell, agent for the West Jersey Society. The writer has a copy of the original writ of ejectment, together with the names of those on whom it was served, dated May term of Supreme Court of New Jersey, 1733. Of the fifty, who on April 22, 1731, entered into a written agreement and solemn compact to stand by each other and test the validity of Dr. Coxe's claim to the 30,000 acre tract, embraced in old Hopewell Township, six were Parkes, Roger Sr., Roger Jr., John Sr., John Jr., Joseph and Andrew.

Dr. Coxe gained the suit, and the settlers who were unwilling to pay the Coxe claim were notified to vacate. Then came the great excitement incident to ejecting the settlers from the farms which they, or their fathers, had purchased in good faith, and on which they had built dwellings, barns and fences, and spent many years in clearing and improving.

At the August term of the Supreme Court, 1735, complaint was made by Mr. Murray, Attorney for Dr. Coxe, that several persons in Hopewell, had, in a "riotous and outrageous and violent manner, and by night assaulted ye persons who by virtue of his Majesties writ, were by the Sheriff of Hunterdon County, put into possession of the several houses and plantations of the persons named in the complaint." Public sentiment among the settlers at the time of this great excitement was largely in sympathy with those who resisted forcible ejectment from their homes.

However it was a lost cause, and their resistance only resulted in their being heavily fined, and bound over to keep the peace. Many of the settlers made the best settlement possible with the attorney of Doctor Coxe, while others sold out their improvements to newcomers from Long Island and elsewhere, for barely enough to give them another start in the wilderness, either in Virginia, Pennsylvania or northern New Jersey.

Nearly all the Parke family left Hopewell Township at that time, and their names are found among the pioneers of northern Hunterdon. They took the early records with them and the writer has been unable to get any definite information concerning their families. From other documents and the records of other families connected with them, the following record is believed to be nearly correct *

Sarah, daughter of Doctor Parke, married Thomas Schooley of Crosswicks, Burlington County, who was doubtless the son of Robert Schooley, a fellow passenger with Doctor Parke in the voyage from England to the land of their adoption. They came in the good ship "The Shield" in 1678, and were among the first European emigrants to be landed at Burlington, as no vessel had previously ventured so far up the Delaware.

Thomas Schooley finally settled in northern Hunterdon County and bought a tract on the mountain near the famous spring, which, in time of the revolution, and later, was such a famous health resort for the aristocracy of Philadelphia. Samuel Schooley bought a tract there including the spring which bore his name. The Schooley family were from Hawsworth, Woodhouse Parish of Handsworth, County of York, England, and were ardent Quakers.

John Parke, son of Roger, married Sarah, daughter of the first Andrew Smith, who bought land in Hopewell in 1688, and his deed is the first recorded document bearing the name of "Hopewell." The Parke family and Andrew Smith, Senior, were also Quakers, but there being no church of their faith nearer than Stony Brook, near Princeton, they all contributed toward the support of the Presbyterian church at Pennington. John Parke was one of the first constables of Hopewell Township in 1705, and served as juror in 1706. In 1721 he served on the Grand Jury with his brother, Roger Parke, Jr., James Stout of Amwell, and David and Freegift Stout of Hopewell.

It would seem that the Andrew, Roger and Joseph Parke, who came on the stage of activity about 1725–35, were the sons of John Parke, but we have no positive evidence. Andrew was doubtless named for his grandfather Andrew Smith. Roger Parke, Jr., re-

*If all these were the children of Doctor Parke, it is quite probable that there were at least two marriages.

sided on the homestead, and in 1722 paid taxes on a part of the land and stock; but we are unable to give any history of his family, as they left this region as early as 1735, if not before.

Anna, daughter of Dr. Parke, probably married William Merrill, Jr., who was by trade a cooper, and they settled on the tract purchased for her by her father in 1697. In 1722 he paid taxes for 130 acres, and in the survey of the road from Stoutsburg to Marshall's Corner in 1723, (given in number 20) the line passes his farm before it reaches Stony Brook.

Grace, daughter of Doctor Parke, married Jacob Stout, son of James, of Amwell.

Their children were: (1) Samuel, married Hannah Drake, and had children, Nathan, John, Elizabeth and Sarah.

(2) Aaron, married Mary Drake and had children, Andrew and Daniel, who owned the farms south of Hopewell, afterward owned by Deacon Benjamin Drake, and Charles and Noah Stout, distillers.

(3) William, married Hannah Hutchinson, and had two children.

(4) John, married Kesiah Brush, daughter of Timothy, and had one child, Sarah, who married Amos Hoagland, the father of John Stout Hoagland and grandfather of our townsman, Simpson Hoagland, Esq.

(5) Elizabeth, married John Vankirk, and had three children, Jacob, Henry and Sarah.

(6) Annie, married her father's cousin, Benjamin Stout, and had three children, Abner, Aaron and Grace.

(7) Sarah, married Azariah Higgins, the ancestor of the family at Ringoes and Wertsville.

(8) Catharine, married Enoch Drake, and had John, Benjamin, William, Anna, wife of Jeremiah Van Dyke, Esq., of Hopewell, and Peter V., who married Rachel Savidge, and had Benjamin, Robert and Alfred.

William, son of Enoch Drake and Catharine Stout, named above, married Achsah, daughter of William Wert, and had Enoch, who is now 90 years of age and a resident of our Borough. (2) John, of Lambertville, now deceased, and (3) Zephaniah, who resides in Trenton.

As an illustration of the heroic measures sometimes resorted to by our forefathers, to stir up the latent energies of timid and luke-

warm patriots of revolutionary times, we give the following incident in the life of the Benjamin Stout referred to above.*

Mr. Stout had a neighbor who, as far as known, had been in
robust health until he received notice that his country needed his
services, and that he had been drafted. On receiving this intelligence, he went to bed at once, and was so ill that the family had to
take his meals to his room. Mr. Stout and one or two of his neighbors called on him, and after satisfying themselves that he was
feigning illness, decided to try the cold water cure, and took him
out to a corner of the house where there was a large cask filled with
rain water. It was frozen over, but to break the ice and plunge
him in was but the work of a moment, and the helpless man was
completely cured of his infirmity and suddenly made as active and
agile as a boy. It is needless to add that he climbed out of that
cask without help and lost no time in getting back in the house, not
even stopping to thank his kind neighbors for performing such a
miraculous cure. Tradition does not state that after his ducking he
obeyed the call of his country, but it doubtless caused him at least
to have a more wholesome respect for his patriotic neighbors.

William, son of Doctor Parke, was the only one of the name
who made a permanent settlement at Hopewell. The records show
that in 1755 he owned the farm where Mr. Robert Brophy now
lives, north of the Borough. Mr. Parke died in 1764, aged 52, and
his widow, Sarah Parke, was granted letters of administration on
his personal estate on March 2, 1764. The rough stone in the old
Parke–Larison family plot on the farm of Mr. C. E. Voorhees with
inscription "W. P. 1764. A. 52." without doubt marks his grave,
as it is in the Parke row.

The old family bible of his son Benjamin is now in possession
of his great grandson William W. Kirkendall, who is the only descendant of Dr. Parke now living on the original tract on Stony
Brook. This bible contains the following entry in the bold, plain
hand of Benjamin Parke. "This book I give to my wife Anna,

---

*It is a fireside tradition that Benjamin Stout was very fond of a practical joke.
On one occasion he found an Indian asleep, and seeing a live blacksnake near by, he
caught it, and placing it in the Indian's bosom under his blanket, he hid himself near by
and waited developments. The movements of his snakeship soon aroused the drowsy Indian, who, instead of giving Mr. Stout a free exhibition of the war whoop and dance, lay
perfectly still, and teased and played with the snake as if it had been a kitten. Mr. Stout
quietly retired, greatly disgusted and disappointed, that his experiment in trying to scare
an Indian had proved such a dismal failure.

during her life, and at her decease to belong to my daughter, Anna Kirkendall." Signed, Benjamin Parke.

William Parke married Sarah Jewell, whose mother was Penelope, daughter of James Stout, fifth son of Richard Stout of Monmouth County. Sarah Jewell's father was doubtless William Jewell, who served on the Monmouth Grand Jury in November, 1715, his name being on the court records.

The record in the old bible is as follows: William Parke, born May, 1711; Sarah Parke, born May 20, 1720. Their children, Penelope and Elizabeth (twins), born October 28, 1738; Rachel, born November 30, 1740; Benjamin, born January 8, 1743; William, born September 25, 1746; Sarah, born January 25, 1749; Naomi, born May 20, 1751; Anna, born May 20, 1754; Zebulon, born January 25, 1757; John, born December 31, 1759; Margaret, born December 17, 1762.

Penelope, the oldest of the twin sisters, married Richard Stout of near Stoutsburg, and had six sons and three daughters, viz: John, William, Jehu, Richard, Elhahan, Nathan, Rachel, Penelope and Sarah. John, the eldest son, was a very prominent citizen of the adjoining County of Somerset, living near Skillman Station. He was known as "Esq. John," and was a justice from 1810–25, and one of the judges of the Court of Common Pleas, 1820–25.

His children were William, Richard, Rachel and Penelope. William, the eldest, married Anna, daughter of Judge Jared Sexton, and had three sons, Richard, Abram Runkle and Zephaniah, who married Abigail, daughter of Jesse Stout, and resided on the homestead until late in life, when he built a comfortable home in Hopewell and spent his closing years in retirement. He was one of the pillars of the First Baptist church, and a very dignified courteous gentleman. He left no children but his death was sincerely mourned by a very large circle of friends, by whom he was greatly beloved.

His grandfather, "Esq. John," mentioned above, was one of the patriots of the revolution and fought in the battle of Monmouth, and doubtless several others. He used to relate an incident of which he was an eye witness at that battle, and which we will publish in this connection.

The chief actor was Sergeant John Swaim, who lived one and a half miles northwest of Hopewell, on the farm now owned by his great grandson, William Phillips. Mr. Joseph B. Schanck of our Borough, is also a great grandson of this old hero of many battles.

The incident of which Esq. Stout was an eye witness, happened near the close of the fight at Monmouth, when he saw Sergeant Swaim pursuing a Tory refugee, who in the retreat of the enemy was considerably in the rear of the column. Sergeant Swaim called to him several times to halt and surrender, warning him that unless the order was obeyed he would shoot. The order was not heeded, the refugee doing his best to get out of range, when the Sergeant put his threat into execution, brought down his man, and carried his gun and knapsack back to his company.

This exploit of Sergeant Swaim was in retaliation for the treatment he had received at the hands of the enemy earlier in the day, when his company was compelled to retreat or submit to capture. A very high five rail post fence stood in the way of their retreat, and Sergeant Swaim thought that he could easily slip through between the top rails, forgetting in his great haste and excitement that he carried a knapsack on his back, and a cartridge box in front. Consequently, to his utter dismay, he found himself wedged fast between the rails, unable to move in either direction. To add to his discomfiture, he could not reach the ground with either hands or feet, and it seemed to be a vain struggle.

Meanwhile he could hear the musket balls striking against the rails, and realized that the British were making a target of his coat tails. Not being aware of their Sergeant's difficulty, his company had gone far to the rear, leaving him to fight his battle with the fence alone, but he finally succeeded in extricating himself, and lost no time in rejoining his company.

In his case discretion was the better part of valor, and the maxim was verified that "He who fights and runs away, will live to fight another day," as he continued in the service until the close of the war and was promoted to Lieutenant before its close.

He served in Capt. Simon Duryee's Company, First Battalion, State Troops, Somerset County, and was in the battles of Brandywine, Trenton, Princeton, Monmouth, and doubtless many others. He was entitled to a pension as a Lieutenant, and would not accept it, under any other conditions. It was not until 1831, that Esq. John Stout found proof of his promotion, and through his efforts the pension was granted. It is said that, including back pay, it amounted to several thousand dollars, and while it was very fortunate that he received it at all, it seemed like very tardy justice to a deserving old veteran, who was then almost four score.

He died September 26, 1838, aged 85 years, and his grave may be found in the rear of the old Baptist Church in the Borough. When we meet on Memorial Day to strew the fresh and fragrant flowers of springtime on the green mounds, which mark the last resting places of the departed heroes of old Hopewell, let us not forget to honor the grave of Lieutenant John Swaim of revolutionary fame.

1905.

NUMBER XXXVI.

Elizabeth Parke, daughter of William, like her twin sister Penelope, had a numerous and honorable progeny, many of whom are still residents of old Hopewell. Elizabeth married Thomas Roberts, who was doubtless a son of Thomas of Long Island, who came to Hopewell Township in 1727, or earlier.

The children of Thomas Roberts and Elizabeth Parke were (1) Sarah, who married James Sutphin and had two children, William and Abigail; (2) Ruth; (3) Elizabeth; (4) Ose, who married Major William Garrison and had five children, viz: John R., Ure, Abigail, Sarah and Naomi. Of this family of Major Garrison, Sarah married Spencer S. Weart of Hopewell, and had seven sons and two daughters, all of whom married and reared families. We hope to give a history of these prominent Garrison and Weart families and something of their ancestors in subsequent articles, and also more of the descendants of Penelope Parke under a sketch of the Stout family.

Benjamin Parke, son of William, the next in order was born January 8, 1743, and his wife Lucy, May 20, 1736. He married second about 1788, Anne, daughter of James Larison and widow of Judge Jared Sexton. She was born February 11, 1743. It has been a popular belief, shared in at one time by the writer, that Benjamin Parke had children by both marriages, but the family record in the hand writing of Mr. Parke explodes this theory, as he mentions but two children, Rachel, born March 17, 1767, and Anna, born August 3, 1778.

Rachel, married John Sexton, and had four children, William Parke, born January 7, 1800; Joseph Rue, born 1806; Ruth, who married John L. Phillips, son of Thomas, of Hopewell, and Catharine, who became the second wife of Mr. Phillips. We reserve a history of this family for a future article.

Anna, daughter of Benjamin Parke, married Adam Kirkendall of Columbia, Knowlton Township, Sussex County (now Warren), three miles south of the Delaware Water Gap. He was born May 15, 1773.* In 1795, Adam Kirkendall, Sr., and his brother David were merchants at Columbia, and judging from the books now in possession of the writer, kindly loaned by Mr. W. W. Kirkendall, they did a very extensive business.

The town of Columbia was the trading point for an extensive territory north and east of the Water Gap, and in old histories is styled the pride and glory of the Delaware Valley between Manunka Chunk and the Blue Mountains.

The Kirkendalls had a store in which they sold not only the lines usually carried in country stores, but being remote from the cities they kept drugs, millinery, jewelry including watches (which they seem also to have repaired), Indian goods, and outfits, etc. They also had saw mills, and men in the woods up the river cutting timber which they rafted to Trenton and Philadelphia, besides supplying their own mills. They also operated the ferry, the books showing charges of two and six pence (30 cents) for carrying over a two-horse vehicle. For shipping rye flour to Philadelphia in flatboats about 40 cents per barrel was charged.

Isaac Devore was given credit for two dollars and seventy-five cents for "making a trip to Trenton with a raft," which was a very reasonable charge for such a hazardous undertaking. In those days the raftmen always walked back, going through Pennington, Ringoes, Pittstown, Hampton and Belvidere.

Benjamin Parke was also a resident of Columbia or vicinity, 1790–1800 or earlier and was one of the township officers in 1798–99. He was a customer of the Kirkendalls, and in comparing the ledger with the handwriting of Mr. Parke in the old bible, it is probable that he did some of the bookkeeping for the firm, as it is in the same bold clear hand.

Adam Kirkendall and Anna Parke were married about 1797,

---

*Jacob Kirkendall was a German and the progenitor of one of the most prominent and patriotic families of Sussex County. He was among the pioneer families and was one of the trustees for a burying ground in 1731, and a Justice for old Hunterdon County in 1738. In 1789 his sons Peter, Henry and Cornelius were among the largest taxpayers in the Minnisink settlement. Peter was a Justice in 1748 and the first marriage ceremony recorded there was performed by him. Capt. Benjamin Kirkendall was appointed by the governor to recruit for the Continental Army and Capt. Samuel one of the officers to report to the Committee of Safety all persons disaffected or dangerous to the government. On the roster of Sussex County are found the names of the two officers named above and also Stephen, Cornelius, William and Samuel, privates.

The Reformed church of Wantage was organized in 1787 and in a membership of 54 charter members about one-half the male members were of the name of Kirkendall.

and about 1800 removed with Benjamin Parke to Hopewell and settled on the farm now owned by Robert Brophy, which was the old homestead of his father William Parke.

Adam Kirkendall and Anna Parke had six children, as follows: (1) Mary A, born March 16, 1798, died in infancy.

(2) Benjamin P., born August 1, 1800, married Rachel Ann, daughter of John Stout of Hopewell, who was born May 3, 1810. They had one son, George W. C. Kirkendall (named for Doctor George Whitfield Case of Hopewell), born November 4, 1830, who was a physician and on December 5, 1856, embarked as surgeon on the ship Cathedral of Philadelphia bound for California. On February 18, 1857, the vessel was wrecked off Cape Horn, and as the Captain was confined to his berth with a very severe illness and unable to leave the vessel, Dr. Kirkendall refused to leave him and they went down to a watery grave together. After the boats were lowered and ready to leave the sinking ship, one of the officers went back to the cabin and pleaded with the doctor to come with them but to no avail. Thus perished a bright and talented young physician who had already distinguished himself in his profession and had he reached his destination would have made his mark in the growing young state.

(3) William Parke Kirkendall, born March 16, 1803, married Eliza, daughter of Lucas Weart of Hopewell, and they had one son William W. Kirkendall who married Rose A., daughter of John, and granddaughter of Sheriff Jacob Kentnor of Kentnorville, Bucks County, Pennsylvania. They had one child Sarah, who married William H. Hart of Pennington. They now reside in Hopewell and their children, Mabel, Grace, Ethel and William Weart, are the seventh generation from Doctor Parke the pioneer.

(4) Samuel P. Kirkendall, born February 4, 1806, never married, and like his brother William Parke was an expert millwright at a time when much of the machinery of our flouring mills was constructed of wood and good millwrights were in great demand.

(5) Cornelius Larison Kirkendall, born November 15, 1809, went to Mississippi in early life but soon returned on account of failing health and died April 15, 1840, unmarried.

(6) Sarah Ann, daughter of Adam Kirkendall, born August 1, 1812, married Lewis Wert and removed to Ohio soon after.

William Parke, son of William, and grandson of Doctor Roger, was born September 24, 1746, and died September 24, 1794. His father resided on the farm now owned by Mr. Robert Brophy, which he owned in 1755 as shown by the records. He was a near neighbor of Col. Joab Houghton, who, as has been previously stated, resided on the farm now owned by Mr. R. J. Birch, one mile north of the Borough.

On the organization of Captain Houghton's Company in 1776, Ralph Guild, son of Rev. John Guild, pastor of the Presbyterian Church of Pennington, was chosen First, and William Parke, Second Lieutenant. On May 3, 1777, when Capt. Houghton was promoted to Lieut. Col. of the First Regiment, Hunterdon County, Lieut. Guild was made Captain and Lieut. Parke First Lieutenant. In 1784, the year following the close of the revolution, Lieut. Parke was one of the trustees of the Baptist Church here as shown by the records.

The wife of Lieut. Parke was Rachel Rowland, born about 1742, died August 15, 1794, daughter of Rev. John Rowland, a noted Presbyterian minister who was a native of Wales, and came to this country in early life with his parents who settled in Pennsylvania near the line between Bucks and Montgomery Counties, north of Philadelphia. He received his education at the famous Log College at Hartsville, Pa., which was the foundation of the College of New Jersey at Princeton. He was licensed to preach by the Presbytery of New Brunswick, September 7, 1738, and the same day application was made for his services by the churches of Maidenhead (now Lawrence) and Hopewell (now Pennington.) He accepted the invitation and a great revival of religion attended his labors.

He also preached with great acceptance at Amwell and on October 4, 1739, they asked the Presbytery to have him installed as their minister to preach for them one-third of his time, but on October 12, 1739, the Presbytery ordained him as an evangelist for which service he was especially adapted. His preaching at Amwell was attended with surprising manifestations and the people flocked to hear him for many miles around. These meetings in Amwell were conducted by some of the most powerful evangelists in the Presbyterian Church and were continued far into the spring of 1739, the farmers leaving their spring work to attend them.

On April 25 of that year, when the renowned Whitfield made them a visit, he wrote in his journal that several thousands were there before his arrival and that Revs. Gilbert Tennent, Rowland,

Wales and Campbell were there and had given them three sermons that day. Rev. John Rowland married June 16, 1740, Martha Anderson, who was probably a sister of Cornelius, Sr., of Hopewell and an aunt of Cornelius, Jr., and of Mrs. William Larison. Mr. Rowland removed to Great Valley, Pennsylvania, about 20 miles west of Philadelphia and took charge of the church at New Providence. His great popularity as an evangelist kept him away from his charge much of the time. He died in 1747, in the prime of life and in the midst of his great usefulness.

John Rowland, son of William Parke and Rachel Rowland, was born about 1770, and married about 1800 Pamelia, daughter of William Larison and Francina Anderson of Hopewell. She was born June 3, 1779. They had two children, viz: Elizabeth Larison, born January 18, 1802, and Rachel Rowland, born December 5, 1804.

John R. Parke was a drover and stock dealer and the certificate of his death in 1807, gives his residence at that time as Knowlton Township, Sussex Co., N. J. Mr. Parke was taken with a very severe illness while on one of his business trips, and we publish the following extracts from a letter written to his father-in-law, William Larison, which will be of interest to his many descendants in this township.

Steubenville, O., April, 1807.

"Sir: I am now to inform you that John Parke came to my house on February 13, and was very unwell. He continued to grow worse until April 17, at six A. M., he took leave of this troublesome world. He had applied to a skillful physician who attended him during the whole time. Five weeks of the time he was confined to the bed. We left nothing undone that we could have done for one of our own family. His complaint was a cough settled on his lungs. He was decently interred in the Steubenville church yard attended by a number of the respectable citizens of the place. I add no more at present. Betsey joins in love to you all.

LEVI REED."

The above states that Mr. Parke was decently interred and the statement was undoubtedly true. One hundred years ago a decent funeral depended vastly more on the character and solemnity of the religious rites and ceremonies than the great display of expensive equipages, and a costly casket. As an item of historical interest in illustration of the above statement, we will publish the total cost of the funeral as exhibited in a bill sent to his father-in-law, William Larison:

Coffin	6.00
5 yds. muslin @ 50c.	2.50
Digging grave	1.00
Proving death	1.00
	—— 10.50

In the estimation of those who had charge of the obsequies the above amount was deemed sufficient to give their friend a decent burial according to the custom of the times and place.

About three years after the death of Mr. Parke, his widow married Jonathan Hunt, and they had one daughter whom they named Francina A. for her grandmother Larison, whose maiden name was Francina Anderson.* We will extend the history of this family in connection with the history of the descendants of James Larison in a future article.

---

*A minute of the death of Mr. and Mrs. Parke is found in the records of the old Baptist Church, stating that they were both worthy members and the maiden name and parentage of Mrs. Parke is also given.

1905.

NUMBER XXXVII.

Elizabeth, daughter of John R. Parke and Pamelia Larison, born January 18, 1802, married January 20, 1820, Asa Titus, son of Samuel, who was at that time a blacksmith at Hopewell.

They resided in Hopewell a short time and then removed to Troy, Miami County, Ohio, where he became a prosperous farmer. In 1852, Mr. Titus returned to New Jersey and settled on the homestead of William Larison near Glen Moore. They had ten children, some of whom had married and settled West before Mr. Titus returned to New Jersey.

(1) Pamelia, the oldest daughter married Job Leming in Ohio, and they came to New Jersey, settled on a part of the Larison tract and reared an enterprising family of children. Asa, the oldest is a well known stock dealer and butcher of Glen Moore; Gilbert H., has extensive mining interests in the Black Hills region; Wilson T., is a farmer of Pennington vicinity; Newell, died unmarried; Elizabeth, married Henry S. Rynearson and died soon after, leaving one daughter Hannah, who married Harry, son of D. Webster Stout deceased; Rebecca, youngest daughter of Job Leming, married Bloomfield Dalrymple and is also deceased.

(2) John Parke, son of Asa Titus, married Elizabeth Smith: (3) Wilson H., married Maria Swager, and (4) Rebecca, married Henry Gearhart, all of whom settled in Ohio or Indiana.

(5) Jane M., daughter of Asa Titus, married Hon. James H. Hill, who at the time of their marriage was a member of the Legislature of this State. Of their children, Homer, Asa T. and Hellena, all unusually bright and intelligent, died just as they were budding into manhood and womanhood, and Elizabeth died in infancy. Kendrick C., twin brother of Hellena, married Anna, daughter of Prof. Alfred Brace, now deceased, of the State Schools, Trenton. They reside in Trenton where Mr. Hill occupies the position of Assistant Postmaster, is Ex-President of the City Council and prominent in the political affairs of the City.

After the death of his first wife James H. Hill married Mrs.
Eure Titus and has since resided in the Borough. The second Mrs.
Hill has been deceased for several years and Mr. Hill has passed
the fourscore milestone, but his mind is still as active and his step as
elastic as many of our "boys" of half his years. Mr. Hill has been
a close student, not only of books, but of men and affairs of his
time. Several years of his life have been spent as a teacher and he
has been an occasional contributor to the columns of the public
press. His maternal grandfather, Benjamin Coles, was a very successful pastor of the Hopewell Baptist Church from 1774 to 1779.
For three score years Mr. Hill has been an earnest and devoted member of the Second Baptist Church of Hopewell at Harbourton.

(6) George W. Titus married Belle Henry and settled in the
west.

(7) Ruth A., married John Sked, a prosperous farmer of Hopewell. They settled at Pennington and reared a large family, all
of whom are well settled in life and nearly all in this township. (1)
Howard, married Laura, daughter of Simpson Van Dyke; (2)
Elizabeth, married Johnson Drake of Pennington; (3) Etta, married Theodore Reed of Pennington; (4) Flora, married Livingston
Atchley; (5) Annie, married Albert Blackwell, son of John; (6)
Homer, married first, Miss Cooper, second, Ida Snook of Pennington; (7) John, married Mary, daughter of George Bunn; (8) Walter W., resides in the West, unmarried; (9) Fred, married Emma,
daughter of Alfred Phillips, deceased; (10) Clarence, unmarried;
(11) Edith, married Robert, son of Charles Blackwell, who is a
merchant in Pennington.

(8) Rachel, twin sister with Ruth, married Asa H. Sheppard,
one of the most repected citizens of our Borough, and their children
are Milton, residing in Elizabeth, N. J., George of Flemington,
Willis of Bordentown, and Hellena residing with her parents.

(9) Catharine E., married J. Britton Hill of Hopewell and had
four sons: C. V. Hill, proprietor of the Hill Refrigerator Works of
Trenton; Samuel C., deceased, Albert and Percy of Trenton. Mr.
and Mrs. J. Britton Hill have both been deceased for several years.

(10) Samuel B., youngest child of Asa Titus married Emily,
daughter of Liscombe T. Blackwell, resided on the homestead and
was a prosperous farmer. He died when in middle life leaving
three children, Viola, wife of Edward Van Doren of Wertsville;

Belle, wife of Samuel Cox of Hopewell, and Liscombe B., who married a Miss Warren of Pennington.

Rachel Rowland, daughter of John R. Parke and Pamelia Larison, born December 5, 1804, married January 25, 1823, Stephen H. Titus, son of Enos, a prominent citizen of Pennington, and for many years a ruling Elder of the Presbyterian church. He was born in 1769 and died February 16, 1840.

Stephen H. Titus resided for a time on the Deacon James Hunt farm, now occupied by Morgan D. Blackwell near Glen Moore. In the spring of 1836 Mr. Titus purchased the farm on the old turnpike west of the Borough, now owned by his son, Edwin S. Titus. Stephen H. Titus and Rachel Parke had nine children, one of whom, Henry B., died in infancy. All the others married and reared families except Charles J., who died at the age of 68, unmarried.

In the writer's early boyhood they all resided at home, their ages ranging from five to twenty-five and one of his earliest recollections is of the evening visits spent with his parents in the near-by home of this happy and hospitable family. It was a time honored custom to make neighborhood visits during the long winter evenings and although they were always surprises, the families visited were always prepared to entertain their friends. The practice of waiting until you were invited, or of sending word that you might be expected on a certain day, had not been thought of among farmer folk, they were inventions of a later period. Neighbors had a standing invitation to drop in and spend an evening whenever they felt like it.

In those good old times farmers were always ready and expecting company, when the walking was good across the fields in winter, and the moon was at the full or in the proper quarter to give light until the small hours of the morning. They went before dusk in those days, or at early candle-light, and they stayed late.

The writer can well remember when the old people prolonged their visits until one, or even two o'clock in the morning, and the younger generation were never censured for following their example. There was a spirit of large open-hearted hospitality abroad in the air in those days and young and old alike were subject to the infection. "Well, we thought it was about time to look for you as you owed us a visit." How familiar this expression sounds to the ears of the old time people of three score and upward, and how vividly they recall the happy faces of dear old friends long since passed away.

And how vividly they recall the old fashioned suppers when you sat down to a table that fairly groaned under the weight of tempting dishes.

It was considered a breach of etiquette to be dainty, and it was far better to go without your dinner in order to do ample justice to the bountiful supper and prove to your hostess that you appreciated her cookery, as it was one of those occasions when actions spoke louder than words.

Then between the supper hour and the time of your departure came another test of your fortitude, as the apples and cider, doughnuts, hickory nuts and mince pie, and perhaps a glass of home-made wine, were passed just to brace you up for the walk home.   Space will not permit, and language utterly fails us in our attempt to describe the old fashioned evening visits with our fathers and grandfathers in the days of Auld Lang Syne, but they ne'er will be forgot while mind and memory last.

William Larison, oldest son of Stephen Titus and Rachel Parke, was a man of more than ordinary ability, well informed on current topics of his day, and in his earlier years was a frequent contributor to the press on matters of political economy, and held several township offices. He married first, Sarah, daughter of William T. Phillips, of Hopewell, and had two children, Oliver, who married Sarah, daughter of Alpheus Phillips, of Harbourton, and Howard, who married a daughter of George W. Bateman of Flemington.

William L. Titus married second, Catharine Phillips, sister of his first wife, and third, Mrs. Abbie Woodruff. Mr. Titus died a few years ago at the age of nearly four score and his widow is a resident of our Borough.

Elizabeth, daughter of Stephen Titus and Rachel Parke, married Judge Enoch H. Drake of Hopewell, and they settled on a farm east of Pennington. Judge Drake served a term in the Legislature and for several years was one of the Judges of the Court of Common Pleas. He has held several other offices of trust and responsibility and discharged his duties faithfully and conscientiously. He is an able public speaker, and the debater who crossed swords with him in the old time debating schools found a "foe worthy of his steel." Mrs. Drake has been deceased several years but the Judge is still with us and one of the oldest and most honorable citizens of our

Township. They had children as follows, viz : Rachel, died single; James Baldwin, married Carrie, daughter of Johnson T. Blackwell; Hallie, Altha and Elizabeth.

Francina, or Fanny, daughter of Stephen H. Titus, married Alexander H. Drake of Titusville and had Cora, Jane, Wilmer, Howard and Georgianna.

Enos, son of Stephen H. Titus, married Mary A., daughter of Samuel Dalrymple of Hunterdon County and sister of John M. Dalrymple Esq., of our Borough. They resided near Lambertville and had two sons, viz : Stephen, an engineer on the Belvidere–Delaware railroad, who married Etta, daughter of John Hunt of Pennington, and Edgar, who married Mary, daughter of William L. Weart of Bound Brook. They reside at Benson, Arizona.

Pamelia, daughter of Stephen H. Titus, married Charles B. Hill and resided near Glen Moore and had children, Mary, who married Franklin Terry of Bucks County, Pennsylvania ; Elizabeth, married William Sheppard ; Elvira, married Freeman Perrine of Glen Moore, and Alice and Bertha, who died in childhood.

James T., son of Stephen Titus, married Anna, daughter of Leonard K. Dilts, a prominent citizen of Ringoes, N. J. They had two children, viz: George, who married Josephine Gallagher of Pennington, and Anna M., who teaches a popular private school in the borough and resides at home with her mother. Mr. Titus resided here several years before his death and his cheerful genial disposition won him many friends who greatly mourned his death which occurred October 1, 1904, at the age of sixty-four. Cornelius L., twin brother with James, married Adelia, sister of the wife of James, and they had Era, who married Alvin Hart of Titusville; James, died in childhood; Rachel and Mary, single; Emily, who died in 1904, and William, who married Fannie Arrowsmith, and resides at Lawrence Station.

All the children of Stephen H. Titus and Rachel R. Parke are now deceased. They were without exception an honorable, upright generation and will be kindly remembered by their old neighbors while any survive to honor their memory. After the death of his first wife Stephen H. Titus married Zeruah Labaw, widow of William Hunt of Woodsville, and although the children of this marriage are not in the Parke line we will mention them to complete the family circle of our old friend. They had four children as follows : (1) Emily, married Emory Hunt, a prosperous farmer of Linvale, Hun-

terdon County, and their children are Charles and Samuel.   (2)
Stephen A., married Anna, daughter of David Bond of Ringoes,
and have children, Albert, David, Zeruah, Harold and Laura. Edna, their second child died in childhood.

(3) Edwin S., the popular merchant of our borough, married
Mary, daughter of L. W. Hartwell and granddaughter of Elder
Philander Hartwell, for many years the pastor of the First Bap-
tist Church of Hopewell. They have three daughters viz : Maud,
Mary Emma and Gladys.   (4) Alfred, married Katharine, daugh-
ter of Augustus Blackwell, Esq., of Pennington.   They reside in
Trenton.

Stephen H. Titus died January 31, 1873, aged 73. Mrs. Titus
still survives and resides with her daughter at Linvale. Mr. Titus
was a kind, peaceable neighbor, a good citizen, a consistent Christian, and greatly beloved in the community where he lived.   In
times of trouble he hastened to offer his services and exerted himself
in every way possible to aid and comfort the afflicted families of his
neighborhood, and his death was an irreparable loss to the community.

Sarah Parke, born 1749, daughter of William Parke and Sarah
Jewell, married David Stout, son of Jonathan Stout and Mary
Leigh, of Hopewell.   They settled at Lexington, Kentucky, and
reared a large family.   After the death of his first wife David Stout
married the widow of Nathan Drake of Hopewell.   Mrs. Drake's
first husband was David Larison of Hopewell.

1905.

NUMBER XXXVIII.

John Parke, son of William, married Charity, daughter of John Stout and Mabel Sexton, and we think removed about 1792 with his wife's father, her uncle Charles Sexton, his brother-in-law Col. William Chamberlin, and a number of Hopewell families to Shimoken, Pa., at the time of the great migration to that region.

Anna Parke, daughter of William, born May 20, 1754, became the second wife of Col. William Chamberlin of revolutionary fame. At the time of the revolution he owned the farm and mills on the Neshanic Creek, near Wertsville, since known as Nevius' Mills. A few years ago the writer made some extracts from a sketch of the remarkable family of Col. Chamberlin which he found in the Pennsylvania State Library at Harrisburg.

Col. Chamberlin was born September 25, 1736, was married four times, was the father of twenty-three children, the youngest of which, Moses, born November 8, 1812, was still living in 1900. The period of time over which his life and that of his father extended was one hundred and sixty-four years. Col. Chamberlin was 76 years old when Moses was born and in 1900 his descendants numbered about one thousand souls scattered in every part of the United States.

Among the persecuted Huguenots who fled from France and found an asylum in England was one "Chambellon," who came to London about two decades prior to the revocation of the Edict of Nantes by Louis XIV in 1685. Owing to the great fire in London in 1666 the refugee removed to Ireland. Like many other Huguenots he changed his French name for an English equivalent, Chamberlin being the anglicized form. Tradition says that three sons of the refugee came to America about the beginning of the eighteenth century, the ancestor of Col. William settling in Hunterdon County.

Col. Chamberlin rendered valuable service to the country during the revolutionary struggle, being Lieut. Col. of the Second Regiment, Hunterdon County, was in a number of battles and skirmishes, and at the battle of Germantown on October 3-4, 1777, he had a most distressing experience. His oldest son Lewis, then 18 years of age, had occasion to visit his father on some business or family affair, and learning that a battle was pending decided to remain with his father, and although a civilian took a position in his father's regiment and went into the action with it. During the engagement he was struck on the knee by a spent cannon ball and for the want of prompt surgical attention he died on the field.

The next month after the battle, when a brave man was needed for the hazardous undertaking of escorting the notorious Tories Ex-Gov. John Penn and Ex-Chief Justice Benjamin Chew of Pennsylvania from Union, now High Bridge, where they had been confined, to Worcester, Massachusetts, for greater safety, the Governor and Council of safety detailed Col. Chamberlin for that service.

The following is a copy of their official action :

Princeton, N. J., Monday, November 24, 1777.

"The Council met at Princeton. Agreed that the officer who is to conduct John Penn and Benjamin Chew to Worcester be directed to purchase 20,000 flints in some of the New England states for use in this state."

"Wednesday, 26 of November, 1777."

"The Council met at Princeton. Agreed that there be advanced to Col. Chamberlin for purchasing 20,000 flints in New England and for defraying his expenses to Worcester in the Massachusetts Bay, whither he is to conduct Messrs. Penn and Chew, the sum of 200 pounds."

That Col. Chamberlin made the purchase of the flints as directed is shown by the following extracts from the minutes of the Council.

March 17, 1778.

"The Council met at Trenton. Agreed that Col. Hathaway receive from Mr. Ogden at Boontown the 20,000 flints, sent or to be sent into this state by Mr. Archibald Mercer from Boston (first paying Ogden at Boontown for the cartage) and to be accountable for them when properly called upon."

In 1791, Col. Chamberlin removed from New Jersey to the Shamokin settlements in Buffalo valley, Union County, Pennsylvania, where he purchased 600 acres of land. He died August 21,

1817, aged 81. A marble shaft marks his resting place in the cemetery at Lewisburg, Pa., overlooking the Susquehanna.

Col. Chamberlin was married four times, having seven children by the first, four by the second, four by the third, and eight by the fourth marriage.

His first wife was Elizabeth Tenbrook, born August 23, 1740, and died April 29, 1770. Their children were as follows: Lewis, killed at the battle of Germantown; (2) Nellie or (Penelope) born 1761, married John Lawshe, through whom comes a great and honorable posterity; (3) Anna, born 1763, married G. Boss; (4) A daughter born 1764, died young.

(5) Lucretia, born December 20, 1765, died January 19, 1841, married Christian Nevius of Clover Hill, who was a revolutionary soldier in Capt. TenEyck's Co., and also served for a time in Major Baird's Co. His father was Peter Nevius of Clover Hill, N. J., and his mother Maria Van Doren, one of the seventeen children of Christian Van Doren and Alche Schenck of Middlebush, N. J. Christian Nevius and Lucretia Chamberlin were married November 16, 1789, and four years later he removed to Shamokin, Pa., where he was a very successful farmer. They had eleven children, all but one of whom lived to old age. He was a very useful citizen in church and state and left a large number of descendants. See genealogy of Nevius family by A. V. D. Honeyman, published in 1900.

(6) John, born 1768. (7) William, born 1770, died in infancy.

The second wife was Anna Parke as stated above. They were married March 6, 1771, and had children (1) William, born 1772; (2) Enoch, born 1774. (3) Ten Brook, 1777. (4) Sarah, 1779, married M. S. Wilson.

Anna Parke Chamberlin died November 12, 1779, and he married her sister, Margaret Parke, 1782. Their children were: Uriah, born 1783; (2) Elizabeth, born 1785; (3) Aaron, 1787; (4) Rachel, 1789.

Margaret died in 1791, and he married in 1794, Mary Ann Kimball, who was born in 1769, and died in 1859, over one hundred and one years after the date of her husband's first marriage. She was of a very distinguished family and among the friends of her childhood were General Washington and other noted men entertained at her father's house. While Col. Chamberlin was a member of the Baptist church his wife was a staunch Presbyterian. Their children were as follows: (1) Lawrence, born 1795; (2) John, 1797; (3) James, 1798; (4) Lewis, 1803; (5) Mary, 1804; (6) Joseph, 1806; (7) James, 1809; (8) Moses, 1812.

Col. Chamberlin's mill near Clover Hill was burned by a foraging party of the British in 1776, and they pressed his colored man and a team into the service to drive a wagon loaded with ammunition. The man pretended that he could not manage his team and told the officers that the horses were not accustomed to being driven behind other teams, but if they were put in the lead they would be more manageable. The officers then placed him in front and coming to a long hill soon after he whipped his horses into a run and succeeded in taking the load into the American lines which were not far distant, although the bullets fell thick and fast around him as long as he was within range.

Kesiah, youngest daughter of Doctor Roger Parke, born about 1700, married James, oldest son of William Larison of Hopewell, who we think owned in 1730 the farm near Glen Moore now occupied by Morgan D. and Ira V. Blackwell. In 1721, his name is found among the township officers as constable for Hopewell township. In 1722, he is assesed for 11 horses and cattle, 9 sheep and 160 acres of land, and the same year his name appears on the account book of Robert Eaton who kept a store near the Old Quaker Church on Stony Brook, west of Princeton.

The town of Princeton had no existence at that time but Stony Brook at the crossing of the King's Highway was known from New England to Virginia. Near the residence of Joseph H. Moore at Glen Moore are still seen traces of one of the first paths or driftways of colonial times, leading down Stony Brook through the woods.

It was a short cut for those who for some time after the settlement attended the Friends Meeting and were also customers of Mr. Eaton, as shown by his ledgers. Letters were left at his store for all the settlers northwest and north for several miles up the brook.

William Larison probably resided at Hopewell until after the death of Mrs. Larison, or near the close of life, when he removed to New Brunswick and probably resided with one of his children. In 1751 his son James owned the tract east of the road along the old driftway as shown by the deed from Joshua Anderson to Hon. John Hart and his brother Daniel on October 4 of that year.

The will of William Larison dated at New Brunswick, N. J.,

April 7, and probated May 30, 1749, is recorded in Libre 6, Folio 70, in the office of the Secretary of State at Trenton and was copied in part by the writer many years ago. This will is remarkable for the deep religious feeling manifested in the introductory sentences, which, although in accordance with the custom of the times, is extended far beyond all precedent, and contains the whole scheme of redemption as revealed in the New Testament.

It is as follows, capitalization preserved: "In The Name Of God Amen. I William Larison of the City of New Brunswick in the County of Middlesex and Province of New Jersey being through the abundant Mercy of God. though Sick & Weak in Body. yet of Sound and Perfect mind understanding and memory Do Make Ordain and Constitute this My Last Will and Testament and Desire that it may be received by all such.

"Imprimis. I most humbly Bequeath my Soul to God my Maker beseeching his Most Gracious acceptance of it through the all Sufficient Merits & Medeations of my Most Compassionate Redeemer Jesus Christ, who gave himself to be an Atonement for my sins, and is able to Save to the Uttermost all that Come unto God by him Seeing he Ever liveth to make Intercession for them and who I trust will not reject me a Returning Penitent Sinner when I come to him for Mercy in this hope and Confidence I render up my soul with comfort humbly beseeching the Most Blessed and Glorious Trinity One God Most Holy Most Merciful and Gracious to prepare me for the time of my Dissolution and then to take me unto himself into that peace and Rest and in comparable felicity which he has prepared for all that Love and fear his Holy Name.

"Imprimis. I Give my Body to the earth from whence it was taken in full assurance of its Ressurection from thence at the Last Day. As for my burial I desire it may be Decent without Pomp or State at the Discretion of Executors hereinafter named—Who I doubt not will manage it with all Requisite prudence as for Such Worldly Goods and Estate as it hath pleased God to bless me with, withall I give and Bequeath in Manner following. To my oldest son James Larison I give and Bequeath the sum of Ten Pounds proclamation Money to be paid to him by my Executors within one year after my decease, and as for the Rest of my Worldly Goods and Estate both Real and Personal I give and Bequeath to be divided Equally between my sons William Larison Thomas Larison John Larison and George Larison.

"I do make and Constitute my beloved son John Larison and son-in-law David Stout to be my executors of this my will and do Empower them to Collect in my debts and dispose of my Estate to the best advantage at discretion of my Executors and after paying my Just Debts Funeral Charges and my aforesaid Legacy to Divide the remainder as aforesaid among my aforesaid sons William Thomas John and George and I do hereby revoke and Disannul all other Wills, Whatsoever heretofore by me made Ratifying and Conforming this and only this to be my Last Will and Testament.

"In witness Whereof I the said William Larison have hereunto set my hand & seal this seventh day of April in the year of our Lord Christ one thousand seven hundred and forty nine

"Signed William Larison

"Witnesses Jediah Higgins–Samuel Wilson and Robert Rolfe"

1905.

NUMBER XXXIX.

John Larison (or Jon Larsen) according to the fireside traditions of the older Larisons was a Danish nobleman who was compelled to flee from Denmark and lose his estates by confiscation in
1660, because of taxes. He fled first to Scotland and hearing that
a large reward had been offered for his capture, he went over to Ireland for a time and finally emigrated to America and purchased a
large tract, about 1700 acres, near Brooklyn, Long Island. His
name is found on the rate list of Newtown, Long Island, in 1683.
When John Larison came to America he left grown sons in Ireland,
who tradition says married and settled there and who have the same
tradition respecting their ancestry.

On May 22, 1683, John Larison, (probably a son of John 1st)
and Jemima Halsey were married at Newtown and on December
20, 1686, a John Larison also of Newtown married Mary Howell, a
widow. She was probably the second wife of John Larison, Senior,
the Dane. The evidence in support of this theory is that the first
husband of Mary Howell was doubtless a brother of Margaret
Howell, who married Rev. John Moore. This was the only family
of Howells at Newtown and this marriage would make the Larisons
a family connection of Nathaniel Moore, the first of the name in
Hopewell, and connect the Larisons with a large circle of the English families who first settled in this region.

This fact will account for Hopewell as the choice of location
for William Larison, who came at the time of the great migration
of Newtown families. Tradition says that of the six sons of John
Larison the Dane, two were killed by the Indians, Roger (the same
as George) went to Pennsylvania, William to Hopewell and the
others settled near Chester in Morris County, and that John the
Dane also spent the closing years of his life there and that after a
very eventful career his body found its last resting place at Chester.

It is said that John the Dane had a very superior education and
that he gave his children the best educational advantages available

at that time, and that in addition to being engaged in agriculture they were a race of school teachers and business men as well. This made its impress on the generations following, among whom have been shrewd business men and educators and leaders in their respective communities.

James, the oldest son of William and grandson of John the Dane, was born in 1695, doubtless on Long Island and died at Hopewell in 1792, aged 97 years. He was buried in the Parke-Larison family plot on the farm where the writer spent sixty years of his life, and his grave, marked by a rough unlettered sand stone, was often pointed out to him by his grandfather, and was carefully protected for 60 years. The location was shown by the writer to Doctor C. W. Larison of Ringoes who has since placed a suitable inscription upon it.

James Larison married Kesiah, daughter of Doctor Roger Parke, and there is a tradition in the family that Dr. Parke found a nugget of silver on the farm while digging a post hole, had it examined and pronounced genuine silver ore. He was very desirous that James Larison should purchase the farm and would not reveal his secret to any one else, and as Mr. Larison did not secure his title of the heirs of Dr. Coxe until after the death of Dr. Parke, his secret died with him.

The old fence was taken up and a trench some six feet in width and several hundred feet in length was dug in order to discover the treasure, and this trench is well remembered by the writer. Along this trench a shaft was sunk and when a depth of ninety feet was reached caved in while the men were at dinner, burying all their tools. They were so discouraged at what they were pleased to consider this ill omen that it was never reopened. Several other shafts were sunk on different portions of the farm, some of them to a considerable depth, but were abandoned on account of the vast accumulation of water which had to be kept out by hand power and necessitated working day and night. James Larison sunk a comfortable fortune in his mining enterprises without realizing any profit whatever on the investment.

David Stout, who married Elizabeth, sister of James Larison, bought out the Parke claims about 1740, but it is not known positively that he ever resided there. That James Larison occupied it prior to 1750 is altogether probable, but the quit claim deed was not obtained from the heirs of Dr. Daniel Coxe until 1765, when they gave a quit claim to David Stout, and on June 10 of the same year he sold the plantation of 243 acres to James Larison for the sum of twelve hundred pounds ($3,000.00.) Both of these old parchment deeds are in the writer's possession and are in an excellent state of preservation, and cover the tracts now owned by C. E. Voorhees, Amos Sked and the Samuel Ege tract, now in possession of E. S. Wells, Esq., of Glen Moore.

There is a tradition in the family that the old log schoolhouse that stood on a part of James Larison's north tract, and at the cross roads near Wm. F. Golden's, was built by James Larison, and that he was the first teacher. It is quite probable that he taught there when a young man, but it doubtless stood there many years before he purchased the Parke tract, and was no doubt built by Doctor Roger Parke, or his son John, who resided on that part of the tract.

The children of James Larison and Kesiah Parke were as follows, viz.: (1) John, born 1737; (2) Andrew, born February 2, 1739; (3) William, born January 24, 1741; (4) Anne, born February 11, 1743; (5) Roger, born 1745; (6) Elizabeth, born 1747; (7) Catharine, born 1750; (8) Achsah, born 1752; (9) Elijah, born 1754;. (10) David, born March 8, 1757. The eldest son John, married Mary, daughter of Benjamin Pelton of Long Island, who about 1740 purchased the farm now owned by John L. Burroughs, between Woodsville and Marshall's Corner. John Larison settled there and kept a hotel for many years. They had no children.

Benjamin Pelton bequeathed the farm to Mary Larison, and in the event of her death without heirs to descend to her nephew, John Pelton, son of her brother Samuel. John inherited the farm and sold it soon after to Moses Quick and joined the great migration to New York State about 1792.

John Larison's will, dated May 8, 1805, proved November 13, 1805, bequeaths his property, including a tract of land in Cayuga County, New York, to his namesake, John Sexton, son of his sister Catharine, who married Benjamin Sexton and resided at Belvidere; to John and Nellie McGee and to Elizabeth Larison, daughter of Catharine Manley of Somerset County. He appointed "Miller" Peter Snook and Jacob Stout his executors and the witnesses are his neighbors, Andrew, George and Anna Smith.

Andrew, son of James Larison, born February 2, 1739, married first a Miss Green who died soon after, and he married second Lavina Severns of a very wealthy, educated and prominent family, who resided near Sandy Ridge, Hunterdon County. His wife inherited a large farm and upon this they settled. Both being well educated they opened a school near their dwelling and taught the higher branches and several young men were here prepared for college and entered the professions, others receiving a good education fitting them for business pursuits.

Their children were as follows: (1) Benjamin, born November 15, 1761, killed by falling from a horse when a young man.

(2) James, born November 5, 1765, married a Miss Holcombe.

(3) Mary, born June 13, 1768, married William Boss.

(4) George, born December 21, 1770, married Catharine, daughter of John Lambert, governor of the State 1802-03. From Gershom, son of George Larison and Catharine Lambert are descended Gershom L. Ege who lives on the homestead of his grandfather on the Delaware below Lambertville, and Horatio N. Ege who resides in Lambertville.

(5) Andrew, born May 17, 1776, married Mary Wilson, and his son Andrew, born October 2, 1803, married Mary Phillips and became the father of our townsman David Larison, who, by his marriage with Sarah A. Wilson, had children, Mary C., John F., Cora M. and Howard W. David Larison married second Rhoda, daughter of Benjamin Drake and widow of Prall Quick of Ringoes.

Benjamin, son of Andrew Larison and Mary Wilson, married Hannah A. Holcombe and became the father of Dr. George H. Larison deceased of Lambertville, Rev. Andrew B. Larison deceased of Ringoes, and Dr. Cornelius Wilson Larison of Ringoes, to whose very interesting history of the Larison family published in 1888, the reader is referred. The Larison family history is given by him in detail in a book of nearly 500 pages, involving an immense amount of labor which should be gratefully appreciated by every descendant of James Larison of Stony Brook.

Lavina, youngest child of Andrew Larison and Mary Wilson, born May 11, 1811, married Samuel R. Holcombe September 12, 1834, and their children were: (1) Sarah J., who married Charles M. Stryker and had children, Margaret, Lavina and Samuel. (2) Thomas, who died in childhood. (3) Mary C., who married first, Samuel, son of Jacob Skillman, and second, George H. Agnew of Titusville, and had children, Raymond H., Robert, Josephine and Olive. (4) Andrew Larison Holcombe, who married Ose Garrison, daughter of Spencer S. Weart, and had children, Thomas, Sarah

and Andrew Larison, died in childhood; Lavinia, married George
M. Taylor and resides in Ewing Township; Ose R., married Joseph
P. Labaw and resides in Utah, and Mary S., residing at home.
Andrew Larison Holcombe is president of the Hopewell National
Bank and is one of the leading citizens of the community.

Benjamin, son of Andrew Larison and Lavina Severns, married Sarah Vanzandt, was a much respected citizen of Bucks County,
Pa., and had two children, Mary and William.

Sarah, youngest child of Andrew Larison and Lavina Severns,
was a teacher. She married Robert Naylor and resided near the
old homestead at Sandy Ridge.

Roger Larison, son of James, was a revolutionary soldier in
Capt. Henry Phillips' Co., 1777, and married and settled near Per-
ryville, Hunterdon County. They had a family of eight children
who married and settled in Hunterdon and Warren Counties in this
State and the Lake Country of New York State.

William, son of James Larison, born January 24, 1741, married Francina, daughter of Cornelius Anderson. He settled on the
farm on the opposite side of the brook from his father and spent his
whole life there. He died October 21, 1816, aged 75, and Mrs.
Larison died November 30, 1811, aged 64. William Larison was
also a soldier of the revolution in Capt. Henry Phillips' Company,
Hunterdon County.

William Larison had two children: (1) Cornelius, born February 14, 1767, married Ure Hunt. They had no children. He
died June 11, 1851, and Mrs. Larison January 19, 1850. For many
years they had resided on a small farm at Marshall's Corner.
(2) Pamelia, daughter of William Larison, married John Rowland
Parke, son of William Parke and Rachel Rowland, and their history is given in Articles 36 and 37. After the death of John R.
Parke, Pamelia married Jonathan, son of "Deacon" James Hunt,
and had one daughter, Francina, who married Charles M., son of
Col. Ira Jewell. By this marriage she had one son, William Larison Jewell, born June 9, 1829, who was a very popular merchant in
Hopewell for many years, associated with his step-father and
brother, Stephen and N. D. Blackwell.

William L. Jewell married Carrie M., daughter of Abraham
Skillman and Henrietta Stout of Hopewell. William L. Jewell
died August 24, 1870, aged 41. His widow still survives, residing
with her daughter at Tolland, Connecticut. William Jewell and Car-

rie Skillman had four children, viz : Dr. Charles A., a graduate of the University of Pennsylvania at Philadelphia, who resided at Lambertville, N. J., where he died June 11, 1900, aged 43. Francina and Henrietta, twins, born 1859, died in infancy, and Mary E., who married Joseph E., son of Judge Joseph R. Baldwin of Paterson, N. J.

Joseph E. Baldwin was a graduate of Princeton University, a law student of Messrs. Calhoon and Gillis of Palatka, Florida. He afterward practiced law at Palatka and was elected mayor of the City and Judge of the Probate Court. On the advice of his physician he gave up his business in Palatka and sojourned for a time in Phoenix, Arizona. A few years before his death he purchased a home in Tolland, Ct., where he resided until his death which occurred January 16, 1902. The children of Judge Baldwin and Mary E. Jewell were Joseph E., died in infancy and Margery Jewell.

After the death of Charles M. Jewell June 20, 1833, his widow Francina, married Stephen Blackwell, merchant of Hopewell, and had three sons, viz.; (1) Hon. Jonathan Hunt Blackwell, wholesale grocer of Trenton, N. J., who married Susan, daughter of Spencer S. Weart of Hopewell. They have four children, Stephen, William Jewell, Henry C. and Clara.

(2) Charles H., a Civil Engineer by profession, married first, Elizabeth, daughter of Ely Moore, and had three children, Edgar, a very talented and popular young man who died at the age of 28, and Carrie and Alice residing at home. Mr. Blackwell married second Lizzie, daughter of Alfred S. Cook of Hopewell. They reside in Hopewell.

(3) Willis B., married Catharine Taylor of Philadelphia. They reside in New York City and have three children, viz.: Willis, Catharine Francina, and Edith.

1905.

NUMBER XL.

In the family of James Larison and Kesiah Parke, the next in order was Anne, born February 11, 1743, married March 28, 1768, Judge Jared Sexton who resided on an adjoining farm. We will give a history of their family in a future article.

Elizabeth, daughter of James Larison, married Aaron Runyan, no doubt a son of Aaron and brother of Catherine, wife of Col. Joab Houghton. Aaron was the son of Thomas the pioneer (whose history is given in previous articles) and a brother of Vincent, whose son Cornelius and grandson John owned and operated Runyan's saw mill for many years. The children of Elizabeth Larison Runyan were, Andrew, John, Aaron and Achsah, and as nothing is known of this family it is presumed that they went to Ohio with others of the family.

Catherine, daughter of James Larison, born 1750, married November 24, 1779, Benjamin Sexton who was a carpenter. They removed to Belvidere, N. J., and had at least two children mentioned in the division of the property of James Larison. Benjamin Sexton died while his children were small, and in his will proved May 14, 1806, directs his wife, to whom he leaves all his property, to put his children to trades when they arrive at a suitable age.

Achsah, daughter of James Larison, was born in 1752, and became the second wife of John Humphrey, son of Stephen, who came to the vicinity of Woodsville about 1740 with Benjamin Pelton, Charles Sexton, and other Long Island families. He settled on the farm now owned by Peter Titus and known as his back farm. This family of Humphrey was high spirited, aristocratic, and like other Long Island families of that period bred and trained race horses, and attended the races near their old homes on Long Island, which was at that time the most popular resort for the sporting fraternity between New England and Virginia. The Humphrey family lived on a farm adjoining that where the writer's grandfather was born and reared, and the varied experiences of the Humphreys in that line were frequently rehearsed in his presence.

The trip to Long Island was made on horse back and sometimes they returned with flying colors, while at other times when
they met with reverses, they would be at home several days before
their neighbors would find it out.   Several families indulged in this
fascinating sport, but after the old settlers who had migrated from
Long Island passed off the stage of activity, the business of breed-
ing horses for racing purposes was discontinued.

John Humphrey, son of Stephen, had three wives, his first
being Pamelia, daughter of Rev. Isaac Eaton, pastor of the Hopewell church, and his last Rachel, daughter of Nicholas Stilwell
Esq., of Woodsville.   They are buried on the farm of Mr. A. L.
Holcombe near the Borough.

John Humphrey and Achsah Larison had one son, born about
April 10, 1777, who was named John Humphrey, Jr.   Achsah
Humphrey died within a few hours after the birth of her son, and is
buried in the Larison plot on the farm of C. E. Voorhees.   Tradition says that the stone which marks her grave was taken from the
Humphrey farm and the inscription engraved by James Larison
when about 80 years of age.   The inscription is quite lengthy, giving the date of her death as April 11, 1777, and her age 24 years, to
which is added the familiar verse, "Hark! from the tombs the dole-
ful sound," etc.

John Humphrey, Jr., married Experience, daughter of Isaac
Dunn, of Hopewell, and their children were as follows, viz:
Achsah, who married John Hortman* of Amwell, whose children
were, Catharine, who married Patrick Riley of Hopewell; Henry,
married Susan Wyckoff, and for several years before his death resided at Flemington; and George, who died at Hopewell, unmarried.   Achsah Humphrey Hortman, married second Philip Riley.

Andrew, son of John Humphrey, Jr., married Susan Primmer,
and had two children, one of whom died in infancy and the other,
Anna, was a teacher at Pennington.   She married John Waters,

---

*In the "Genealogy of New England Settlers," is found the name of Timothy Hort-
man who was doubtless the ancestor of this family.   In 1675 he served seventeen weeks as a
soldier in King Philip's war, and was then discharged on the petition of his wife representing that he had two children to support.   From a later petition we learn that he had three
children but their names are not given.

Peter Hortman was an early settler in Amwell Township, and was a Justice of the
Peace.   He had sons, Gabriel of Snydertown, a miller; Amos, a teacher, and John.   One of
his sisters, Christiana, was the wife of William Golden, Sr., in 1780, and another, Charity,
was the wife of James Sutphin of Amwell.

son of Philemon, of Hopewell, and resided in Washington. Their two children both died in childhood.

George, son of John Humphrey, Jr., married Emily Gorcher, and they resided at Conshohocken, Pa.

Samuel, son of John Humphrey, Jr., went to Milwaukee, Wisconsin, when it was a small village. He owned the first flouring mills there and made a comfortable fortune.

Elizabeth, daughter of John Humphrey, Jr., married Edward Noyes of Princeton, N. J.

Stephen, son of John Humphrey, Jr., married Elizabeth, daughter of John L. Phillips, of Hopewell, and had one son, Edgar. They went to Cordova, Illinois, where Elizabeth married second, William Golden Marshall, a wealthy farmer and grain dealer of Cordova, who is now deceased. His widow is living at Cordova. Mr. Marshall had no children and devised the bulk of his large estate to Edgar Humphrey, who resides at Cordova. Mr. Humphrey married Elizabeth, daughter of Thomas Karr.

After the death of his first wife John Humphrey, Jr., removed to central New York, taking several of his younger children with him. By a second marriage he had a family of children. He died in 1870 aged 93, and his body was brought to Hopewell and interred in the old cemetery.

Elijah, son of James Larison, born in 1754, married Eleanor, daughter of James Stout and Jemima Reeder, of Amwell. She was born in 1749, and her grandfather was James Stout the pioneer of the name in Amwell. Elijah Larison settled on the homestead of his father on Stony Brook, and tradition says that while engaged in the mining operations referred to in previous articles he received an injury which incapacitated him from managing his farm.

His young wife proved herself equal to the emergency, and her industry and good management has seldom been equaled by one of her sex. With her own hands she planted and grafted with the best varieties one of the largest orchards in the county, which was the pride and admiration of the horticulturists of the whole region. This orchard was planted about 1780 or earlier, and some of the varieties grew to be immense trees attaining a diameter of thirty to thirty-six inches, and rounded out a century of usefulness, a few still bearing fruit in 1900. Elijah Larison died October 26, 1827, aged 73, and Mrs. Larison December 30, 1828, aged 79.

They had children as follows, viz: Jared Sexton, born June 6,

1786, died in infancy. Catharine, born June 23, 1789, married February 8, 1808, William Marshall Esq., born January 10, 1789, whose brother, Philip Marshall, was the father of James Wilson Marshall, the discoverer of gold in California in 1848. (See sketch of the Marshalls in article 16). William Marshall was a Justice and known all over this region as "Esq. Marshall." He represented this district in the Legislature 1830-36.

On May 5, 1829, William Marshall and Catharine his wife conveyed by quit claim deed their right and title to the Stony Brook farm to Elizabeth Cool, and in 1837 Elizabeth Cool sold out to John Ege. In the spring of 1838 the large families of Marshall and Cool, together with Joseph Rue Sexton and perhaps others, left Marshall's Corner with quite a caravan of large farm wagons especially fitted up for the purpose. They set their faces toward the setting sun, and after a journey of fifty three days they came in sight of the great "Father of Waters" where Cordova, Illinois, is now located. Here they settled on the broad uncultivated prairie which soon became a wealthy and prosperous community. When the writer first visited there, over 46 years ago, he found the Jersey settlers the leading citizens of the place, and everything both indoors and without bore such an unmistakable impress of Old Hopewell thrift, culture, and refinement, that he could scarcely realize that he was over one thousand miles from home.

The children of William Marshall and Catharine Larison were John, born October 1, 1808; Jared Larison, born August 26, 1810, died in infancy; Jonathan Larison, born November 11, 1811, was a physician in Keithsburg, Illinois, and died there aged 76; George W. C., named for Dr. Case of Hopewell, born August 23, 1813; William, born November 22, 1815; Charles B., born December 14, 1817, married Lucretia Bailey, and had a daughter, Catharine Marshall; Rebecca, born October 14, 1819.

Elizabeth, daughter of Elijah Larison and Eleanor Stout, born July 23, 1791, died January 12, 1871, married William Cool in 1809. Their children: Jared Larison, born February 1, 1810, married November 5, 1832, Margaret Smith of New Jersey, whose children were Sarah, married J. J. Johnson; Mary, married J. V. Bailey; Jonathan, married Julia Withrow; Robert Condit, married Ellen Harding; Edward, married Elizabeth Vandeburg.

Jonathan Smith Cool, son of William and Elizabeth, never married.

Elijah Stout Cool, son of William and Elizabeth, born June 10, 1814, married Elizabeth Marshall of Ohio, and their children are Theodore, married Rachel Davis; Albert, married first Ella Wressle, second, Agnes Walker; Jane, married Simpson Quick of New Jersey; Annetta, married Thomas McCarm; George, married Esther Reynolds.

Mary Eleanor Cool, daughter of William and Elizabeth, born July 9, 1819, married John Marshall, of Trenton, N. J., and their children are: Harmon, married Virginia Hoff; Jerome, married Minnie Withrow; Elizabeth, married Joseph Cranston; Charity, married Paul Dewitt Ege; Jonathan, married Sarah Crawford; Edward; Samuel, married Emma Seeley; Clara, unmarried; Robert, married Mary Burlingame; Horace, married Sarah Crawford Marshall, widow of his brother Jonathan; and Minnie, married Charles Wells.

Isaac, son of William Cool and Elizabeth Larison, born February 15, 1822, died August 24, 1897, married August 15, 1861, Nancy Jane Hatchner, of Prestonburg, Kentucky, who was born June 19, 1832, and died October 19, 1901. Their children are: Amanda Elizabeth, unmarried; Eleanor Larison, married William S. Block; and Anna Gertrude, who married Prof. William H. Plymire, principal of the schools at Cordova.

David, youngest child of James Larison, born March 8, 1757, married September 15, 1780, Jerusha, daughter of Ethan Smith, and sister of Temperance who married Hart Olden, and became the mother of Charles Smith Olden, afterward governor of New Jersey. She also had a brother Dr. Charles Smith, a wealthy and prominent citizen of New Brunswick. David Larison settled on the farm adjoining the James Larison tract on the north, now the property of Mr. E. S. Titus of the Borough. They had four children, viz: Jonathan, born September 1, 1781; Amos, born May 7, 1784, resided in Ohio and had two daughters, died in 1839; Charles, born July 24, 1793, resided in Cass County, Indiana, had twelve children and died in 1841; Enoch, born November 2, 1796, removed to Cincinnati, Ohio, when it was a small town, grew up with the place, and also had a family.

David Larison died November 29, 1800, aged 43, and his widow married second, Nathan Drake and removed to Lexington, Ky., where he died, and his widow married third, David Stout, son of Jonathan Stout and Mary Leigh, of Hopewell. David Stout's first wife was Sarah, daughter of William Parke and Sarah Jewell (see number 37).

The will of David Larison, dated November 19, 1800, bequeaths the homestead farm to his widow and four sons, directing that his son Jonathan work the farm, and the children, all of whom are under age, be kept together. One item reads as follows: "At the expiration of my wife's widowhood the farm is to be sold, and the proceeds divided between my four sons, Jonathan, Amos, Charles and Enoch." He appoints his wife Jerusha, and his neighbor John Sexton, executors.

James Larison, the father of this large family, was the executor of his own will, which he made in the form of a deed to his two youngest sons, Elijah and David. The old patriarch was then 94 years of age, and his four eldest sons were well advanced in life. He had doubtless given them their portion many years before, and they were well established in business. It only remained for him to deed the homestead farm of 243 acres to the two youngest, and make some provision for the three remaining daughters who had doubtless been given a start in life at the time of their marriage many years before.

This deed is dated February 14, 1791, and is a very lengthy document. It states that in consideration of his natural love and affection for his two sons, Elijah and David, and also for and in consideration of the sum of two hundred and thirteen pounds to be paid by the said Elijah and David Larison unto his daughters and their children, and names them in their order as given above, not forgetting the young grandson, John Humphrey, Jr., son of his deceased daughter Achsah. The boundaries of the tract are then given in detail, commencing in the middle of Stony Brook, and bounded by lands of Charles Sexton, deceased, on the west and north, James Hunt on the east, and lands of Ralph Hunt and the several courses of Stony Brook on the southeast and south.

After the death of James Larison, Elijah and David divided the tract as equally as possible and each gave to the other a quit claim deed. All these deeds and also a map of the tract as divided, made by Wilson Stout December 7, 1796, are in possession of the writer.

After the death of David Larison the administrators sold their tract to Samuel Ege, who divided it between two of his sons, John and George.

1905.

NUMBER XLI.

After the death of David Larison the family continued to reside on the old farm described in our last, until the marriage of Mrs. Larison with Nathan Drake, when the farm was sold to Mr. Drake, the deed bearing date May 15, 1807. The same spring Jonathan, the oldest son of David, removed to Ohio, settling in Hamilton County, twelve miles north of Cincinnati, which was then about the present size of the Borough of Hopewell. Here Mr. Larison cleared and improved a fine farm on which he resided for a period of fifty years, and being within a few hours drive of the most rapidly growing town in the country at that time, he found a ready market for his products and became very prosperous.

Mr. and Mrs. Larison lived to celebrate the sixty-fourth anniversary of their marriage, and had a family of four boys and four girls, to each of whom he left a comfortable competence from the stand point of a western farmer of that period. One very remarkable characteristic of this large family was their longevity, several of the family reaching the age of 90, and one daughter (Mrs. Margaret Fitch) reaching the age of her paternal grandfather, 97 years.

We cannot give the history of this large family but will mention the oldest, Jerusha, who married a Hopewell boy, Nathaniel B. Hoff, a nephew of Capt. Ely Moore. They settled on the Ohio river at New Albany, Indiana, on the opposite side of the river from the thriving town of Louisville, Ky.

Two letters written by Nathaniel Hoff to Hopewell friends are in the writer's possession, one dated August 24, 1818, announcing his marriage, and the next dated October 3, 1819, announcing the birth of a son, whom he states he has named Joseph Moore for his cousin of Glen Moore. These letters give both the bright and the dark side of life on the frontier, relating minutely some of the hardships and privations suffered by the pioneer in a part of the country then known as the "far west."

The letter of 1819 gives an account of the great losses and in-

conveniences caused by the great drought of that year. They depended on the New Orleans Packets for their supplies and for an
outlet for their produce, and the letter states that no boats had nav-
igated the Ohio since June 1, and they were suffering for many of
the necessaries of life in consequence. Money had no specific value as a medium of exchange. A bank bill good one day
would not pass current the next. Merchants were failing on every
hand and farmers losing their lands after having them nearly paid
for. It seems difficult to imagine that these conditions prevailed in
a region that about thirty years later was within a day's ride by rail
from New York City, and in a community where the population
within a radius of five miles now numbers over two hundred thousand
inhabitants and includes some of the largest and most flourishing
manufactories in the country.

In 1814 Nathan Drake sold the undivided tract of the David
Larison farm to Benjamin Blackwell of Hopewell for the sum of six
hundred and fifty pounds, the deed stating explicitly that it was
"equal to one thousand seven hundred and thirty-three dollars and
thirty-three cents." The removal of the family of Nathan Drake to
Lexington, Ky., and the subsequent marriage of Mrs. Drake to
David Stout, of Lexington, is given in our last.

The name of Judge Jared Sexton has been frequently referred
to in connection with the settlement of estates, etc., in previous
articles, and after the death of Hon. John Hart, Judge Sexton was
one of the most conspicious public men in this part of Old Hunterdon County. He was born in 1737 and married March 28, 1768,
Annie, daughter of James Larison, as stated in the opening paragraph of our last article. He was soon after elected a Justice of the
Peace, and in 1777, or earlier, was elected Surrogate of Hunterdon
County.

A copy of the Duties of Public Officers with forms of Warrants,
Executions, etc., published in the early part of the reign of King
George the Third, and used by Judge Sexton, has been in possession of three generations of the writer's family, and has neatly in-
scribed on the front cover "Jared Sexton his hand." As there is
no tie of relationship between the families it probably was purchased
with other old books at a sale.

In Evart and Peck's History of Hunterdon County, page 203
in the list of Judges and Justices for Hunterdon County, the following paragraph appears: "During the revolutionary period the bench

presents to our notice among others the honored names of Samuel Johnson, Robert Reading, Moore Furman, John Mehelm, Robert Hooper, Nathaniel Hunt, James Ewing, Joseph Beavers and Jared Sexton.''

The first member of the Legislature from this part of Hunterdon County, 1776 to 1779, was Hon. John Hart, and a few days after his death, which occurred on May 11, 1779, a notice was given in the Trenton Gazette of a special election for the purpose of filling the vacancy.

The following is the notice in full:

"May 27, 1779.

"To the Electors of Hunterdon County.

"Being duly authorized I do appoint the twenty-first day of June next for the election of a fit and qualified person to represent said county in the room and place of John Hart, deceased.

"Election to be held at Henry Mershon's in Amwell. Ringo's Old Tavern.

"Signed, JOSEPH INSLEE, Sheriff.''

At this election Jared Sexton was elected as the successor of of Hon. John Hart and at the expiration of the term was appointed Judge of the Court of Common Pleas, which he continued to fill until his death in 1785.*

In 1777 Jared Sexton, Esq., and Joseph Chamberlin were appointed to procure clothing for the revolutionary soldiers of Hunterdon County, and also served as one of the committee appointed to report to the committee of safety all persons in the County who were disaffected toward the government or disloyal to the patriot cause. He also served as one of the commissioners appointed by the Governor to sell the confiscated lands of the Tories. On August 8, 1778, a meeting was held by the committee, consisting of Jared Sexton, chairman, Nathaniel Hunt and Peter Bruere, and notice was given that Inquisitions be found against a large number of the citizens of Hunterdon County.

A very large number of those whose names are given in the list were members of the Society of Friends who were conscientiously opposed to the shedding of human blood, many of them living in

---

*Judge Sexton died May 10, 1785, and is buried in the family plot on the farm. On October 5, 1785, Gen. Peter Gordon and William Larison of Hopewell were granted letters of administration on his estate. Judge Sexton was Surrogate until his death, one of his last acts being the probate of the will of the writer's great great grandfather, John Titus, in April, 1785.

the vicinity of Quaker Churches at Princeton and Quakertown. Not all were Quakers, however, as some had "gone over and joined the army of the King of Great Britain." It may be added that many of the sons of these old Quakers were not so conscientious on the war question as their fathers and were fighting as privates in Washington's Army, and while not accepting commissions, were among the most ardent patriots.

In the Trenton Gazette of November, 1778, is also found the following notice:

"On Thursday, November 12, 1778, a Court of Appeal, consisting of two magistrates and one field officer, viz.: Rensalear Williams and Jared Sexton, Esq's., and Col. Joab Houghton will set at the house of Thomas Bullman in Pennington to determine the appeals for excessive fines for delinquents belonging to the First New Jersey Regiment."

When the American Army lay at Morristown in the winter of 1779-80, and when the Continental Currency had so depreciated that the pay of the soldiers was insufficient to supply them with the barest necessities, the ladies of New Jersey came to the rescue and organized a committee, "for the purpose of promoting subscriptions for the relief of the brave men in the Continental Army who, stimulated by example, and regardless of danger have so repeatedly suffered, fought and bled in the cause of virtue and their oppressed Country." Among the prominent ladies from this portion of the State who were appointed to solicit subscriptions is found Mrs. Vice President Stevens, wife of the Vice President of the Legislative Council, Mrs. Attorney General Paterson, Mrs. Robert Stockton, Mrs. Jared Sexton and Mrs. Benj. Van Cleve.

The children of Jared Sexton and Anna Larison were: (1) John, (2) Sarah, (3) Achsah, (4) Margaret, (5) William, (6) Elijah, and (7) Anna.

After the death of Judge Sexton his widow married Benjamin Parke as stated in a previous article. She lived to the age of 92, and retained her faculties of mind and memory to a remarkable degree. She was eminently social, an entertaining conversationalist and as she was on terms of intimacy with the wives of many of the leading men of the revolutionary period she was considered authority on reminiscences of the war for fifty years after its close. She died in 1835.

The first of the Sexton family in America of which we have

any knowledge was George, who emigrated from England in 1663, and died at Westfield, Conn., in 1690. Dr. T. C. Sexton of Fremont, Nebraska, is authority for the statement that Allan Hale Sexton of Albany, New York, had visited the British Isles and had found authentic records as far back as between 1400 and 1500 A. D., but so far as I have been able to learn his sketch of the family is as yet only in manuscript.

George Sexton of Connecticut had a son George who crossed over to Huntington, Long Island, in 1689. Charles, son of George second, born at Huntington about 1690, was married twice. He mentions 14 children in his will and there may have been others who died in childhood. Many of the children were born and some of them married on Long Island and probably remained there.

Charles Sexton came to Hopewell about 1745 and settled on the northern half of the Doctor Parke original tract, now owned by W. W. Kirkendall, W. C. Velit, and the lot north of the old turnpike owned by N. S. Voorhees. 'He purchased a much larger tract however, adjoining the homestead farm on which some of his sons and sons-in-law settled about the same time. These farms are now owned by E. S. Titus, R. J. McPherson and John S. Van Dyke. In his will dated January 24, 1751, proved April 13, 1752, he mentions his six sons and eight daughters in the following order: (1) Charles, (2) George, (3) Joseph, (4) Nathaniel, (5) Nehemiah, (6) Jared, (7) Japath, (8) Hannah Platt, (9) Sarah Hallock, (10) Esther Rogers, (11) Elizabeth Adams, (12) Kesiah Brush, (13) Bathsheba Hill, (14) Mabel Stout. He also leaves 60 acres to the two sons of his son Charles, viz.: Charles and Nathaniel, and leaves his other sons the balance of the 219 acres.

Charles, the first named in the will, married first probably on Long Island or soon after coming to Hopewell, as in a deed given to his brother-in-law Timothy Brush, and Henry Wollsey in 1765, he mentions two sons Charles and Nathaniel. He married second Elizabeth, daughter of Benjamin Pelton, and settled within a few yards of his father-in-law on the farm then owned by Mr. Pelton and now owned by Joseph B. Horn, Esq. Besides the farm, Benjamin Pelton owned the farms now owned by John L. Burroughs and N. Stout Voorhees as shown by the division of his lands in his will dated in 1775. Benjamin Pelton kept a hotel in the old house which stood on the site of Mr. Burroughs' mansion, and as it was located on the top of a very long hill and on the Great Road leading from Trenton to Sussex Co., he did an extensive business in his line.

Tradition says that Charles Sexton (like most of the Sexton family) was by trade a blacksmith and did a thriving business for the emigrants and teamsters that constantly filled the road at nearly all seasons, which was at that time the only avenue or outlet for all the rich country lying north for sixty miles. Charles Sexton was a soldier in Capt. Henry Phillips' Company and also in Capt. Carle's Company Light Horse 1777.

In 1780 he built the house in which Mr. Joseph B. Horn now resides. John Stout, the husband of his youngest sister, Mabel, was the mason and cut his name and the date on the west end of the house. This farm of 57½ acres was sold to Charles Sexton, July 5, 1776, by Adam Ege, the surviving executor of the will of Benjamin Pelton, and was bounded by lands of John P. Hunt on the south, Seth Field on the west, Nathaniel Hunt on the north and Stephen Humphrey and Benjamin Pelton, deceased, on the east.

On October 10, 1791, Charles Sexton sold this tract, together with a wood lot on Stony Brook, now owned by Joseph Horn, to Amos Corwine, and Mr. Sexton joined the large company of relatives and neighbors who, in the spring of 1792, formed the caravan which went to Shimoken, Penn., and settled at the great forks of the Susquehanna. In the spring of 1793, after a sojourn of one year, Amos Corwine caught the western fever and on May 8, sold this land to Mary Humphrey and went to Mays Lick, now Maysville, Kentucky. The wife of Amos Corwine was Sarah, daughter of Col. Joab Houghton. They became quite a distinguished family in the West and their history as editors, artists and politicians will be found in the Houghton Genealogy, No. 5 of this series, where is also a sketch of the Corwine family.

1905.

NUMBER XLII.

The next in order in the family of Charles Sexton, Senior, was George, who probably never resided in Hopewell Township, as nothing is known of his family. He owned property here, however, and on May 15, 1759, sold 130 acres to his brother-in-law, Timothy Brush. This tract doubtless came into his possession in the division of his father's estate, and is the farm described in our last as the home of David Larison. The survey of this tract commenced at a corner of Joseph Golden's land, in the road now leading from M. Montag's to the mountain, thence to James Larison's corner, and thence by his line, now the line between E. S. Titus and Amos Sked, to the corner of Nehemiah and Jared Sexton's lands, now W. C. Velit's, thence north to Charles Sexton's land, and by his lands to the place of beginning.

The other tract owned by George Sexton was the Col. Joab Houghton farm north of Hopewell. About 1750, Philip Rogers, another son-in-law of Charles Sexton, purchased quite a large tract, or two or three adjoining tracts of the heirs of Dr. Daniel Coxe as a part of the 30,000 acre tract, and sold 125 acres to another brother-in-law, John Stout, and he in turn sold it to another brother-in-law, George Sexton, who in 1765 sold it to Col. Joab Houghton, whose history is given in previous articles.

Joseph Sexton, the next in order of the children of Charles, Senior, was born at Huntington, on Long Island, on January 4, 1730, and married Phebe Campbell. Tradition says that he was a wheelwright and lived first two miles west of Hopewell on the farm owned by Wm. S. Stout, deceased, and recently sold by his heirs to Daniel A. Northrup. The old house stood a few yards in front of the present mansion, and directly on the present line of the old turnpike, and the wheelwright shop east of the house and near the mountain road. This was over sixty years before the old turnpike was opened.

On June 1, 1759, Joseph Sexton sold this tract of 95 acres to

James Slack of Amwell, bounded on the north by the north line of Dr. Coxe's 30,000 acre tract, purchased of the Indians March 30, 1688; east by lands of Timothy Brush, recently purchased of Henry Mathews, south by lands of Nehemiah and Jared Sexton and the middle of Stony Brook, and west by lands of William Snook, Senior. After the sale of this tract Joseph Sexton removed to Princeton where he followed his business of wagon and coach building at the time when there was an immense travel over the King's Highway, which led from the New England States through Princeton to Philadelphia, Baltimore and the South.

Jared, one of the sons of Joseph, born about 1755, married February 15, 1779, Mary, daughter of David Stout and Charity Burroughs, who lived on the farm near Stoutsburg now occupied by David Moore. This David Stout was the son of David Stout and Elizabeth Larison, and grandson of Jonathan the pioneer. It is a family fireside tradition that when General Washington had his headquarters in the old Col. Joseph Stout mansion, which stood on the site of the present residence of George E. Weart, that this Mary Stout picked a basket of strawberries in the fields near by and presented them to General Washington in person.

Jared Sexton resided at Princeton and later removed to Philadelphia. The children of Jared Sexton and Mary Stout were Joseph, Jared, Silas, Stephen and perhaps others. Joseph married and had three children, Alfred, Joseph and Emma. Silas married and had at least one son, John W. Sexton, of the firm of Burnet & Sexton in Philadelphia. Many now living will remember Mr. Sexton as cashier for the banking firm of Jay Cooke & Co., the famous financiers of the civil war period who did more than any other, or more than all others combined to pull the country through the grave crisis. The writer was personally acquainted with Mr. Sexton and in an interview with him in the office of Jay Cooke & Co. in 1871, gave him some of the facts relative to his Sexton ancestry. The writer will always remember Mr. Sexton as his ideal of a perfect gentleman in appearance and manner. He was tall, very dignified and courteous, very social and proud of his Hopewell ancestry.

Thomas Sexton, son of Joseph, was born at Hopewell, January 8, 1764, and married Charity Currant. He removed in early life to the Shenandoah Valley in Virginia, and had a family of eleven children. A few years after his settlement there he again removed, this time to Smythe County, Va., and was one of the pioneers of that county. His ninth child was John G. Sexton, born at Shenandoah May 19, 1808, married February 23, 1836, Sarah B. MacDonald of Smythe County. One of their children, Dr. Thomas C. Sexton, born at Chatham Hill, Va., August 24, 1843, served in the Confederate Army and after the war studied medicine and married December 4, 1872, Emma Peters in Ohio. In 1868 he removed to Fremont, Nebraska, and became a successful physician, an extensive dealer in real estate and was reputed wealthy.

Nathaniel, the next in order of the family of Charles, probably removed to Virginia also, as nothing is known of him except that he received a legacy by his father's will and was living in 1751.

Nehemiah, the fifth son of Charles, born about 1735, was twice married and had children nearly grown when he married Elizabeth Campbell, April 15, 1779. She was doubtless a sister of Phebe, the wife of his brother Joseph. He owned the old Sexton homestead in partnership with his brother Jared for several years, and I think until the Major Ralph Hart farm at Marshall's Corner was sold in 1782, when he purchased it and lived there nearly forty years and was one of the prominent citizens of the community. He died September 30, 1819, aged 83, and his widow March 2, 1828, aged 81. They are buried near the Presbyterian church at Pennington. His will, proved March 13, 1819, names Mary, the wife of Charles Welling of Pennington, to whom he leaves $1,200, and the balance of his estate to his wife and son Joab, who lived with him on the farm.

Joab married a daughter of Benjamin Clark, who resided near the Ewing church at the time of the battle of Trenton, and was a much respected citizen. Joab was an ensign in Capt. Andrew Phillips' Co. in 1811, and a Lieutenant in 1814. After his father's death he removed to the Lake Country of New York State.

Mary, daughter of Nehemiah, married Charles Sexton, son of John Welling, Esq., of Pennington and settled on the farm now owned by his granddaughter, the widow of Col. Wm. B. Curlis of Pennington. They had children as follows, viz.: (1) Robert, who married Ruth Hunt; (2) George, died young; (3) William, married Charity Spencer; (4) Nehemiah Sexton, married Maria Sansbury; (5) Charles, married Elizabeth Docherty, and removed to Missouri; (6) Isaac, a graduate of Princeton College, died unmarried; (7) Israel, married Elizabeth Thomas; (8) Asa; (9) Elizabeth; (10) John, died unmarried.

Nathaniel, son of Nehemiah Sexton, born 1767, when a young man went to Flemington, and was for several years a deputy in the office of the County Clerk, and studied law at the same time. He was admitted to the bar in 1804, and became one of the ablest lawyers of his time. His biographer says of him that in the chancery line he was without a peer in the State. In 1834, he served a term in the State Senate. Hon. L. Q. C. Elmer in his "Reminiscences of the Bench and Bar of New Jersey," page 183, speaks of "Natty" Sexton, the "Chancery Reportor," as one of the leaders in the fun at the "Rising Sun Tavern," (which stood on the site of the American Hotel in Trenton) where songs were sung, old stories revived and flashes of wit sparkled, each one deeming it a duty to contribute as well as he could to the general amusement. Mr. Sexton never married. He died in 1847 and is buried in the Presbyterian church yard at Flemington.

In the last article is found a sketch of the public life of Judge Jared Sexton, the youngest son of Charles, Senior, and also the maiden name of his wife, date of marriage and names of children. Their oldest son John, married Rachel, daughter of Benjamin Parke, and their oldest son William Parke, born January 7, 1800, married first, Sarah, daughter of Joseph Hagaman. The name of her first husband was Booream, by whom she had one son, Joseph Hagaman, who in early life went to Jerseyville, Ill., and made a very comfortable fortune.

William Parke Sexton and Sarah Hagaman Booream had two children, Jared, born November 28, 1828, and Lucy, born April 3, 1831. Jared married November 1, 1850, Achsah, daughter o John Wert, who was born November 12, 1831. Mr. Sexton resided on the homestead farm a few years, working it for his father, who was a drover and stock dealer, spending much of his time away from home. In the autumn of 1859, he removed with his little family to Illinois, settling at Cordova, Rock Island County, among the large colony of Hopewell Township families who had preceeded him, and many of whom were his relatives.

The children of Jared Sexton and Ashsah Wert were: (1) John William, who married Isola, daughter of George Marshall. He is an express messenger on the Chicago, Milwaukee and St. Paul Railroad and resides in Chicago; (2) Mary A., married George W. Gale and resides at Fulton, Ill.: (3) Lucy C., married Oscar H., son of James Marshall; (4) Sarah E., married Elwood H., son of

Garret Quick of Cordova; (5) Joseph, who was an operator and agent at Rapid City, Ill., and died in 1900 unmarried; (6) Annie M., married Frederick Smith and resides in Cordova. Jared Sexton and wife reside at Cordova, and he is still actively engaged in business at the age of 76. They have celebrated the fifty-fourth anniversary of their marriage. He has served as Justice of the Peace and Township collector for several years and has proved a reliable official.

His sister Lucy, married Zephaniah S. Drake of Hopewell and for several years they resided on the old Sexton homestead. After the death of his wife Mr. Drake sold the farm and removed to Florida, where he resided a few years, when he returned to New Jersey. He is one of the very few honored veterans of the Civil War who still survive, and is well and active at the age of seventy-five, residing with one of his daughters in Trenton.

The children of Zephaniah Drake and Lucy Sexton were: (1) Sarah M., who married Henry Higgins of Amwell; (2) Mary, wife of William Phillips of Hopewell; (3) Josephine, married Augustus Bodine and resided in Camden where he died a few years ago; she now resides in Trenton; (4) Roxanna, married Samuel Smith, who is now deceased and his widow resides in Trenton; (5) John William, who died unmarried in Florida, and (6) Katie.

William P. Sexton married second Hannah, daughter of Andrew Wyckoff, and had three children; (1) John William, who died in infancy; (2) Susan A., who married a Mr. Alburtus and resides in Los Angeles, Cal., and (3) Sarah, who married a Mr. Cody, by whom she had one daughter, Lida. They reside in Trenton.

Misses Susan and Sarah Sexton operated the old Sexton homestead farm very successfully for some years after their father's death when they sold it to their brother-in-law, Mr. Z. S. Drake. They removed to Hopewell and started the first drug store here, which they managed for some years before they were married. Very many of our readers will remember them not only as women of business ability, but as ladies of culture and refinement and very accomplished singers, who were in demand at all the social events in the village, and were indispensable at the entertainments where vocal music was one of the features.

1905.

NUMBER XLIII.

Joseph Rue, son of John Sexton and Rachel Parke, was born November, 1806, and married about 1835, Mahala, daughter of Esq. George Smith and Anna Ege. In the division of the homestead farm after the death of his father, Joseph R. took the southwest half bordering on Stony Brook, now the property of W. W. Kirkendall, and erected the buildings which are still standing in good repair.

In the spring of 1838 Mr. Sexton caught the western fever, and cast in his lot with his neighbors, the Marshalls, Cools, and others, and removed to the state of Illinois, locating at Cordova on the banks of the Mississippi, as has been previously stated. Mr. Sexton was one of the sturdy pioneers who contributed so much toward making that remote outpost of the United States a model community. It was very remote at that time, with no means of communication with the Atlantic States except by long pilgrimages by wagon road, or a trip of nearly three thousand miles by way of the river to New Orleans, and thence by ocean steamer to Philadelphia or New York.

Joseph R. Sexton and Mahala Smith had but one child, Phebe A., born 1837, married December 8, 1859, Peter Swallow, a native of New Jersey. Mrs. Swallow died October 20, 1862.

Ruth, daughter of John Sexton, married John L. Phillips of Hopewell, who owned and operated a tannery at Hopewell, on lands now occupied by Mr. E. W. Drake, and the lot of Mrs. Sheppard adjoining on the east. This long forgotten Hopewell industry was subsequently conducted for many years by his brother Enoch Phillips, and abandoned nearly sixty years ago.

John L. Phillips and Ruth Sexton had children, Catharine, Ruth, Elizabeth, John Sexton, William and perhaps others. They also removed to Cordova, Ill., where some of their descendants still reside.

Sarah, daughter of Jared Sexton and Anna Larison, married Moses Quick of Amwell, the man of affairs and extensive real estate dealer previously referred to in these articles. They had children, Jared S., a teacher in early life, died February 15, 1871, aged 78 ; Elijah, died June 5, 1839, aged 34 ; John B., died in 1812. Moses Quick died December 3, 1847, aged 81, and his widow, June 27, 1853, aged 83.

Achsah, daughter of Jared Sexton, married Charles Stout, son of James, and grandson of David Stout and Elizabeth Larison. They had at least four children, Lewis, Charles, Dr. John and Elizabeth. Lewis, never married. Charles, married Rachel, daughter of David Manners of Wertsville, and had two sons, Lewis David, who married a Miss Young of Wertsville, and W. H. Harrison, who married Helen, daughter of Jonathan H. Blackwell, and was for a time in the mercantile business with his father-in-law in the building now occupied as a general store by Messrs. Holcombe and Titus. Dr. John went to Illinois, married and settled first at Fairview, Fulton County. He had two sons, who were known to the writer in 1859, but as they removed farther west, he has lost trace of them.

Elizabeth, daughter of Charles Stout and Achsah Sexton, resided until her marriage in the family of her "Aunt Kitty" Weart at Hopewell. She married Isaac Moore, brother of Abraham Moore of Stoutsburg, and removed to Illinois, settling near Canton, some ten miles east of Dr. John Stout. Mr. Moore, although nearly fifty years of age when the Civil War broke out, enlisted in an Illinois Regiment, went to the front, and soon after was killed by a tree falling across his tent.

Margaret, daughter of Jared Sexton, born 1776, married 1793, William, son of Col. Joab Houghton. They resided on the Col. Houghton farm for about ten years, when Mr. Houghton sold it to William Suydam and removed to the Lake Country of New York state, settling on a beautifully located farm of 400 acres near the present site of Homer, Cortland County. They had nine children, several of whom were born in New Jersey. The record of this family is given in the sketch of Col. Houghton's family in number 5 of these articles. William Houghton died June 29, 1835, aged 78, and his widow March 6, 1864, aged 88.

William, son of Jared Sexton, like most of the Sexton family, was a blacksmith, and went to Sussex County, where he died in 1801, aged about 25. In his will dated 1801 on file in Trenton, he mentions his brother Elijah, and sisters "Sarah, wife of Moses Quick, and Margaret, wife of William Houghton."

Elijah, son of Jared Sexton, we think also was a blacksmith and resided in Sussex County.

Anna, youngest child of Jared Sexton, married William Stout, son of Judge John Stout of Somerset County, near Skillman's Station, and their children were Richard, Abraham and Zephaniah, a sketch of whom is found in number 35 of these articles.

As stated in number 41 of this series, many of the eight daughters of Charles Sexton, Sr., married and remained on Long Island. Esther, one of his oldest daughters, born about 1715, married January 14, 1735, Philip Rogers, on Long Island. He is named in our last in connection with the real estate transactions of his brothers-in-law in the Sexton line, as owning the tract north of Hopewell, a part of which was sold to Col. Joab Houghton, and on which he resided at the time of the revolution. Nothing further is known of Philip Rogers, but he probably sold out the balance of his tract to his brother-in-law Timothy Brush, who, in 1790, owned the farms now owned by William Phillips and the Hankins brothers.

Kesiah, daughter of Charles Sexton, Sr., married Timothy Brush and they became residents of Hopewell. On May 15, 1759, he purchased the tract of his brother-in-law, George Sexton, described in the last article, now the property of Mr. E. S. Titus, which was the home of the Brush family for several years. His son Timothy Brush, Jr., was a member of Capt. Joab Houghton's Company in the revolution, but how much time he spent in the service is not known. He married December 16, 1769, Catharine Lane of near Stoutsburg. Near the close of the revolution he had a store in Hopewell, and tradition says that it was located on the corner of Greenwood avenue, where Mr. Simpson Hoagland now resides. He doubtless succeeded in the store, Major Peter Gordon, who was Brigadier Major in Captain Toman's Battalion and in the Quarter Master General's Department.

On March 14, 1780, Major Gordon "Quarter Master" advertises horses and cattle in the Trenton Gazette and gives notice that he will be in Trenton on Mondays, but the balance of the week on his farm near the Baptist House in Hopewell. He refers buyers to Timothy Brush, Jr., in Hopewell.* Major Gordon's farm is now owned by Charles Durling, Esq., on the north line of the Borough.

---

*November 22, 1780, the following advertisement appears in the Trenton Gazette:
"To be sold cheap.
"By the subscriber in Hopewell 5 blooded colts cheap also Cyder Spirit and Cyder Royal by the hogshed or less quantity.
"Timothy Brush."

In 1778, Doctor Ephraim, the bachelor brother of Capt. Ely Moore, sold to Timothy Brush a lot in Pennington adjoining Jonathan Furman, who kept the hotel opposite the church yard. Rev. Abner Brush of New York State was doubtless a son of Timothy, and on December 16, 1778, advertises a farm of sixty acres near Hopewell, and on the Amwell line, occupied at that time by John Allen. Rev. Mr. Brush announces that he will return to New York state in a few weeks and desires to dispose of the farm before leaving New Jersey. The Israel Brush who was a member of Capt. William Tucker's Company, state militia, and also of Capt. Polhemus' Company Continental army, was doubtless a son of Timothy and was afterward an inn keeper at Nine Partners, Dutchess County, New York.

Kesiah, daughter of Timothy Brush, Sr., married John, son of James Stout and Grace Parke of Amwell, a sketch of whose family will be found in number 35 of these articles. This John Stout was known as "Tailor John" to distinguish him from the host of John Stouts in Hopewell and Amwell who were contemporary with him. They resided on a small farm about two miles northwest of Hopewell. He was enrolled in Capt. Wm. Tucker's Company, First Regiment, as Tailor John Stout, and was a revolutionary soldier. They had one child, Sarah, who is well remembered by the writer and who married Amos Hoagland of Amwell, and about 1833 settled on the Miller James Hunt farm, now the railroad quarry farm, southwest of the Borough. The descendants of Amos Hoagland and also a list of his ancestors are given in a foot note to number 19.

The only descendant of this Brush family, who at one time owned so much real estate here and was prominent in business affairs in this region, is Mr. Simpson Hoagland, who by a strange coincidence has his residence on the spot where Lieut., afterward Capt. Brush had his store in revolutionary times.

The Stout history states that Jacob Stout, father of John, above mentioned, was born in 1721, and in the records of the Baptist church of Hopewell is found the following entry. "Jacob Stout died September 20, 1785, aged 64 years. He was a useful and valuable member of this church for many years."

The only remaining child of Charles Sexton, Senior, of whom we can give any account was Mabel, who married John, son of Zebulon Stout and Charity Burroughs, and grandson of Jonathan, the pioneer Stout in northern Hopewell. John was born about 1730, and owned, 1760–65, the old Col. Houghton farm north of Hopewell. John Stout and Mabel Sexton had seven children as follows, viz.: Zephaniah, Amos, Elizabeth, Mabel, Kesiah, Rachel and Charity.

Zephaniah, married about 1776 Rhoda, daughter of Nathaniel Stout and Charity Furman, and resided on the farm of his father-in-law, now the farms of the Haynes family and George Stilwell east of the borough. They had two sons, Ebenezer, born about 1777, and one who died in childhood. Zephaniah died soon after the birth of these children, and his widow married Rev. Burgess Allison of Bordentown, one of the most eminent clergymen of the Baptist denomination, who supplied the Hopewell church in the spring of 1780, before the installation of Oliver Hart. He was born August 17, 1753, and was educated at the celebrated school of Dr. Jones in Pennsylvania, and of the Rhode Island College. He resided in Bordentown where he had a very select school (or academy it was called) for boys, which he opened in 1778 in the building which is now the hotel adjoining the Penna. Depot.

Mr. Allison's biographer says of him that he "was a very remarkable man, not only a thorough and accomplished scholar, but also a skillful and ingenious mechanic. Much of his school apparatus for the study and experiments in National Philosophy, astronomy, geography, such as globes, instruments, etc., was the work of his own hands. His extensive acquaintance with several of the living languages, especially French, Spanish and Portuguese brought him many scholars from foreign lands." Under these very advantageous circumstances his little stepson, Ebenezer Stout, was reared and became an accomplished scholar, and after a course in the study of law, an able lawyer.

Mr. Allison transferred all his interests in the academy in 1796 to William Staughton, a licensed minister, and devoted all his energies to the ministry in which he was singularly successful. In addition to other duties he was chaplain of the House of Representatives in Washington.

Mrs. Rhoda Allison died January 3, 1798, aged 40 years, and her remains were brought to Hopewell and interred among her Stout relatives in the old church yard. She was the only child and heir of Nathaniel Stout, but did not live to heir her property as her father died about the same time, and Ebenezer, her only child that lived to maturity, inherited the south half of the Benjamin Stout tract, which had originally extended from the Trenton road to the Sourland range, including the Hezekiah tract now owned by James R. Voorhees.

On February 10, 1800, Ebenezer Stout advertised in the Trenton Gazette the farm which is described as the property of the late Nathaniel Stout. "A house large enough to be convenient for two families, to enable a farmer to live in the house with the owner and carry on business."

The farm was not sold, however, and Mr. Stout having married about that time Miss Ann, daughter of Hon. Francis Hopkinson of Bordentown, came to Hopewell and resided on the farm, Dr. Benjamin Van Kirk of Stoutsburg having it worked for him on half shares as shown by the account books of Dr. Van Kirk at that time.

1905.

NUMBER XLIV.

The history of Hon. Francis Hopkinson, the father-in-law of Ebenezer Stout, is too well known to every student of history to be repeated here. His record as one of the signers of the Declaration of Independence, and as poet, artist, accomplished musician and statesman, won for him imperishable fame, and placed him in the front rank of the distinguished men of his time. He was one of General Washington's most intimate friends, and was so popular as a writer that it has been said that few pens effected more in educating the American people for independence than that of Francis Hopkinson. As soon as General Washington entered upon his duties as President of the United States, he addressed Mr. Hopkinson a highly complimentary letter and enclosed him a commission as United States District Judge for Pennsylvania.

Soon after the marriage of Ebenezer with his accomplished and aristocratic bride, they came to Hopewell and made the old farm their home for several years. We can give no account of their family, but that they had two children while at Hopewell is pretty conclusive from the day books of Doctor Van Kirk, who enters a charge against Ebenezer Stout with "visits to Joseph and Annie," the name Joseph being for Mrs. Stout's grandfather, who was the distinguished Col. Joseph Borden, one of the most active patriots of the revolution, and the father of Borden Town—as it was named in his honor—and Anne, named for her mother, Ann Borden Hopkinson, one of the foremost ladies of the United States.

Not being a practical farmer Mr. Stout soon tired of his Hopewell estate and in 1808 sold it to Cornelius Skillman of Harlingen and returned to Bordentown. In the old Borden-Hopkinson cemetery at Bordentown, near the tomb of Judge Joseph Borden, is a tombstone bearing the following inscription: "Ann, daughter of Francis and Ann Hopkinson, and relict of Ebenezer Stout, born at Bordentown, October 19, 1777, died September 22, 1868, aged 91 years.

Amos, son of John Stout and Mabel Sexton, married a Miss Morgan and removed to New York State.

Elizabeth, daughter of John Stout and Mabel Sexton, married Nathaniel, son of Hon. John Hart, signer of the Declaration of Independence from Hopewell, whose record, like that of Hon. Francis Hopkinson, is too well known to be repeated in these articles. Nathaniel Hart was born October 27, 1747, and married Elizabeth (known in history as Betsy) Stout, May 2, 1770. So far as known Nathaniel Hart and his brother Jesse, the two oldest sons of Hon. John, remained on the homestead farm until about 1792.

During the revolutionary period their home was frequently visited by British scouts, who were in search of the illustrious father of Jesse and Nathaniel Hart, for whose capture a large reward had been offered. On such occasions their stock was driven off, their crops destroyed, and everything of value taken away that could be conveniently carried. Their home was at times an asylum for sick and wounded soldiers, as may be seen by the books of Doctor Benjamin Van Kirk, who attended them, and charged the visits to the United States.

Tradition says that these Hart brothers guided the army of General Washington from Coryell's Ferry to Hopewell, and to their father's farm, where they encamped on June 23 to 25, when they resumed their march to Monmouth. It rained constantly and the roads and fields were in a very miry condition, but the crest of the hill north of the borough afforded a reasonably dry and solid location for their encampment.

The children of Nathaniel Hart and Elizabeth Stout were as follows, all of whom were doubtless born at Hopewell: (1) Sarah, married Henry Voorhees at Hopewell, and as far as known remained in New Jersey; (2) Mabel, named for her grandmother, and tradition says remained with her in New Jersey; (3) Zephaniah, married in Kentucky Mary Arms, and removed to Ohio; (4) Betsy, died single; (5) Mary, wife of Stephen Bayliss of Mason County, Kentucky, with one of whose descendants, Mrs. Mary E. Mitchell of St. Louis, the writer has had some correspondence concerning the family; (6) Charlotte, married Elijah, son of Col. Joab Houghton, and resided for a time in Mason County, Ky., a sketch of whose family is given in the Houghton history, number 5 of these articles; (7) John, known as Judge John Hart, lived in Lebanon, Ohio, where he married first, Mary Corwine, and had children: Zephaniah,

William and Francis. His second wife was Hannah Pumes by whom he had one son, Jeremiah P.; (8) Zebulon, married Nancy Thomas of Kentucky, and had children: Alanson, Joseph and Jeremiah; (9) Nathaniel, married Jane Marshall and resided near Columbia, Missouri. He had sons, Joseph and Alfred, and in 1903, one of these was still living. Nathaniel, their father, died at Columbia at a very advanced age.

Of the other children of John Stout and Mabel Sexton we know but little.   Mabel, married James Campbell; Kesiah, married Lewis Gordon; Rachel, married Jonathan Stout, and Charity, married John Parke, son of William.

The above completes the record of the family of Charles Sexton, Senior, and we pass to the farm adjoining the Sextons on the north, and will mention Captain Philip Snook, who received his commission as Captain in the Regiment of Col. William Chamberlin in 1776, and was a very brave and daring officer. He was first ordered out with the regiment to Hackensack in 1776, and next to Bound Brook where they were surprised by the enemy from New Brunswick and driven into the mountains.   On October 4, 1777, he was at the battle of Germantown, and in June, 1778, went with the army to Monmouth, where he was severely wounded. At the battle of Monmouth his company was attached to a Virginia Regiment.

He married Mary Heavener of Amwell, April 1, 1773, who was probably a sister of Rev. Mr. Heavener of Amwell, who soon after the revolution became a very active and influential evangelist of the Methodist church, organizing several churches in Hunterdon and Warren Counties.   In 1792, Capt Snook, with Charles Sexton, Jr., Minnie Gulick and others from this vicinity, removed to the Jersey settlement at Shimoken, Pa.   The writer has corresponded with Hon. John S. Snook, member of Congress from Paulding, Ohio, in reference to the descendants of Capt. Snook, but for the want of some of the connecting links, has made slow progress.

William Snook, the father of Capt. Philip, was naturalized with Hendrick (his brother doubtless) July, 1730, and came to this region in 1744. He came with other Dutch emigrants up the valley of the Raritan into Somerset County, and had the choice of two large tracts.   One of these was at the present site of the village of Blawenburg, three miles east of Hopewell, and the other at the confluence of Rocky and Stony Brooks, near Woodsville. While it was his preference to settle among the people of his own nationality,

(Holland Dutch) he selected the Stony Brook tract for the reason that the timber was much larger and taller, indicating a greater depth of soil. Another reason was that the brooks would afford a good mill site, and having their source in the rocky and heavily timbered mountain range, would afford a never failing supply of water.

Having decided in favor of Stony Brook, he built his cabin along the north line of Doctor Coxe's 30,000 acre tract, where the buildings on Mr. A. S. Golden's lower farm are now located. It was also on the old path or driftway that was cut through the wilderness when the 30,000 acre tract was surveyed. This old road came to be known in later years as "the way to Bungtown," now Lambertville, and was a much travelled road until the turnpike was opened in 1822. In 1744, Mr. Snook purchased of William Willett and Margaret, his wife, late widow of Rev. John Thomas, Rector of the Parish of Hempstead, Long Island, 675 acres, lying on both sides of Rocky Brook, and running a considerable distance "back in ye rocks," with Stony Brook as the southwest line.

This tract was conveyed to Rev. John Thomas in 1706 by James Bennett, Linen Draper, of London. Another tract of 160 acres adjoining the above, was sold to Rev. John Thomas October 28, 1708, and the deed locates it on the "north side of a brook, called Stony Brook, and next to Thomas Smith's." The survey of the Thomas Smith tract in 1699, described it as "commencing at an elm tree at the northwest corner of Roger Parke's 400 acres," described in previous articles of this series.

The writer has a copy of the survey of this original tract of 675 acres, giving the lines and courses as surveyed in 1706-08, and it may be described as comprising most of the large tract extending from a point on Stony Brook about half way between the old turnpike and Linvale, thence to a point a half mile northeast of Snydertown, thence northeast about one and a quarter miles to the Hopewell line, a few rods south of the residence of Isaac Horn, Esq., thence following the Hopewell and Amwell line, south one and one-sixth miles, thence southwest to Stony Brook, and up the same to the place of beginning. The allowance for "ways and waste lands" in the above tract brought it to about 800 acres, about 500 of which was cleared and improved by Mr. Snook and his four sons, John, Philip, George and William. They also built the mill which was known as "Snook's mill" for one hundred years, and was owned by four generations of the family in succession.

During Washington's march from Coryell's Ferry to Hopewell June 22, 1778, a detachment of the army (cavalry doubtless) came over the old Bungtown road, and four of the soldiers became so ill on reaching John Snook's (who then occupied the place described above as the property of A. S. Golden) that they were taken in there and cared for. Two of them recovered, but the others died, and were buried in a corner of a field southwest of the house.

When the old turnpike was located, it passed directly over the graves of these two old patriots, whose last resting places should have been too sacred to be thus desecrated. The location of the graves is in the middle of the road just opposite the west end of Mr. Daniel Stout's garden, about two and a half miles west of the Borough. The spot was pointed out to the writer when a small boy, and is published in this connection that, although their names may never be known, and the gallant services rendered to their country unrecorded and forgotten, their last resting places beneath the trodden road may not be unknown, nor their memory unhonored by the patriotic men and women of this and succeeding generations.

William Snook in his will dated May 6, 1760, divides the above mentioned tract among his large family as follows: To his wife "Catron" (Catherine), 120 acres; to son John, 102 acres on the south side (this included the mill); to his five daughters the northern part of the plantation, which he describes as "coming down to the wall of rocks"—now known as "wall rock"—extending southwest from Runyan's saw mill a half mile or more. The names of these daughters were Catron Steenman, Elizabeth Talbert, Christian Ketcham, Ann Wambaugh and Mary Abbott. The balance of the plantation he leaves to be divided between his three sons; Philip, the eastern part now the upper farm of A. S. Golden; William, the middle part, and George, the westerly part. If any dispute arises as to the boundaries, they are to choose three of their neighbors to settle it. The will is witnessed by Timothy Smith, (who doubtless wrote it), Timothy Brush and Jeronious Mingo, who were his next neighbors on the east and north. The executors were his wife Catron and son John, and the will was proved June 18, 1760.

The will of his widow Catron, dated January 30, 1763, leaves all her property to her daughters as follows: Catherine, wife of

Randolph Steenman; Elizabeth, wife of William Plutphin (Sutphin probably); Christian, wife of Jacob Ketcham; Ann, wife of Henry Wombock, and Mary, wife of Benjamin Abbott. The witnesses are Hon. John Hart of Hopewell and her neighbors on the west, Richard Reed and George Corwine.

In the absence of the family records of this old pioneer, we can only give the family as recorded in the will. As stated above, Capt. Philip went to Pennsylvania and all trace of his family has been lost. George left a will dated October 15, 1803, and mentions fourteen children as follows: William, George, Peter, Samuel, Richard, Nathaniel, Elizabeth Marts, Catherine Field, Sarah Bozenbeck, Mary Young, Hannah Golden, Deborah, Achsah and Rachel. He left his farm, with all the stock and utensils, to his wife Anna, for her use and maintainance, and education of his children that may choose to remain with her after his decease. Of this family George Jr. was the grandfather of George W. Snook, a former resident of our Borough, now of Philadelphia, who, with his sons, Herbert and Alvin, is a frequent visitor here. They have corresponded with various branches of the family with a view to obtaining reliable data of their respective branches. 'Samuel is the ancester of the family who resides on the Millstone between the aqueduct and Kingston, of which State Fish Commissioner George E. is a worthy representative. The Pennington and Titusville families are also of this large family of George Senior, and also Richard of Rileyville. The family of Amos, now deceased, of Linvale, is descended from William, who inherited the middle part of the tract.

"Miller Peter Snook," who for many years was the sage, philospher and oracle for the surrounding community, was a son of John, who inherited the southern part of the tract. "Miller Peter's" wise maxims and proverbs were often quoted long after his decease. His old almanacs from 1789 to 1840 came into the writer's family with some old books bought at auction, and are interesting relics, as they contain on the margins his observations concerning the weather conditions one hundred years ago, and also several accounts of business transactions with his neighbors. His sons, Enoch and John, succeeded him in the mill as partners for a time, when Enoch sold out and removed to Trenton. John married Mahala Hunt and they had children Alexander and Emley, millers, and also Peter Johnson and Rebecca. The old family was largely Presbyterian and the names of John, Peter, Philip Jr., Elizabeth, Daniel, George and

Charles, are found on an old subscription list of the Amwell Presbyterian church, which stood in the cemetery on the York road, about half way between Ringoes and Reaville, in Hunterdon County. This is now the "Amwell First" Presbyterian church, at Reaville, the church at Pleasant Corner—or "Larison's"—being known as the "Amwell United First."

1905.

NUMBER XLV.

The first farm east of Hopewell on the south side of the road was for about a century the home of one of the most prominent branches of the Stout family in the Hopewell valley and furnished two, if not three, brave soldiers for the patriot army of '76.

Samuel Stout, youngest son of Jonathan the pioneer of northern Hopewell, was born in 1709, and in 1729 married Catharine Simpson, the widow of his first cousin, James Stout, of Amwell.   They had one son, Samuel, born in 1730.   (The published history of the family gives the date of his birth as 1732, but the inscription on his tomb in the old cemetery near the Baptist church gives the date of his death as September 24, 1803, and his age 73, which is undoubtedly correct.)

Catharine Simpson married James Stout, son of David, in 1712, in Monmouth County, and they soon after removed to Amwell Township, Hunterdon County, and settled on a tract of 700 acres near the present location of Wertsville, about five miles north of our Borough.   By this marriage they had a family of six sons and one daughter, the oldest born in 1713, and the youngest in 1725.   We are unable to give the date of the death of James Stout, but the "Stout History," written by his grandson, Captain Nathan, gives his age as thirty-six, and in all probability his death occurred about 1726.

Neither history nor tradition has left us any further account of Catharine Simpson who was thus bereaved and left with this interesting family to rear and educate, but judging her by the characteristic traits of her family, she was above the average in intelligence and ability, and was equal to the emergency.   At all events the bewitching charms of this fascinating widow of Amwell, proved absolutely irresistible to the Hopewell Samuel, or he would not have volunteered at the age of twenty to take her brood of six Stout stalwart sons under his sheltering wing.   His eldest stepson was but four years his junior, but subsequent events proved that there had been good discipline in that household, and that the family had been reared in the wholesome atmosphere and environment which tends to develop just the kind of sturdy manhood which was one of the marked characteristics of this family of pioneers.

The eldest of the family, John, was the father of three revolutionary soldiers. Captain Nathan and Moses were officers of distinction, and their older brother Abraham might also have been as prominent had he not been stricken with a fatal illness in the early part of the struggle. Abraham and his son Solomon fought side by side at the battle of White Plains, and they were doubtless both at the battle of Long Island a month previous. At the battle of White Plains October 28, 1776, Solomon was killed by a cannon ball, and his father returned home and died soon after at the age of 42. Abraham was a brother-in-law of Captain, afterwards Colonel Joab Houghton, and Abraham and his son were no doubt in Capt. Houghton's company in both of the above engagements.

The residence of Abraham Stout was two miles west of the Borough of Hopewell, and stood directly on the Hopewell and Amwell line, now the middle of the old turnpike, a few yards in front of the present residence of Daniel Northrup. The early history of this farm has been given in previous articles, and it was the home of four generations of this Stout family within a period of one hundred and forty years, viz: (1) Abraham, died in 1777; (2) Joab Houghton, died in 1845; (3) Benjamin Bryant, died in 1880; (4) William Schenck Stout, the last of his generation, died in 1904.

We hope to give a sketch of this Amwell family of James Stout and Catharine Simpson in subsequent articles, as many of their descendants became residents of Hopewell Township, and a large number being connected with Hopewell families by marriage, their interests have always been so closely indentified with Hopewell in church and society, that it is a difficult matter to draw a line between the pioneers of old Hopewell and those of old Amwell.

Jonathan Stout, the Hopewell pioneer, died in 1723, and in his will proved March 25, 1723, he bequeathed to his two youngest sons, Samuel and David, (who were at that time aged 14 and 17 respectively) the tract on which Jonathan resided at the time of his death. This was the tract lying south of the Col. Joseph Stout farm, now George E. Weart's, and extended south about one mile along the Province line, and west to the mountain road. This tract now includes the farms of P. W. Sheppard, Harry Van Dyke, David Moore, Miss Sarah Stout, Peter O. Voorhees, and the northern half at least of the David Stout and Amos Bond farms. The will states that these two sons were left "one full equal undivided sixteenth part of a proprietary," and one standing on the hill near Mr. George E. Weart's dwelling and viewing this whole tract spread out like a panorama at his feet can but exclaim in admiration, "What a magnificent inheritance was theirs!"

David, the oldest of these two sons, settled on the north side of the road where P. W. Sheppard now lives, and Samuel in the old house which stood a few yards west of the residence of Mr. Peter O. Voorhees. Samuel Stout was not a man of so much prominence as his brother Col. Joseph, but the records show that he was a Justice in 1745 and in 1754, one of the Judges of the Court of Common Pleas. In 1753, Samuel Stout, Esq., was the second largest tax payer in Hopewell Township, the name of Wilson Hunt heading the list. After the death of his first wife, Samuel Stout married second, a Mrs. Timbrook, and by this marriage had two sons, Jonathan and Andrew. Andrew died single, and Jonathan married Sarah Phillips, a daughter probably of Capt. Henry of revolutionary fame, and they settled on the Delaware at the foot of "Bellmount, and founded the family widely known as the Bellmount Stouts."

Samuel, only son of Samuel Stout and Catharine Simpson, married about 1754 Anne, daughter of John Van Dyke, of Beden's Brook, Somerset County, N. J. She was born in 1733, died September 12, 1810, aged 77, and is buried beside her husband in the old cemetery. Samuel Stout was one of the most prominent public men of this valley, serving as a Justice many years, and in 1793, at the age of sixty-three, was elected a member of the Legislature, fulfilling the duties of the position to the great satisfaction of his constituency. He resided on the farm now owned in part by Mr. Gustav Johnson, which at that time extended to, and included a part of the eastern section of the Borough.

The old house in which he resided is well remembered by many now living as a typical old colonial structure, covering a large area, but with eaves so low that a person of ordinary height could reach them from the ground. To the writer's youthful imagination, the old house was located on a very romantic spot. It stood on a high ledge of rock, overgrown with moss, ferns, vines and shrubbery, and was almost hidden from view by a thicket of rose bushes and lilacs. It was an old colonial mansion, which sheltered a family of ardent patriots of the revolutionary period, and should have been preserved in its original condition as a much prized relic of ye olden time.

Samuel Stout and Anne Van Dyke had seven sons and three daughters. Abraham, born 1755, was a Captain in ——Regiment, Hunterdon County, and served with distinction all through the war of the revolution. He married Jane Pettit, and as we have been unable to get any trace of his family, he probably removed to Ohio and settled on a large tract which his father had purchased some years previous. It is stated in the Stout History that he had a large family.

Samuel, the second son of Samuel, was also a patriot of the revolution, enlisting first in Captain Joab Houghton's Company, First Regiment, Hunterdon County. At the battle of Long Island, August 27, 1776, he was in Col. Philip Johnston's Battalion, Heard's Brigade, State Troops, and was taken prisoner. He was confined in one of the vile prison pens in New York, where with hundreds of other brave men he suffered indescribable tortures for a period of two months. We will publish in this connection a letter written by his father to his son, Capt. Abraham, which expresses in pathetic language the great sorrow that had fallen upon the home, as they could get no reliable information concerning him.

The letter is as follows:

"Hopewell, N. J., Sept. 1776.

"Dear Son—These are to let you know that thro the favor of ye Almighty we are all in reasonable health at present and have received your letter Dated ye 26 of August and are sorry to hear of ye destruction of the country as you have related. And ye next news was on the 28 at 11 P. M. Ye news came to me that you had a general engagement on ye 27th and that thousands were killed on both sides and one Regiment taken prisoners that belonged to New England, and that Major Gordon's Company had suffered very much.

"Ye next morning being ye 29th there seemed to be a general mourning in ye neighborhood. In ye afternoon I went to Princeton and there I found many people all enquiring of every person that came from New York on that day. At length Captain Moulder of Philadelphia came up from ye Blazing Star and gave me ye best account, that was that we had forty killed and fourteen wounded, and none taken prisoners. Ye 30th in ye afternoon John Barton's letter came to hand and gives account that James Merrill was shot just by his side and that cousin Zephaniah Stout* was wounded and not heard of since.

"At 11 o'clock at night Henry Drake's account came to me by my son John, that my son Samuel was missing and supposed to be taken prisoner, and therefore no probability of sending any letter to you at present. We are waiting in hopes of learning of your safe arrival in some part of our army. Ye 31st news came that our people had retreated from Long Island and September 1 at 7 A. M. James Hunt saith that he had a certain account that my son Samuel and Zephaniah was slain at Long Island and confirms ye account of ye Island being left and that ye Regulars had full possession.

"At 11 A. M. September 1 Doctor De Camp's letter came to hand and confirms the foregoing account only saith that my son and Zephaniah Stout were missing and it was thought they might be taken prisoners. Ye Wednesday before the fatal day of ye battle of ye 27th of August, there was several persons killed by lightning in New York and other places, and several buildings burnt. It seems as if ye artillery of heaven and earth was leveled against the inhabitants of this part of the world. May God in his infinite mercy interpose and put a stop to ye effusion of any more human blood.

"Ye 2d of September I dreamt I was in some place where ye water had got obstructed from its natural channel and came rolling over the earth about two foot deep. It was white as froth and one of my little boys was overtaken in it, but I didn't apprehend him to be in any danger and I concluded from my dream that my son was not dead. September 4 John Disbrow came home from Amboy and saith that several persons had told him that they had seen Samuel laying down sick and Zephaniah wounded and that it was thought they were both prisoners.

---

*"Cousin Zephaniah" was the son of John Stout and Mabel Sexton of whom a sketch is given in No. 43. He died probably soon after his release from imprisonment.

"September 5 Moses Randal returned sick, and John Hunt and David Merrill and brought my son's Knapsack, and the 6th, William Jewell returned, yt no further account of him. Had made all ye enquiry from New York and saith that he had made all ye enquiry he possibly could and that James Boden says that he saw Samuel on ye way home and that is the last that any person saw him. Ye 11th of September word came by Capt. Hoppock that there was one Samuel Stout that had been missing came into New York last friday.

"Ye 13 Gideon Lyon came in from ye camp at Fort Washington and says that Sam. had not been heard of when he came away. September 1 at 11 A M after writing ye within Dr. De Camps letter came to hand and seems to give some encouragement that my son and Zephaniah may still be in the land of ye living. I make no doubt but you will take all ye possible care to find out what may become of them.

"From your father Samuel Stout."

Samuel Stout, Jr., regarding whose fate there was so much painful solicitude was at length released from his imprisonment which had been a living death for so many weeks, and as we published his father's letter in full, we will also publish his first letter to the home folks, which is as follows :

"New York December 4 1776

"Honored Father and Mother

"I take this opportunity to let you know that I am in good health and that I have got out of prison and have got to work at my trade* I long to see you but I cannot come yet as I have engaged to stay two or three months with Mr. Reeves the Golde Smith with whom I have to work. I have been a prisoner from August 27 to Novem. 24, and in that time I suffered more than I can express. I long to hear from you. I expect matters will be made up soon and we will once more have peace. I have just heard that the Kings Troops are at Trenton. I think it best to stay here part or all of this winter, as work is very plenty in New York.

---

*Samuel Stout, Jr., was only 20 years of age at this time but had worked some at the jewelry trade in Princeton before his enlistment. J. Hervey Stout of Stoutsburg, who is a great grandson of Samuel the soldier, has in his possession a silver spoon, made by him about the time of the revolution, which is much prized as a souvenir of his handiwork. Mr. Stout has also the originals of the two letters published above and also a large collection of other relics of revolutionary times.

"I was almost naked when I got to work, but hope with Gods blessing to be able to have some good clothes in a short time. Give my respects to all my friends.

"To conclude Your loving son,

"Samuel Stout, minor."

"N. B. Zephaniah is well and writes his father that he has lost the sight of his right eye. There is a neighbor of Andrew Smith among the prisoners, his name is Cornelius Maloby. Please send word to his family that he is alive, and also to the family of John Docherty who lives near Ralph Guild. James Merrill is alive and his wounds are almost well.* Write to me the first opportunity. Please take care of my tools. If it is Gods will I intend to use them once more."

*James Merrill died from his wounds soon after.

1905.

NUMBER XLVI.

The will of Samuel Stout, Esq., dated September 12, proved October 5, 1803, is on file in the office of the Secretary of State at Trenton. The order in which he names his children we accept as correct. The name of his second son, Samuel, is omitted in the will as his death had occurred about eight years previous, and the writer has inserted his name in its proper place. Some of the birth dates are known to be correct as given, others are conjectural but approximately correct.

Abraham, born 1755, married Jane Pettit; Samuel, born 1756, married Hellena Cruzer; Jonathan, born 1758, married Rachel Stout; Catharine, born 1760, married Rev. Peter Smith; Anna, born 1762, married Benjamin Stout; Sarah, born 1764, married John Wykoff; John, born 1766, married Rachel Rosencrans; Jacob, born 1768, married Anna Burtis; Ira, born 1770, married Sarah Burroughs; Andrew, born 1772, married Sarah Stout.

We will publish an abstract of the will of Samuel Stout as an item of historical interest to his numerous descendants. His son Ira resided with him on the homestead and he leaves him the use of the farm on the following conditions, to wit: "I bequeath to my son Ira, the farm whereon he lives as long as my wife Anna—his mother—lives. After her decease I will and ordain that the farm, together with three wood lots, be sold by my executors, empowering them to make sufficient deeds. As one-half of the stock and farming utensils (except one mare and colt and one cow) belong to my son Ira, who lives with me, I have thought sometimes to have my part valued by some indifferent person or persons and to make the whole over to my son Ira, by taking his bond for the valuation or amount of such appraisement, but if this should not be completed before my decease, I will that my part, except a cow and mare and colt, hereinafter mentioned be sold by my executors after my decease.

"I give to my wife Anna a mare and cow to be chosen by herself out of my part of the stock. If the above mentioned valuation and disposal goes on she is to have her choice after it, also I give her twenty-six dollars and sixty-seven cents per year during her natural life, to be paid her yearly by my son Ira, out of the produce of the farm, he also to leave her one room, bed, bedding, Dutch cupboard and such books as she may choose, and further, if she chooses to live with my son Ira, I will and appoint that he shall maintain her over and above what I have bequeathed her, but if she shall choose to live at some other place I will that my said son, Ira, shall pay for her maintainance, one hundred dollars a year, out of the produce of the farm, over and above the yearly sum above mentioned, it being understood that I leave the farm to Ira, (as I have above expressed) that she may be well provided for in health and sickness as long as she lives.

"I will that as soon as may be after the decease of my wife, not only my farm, but all my household furniture, not herein otherwise provided for, be sold by my executors." The testator then leaves cash legacies to seven of his children in amounts from five hundred to twelve hundred dollars each, to Abraham Stout, Jonathan Stout, Catharine Smith, Anna Stout, Sarah Wykoff, John Stout and Jacob Stout, stating that these bequests are to be considered as over and above all other gifts they have received from him. He leaves his agate stock buckle to his son Jacob.

"I give to the Baptist Church (meeting near where I live in Hopewell) one hundred dollars, the interest of which the trustees of said church are to pay the minister thereof. That no misunderstanding of intention to leave out my sons, Ira and Andrew, in the distribution of the above specific legacies may remain on their minds or on the minds of any of the children as if they had offended me, I declare that the plantation that I divided between them and for which I gave them deeds is to be considered by them as in lieu of any such specific sum in my will.

"After the above legacies are paid I will that any balance that may remain is to be divided between my children now living (or reputed to be living,) viz.: Abraham, Jonathan, Catharine, Anna, Sarah, John, Jacob, Ira and Andrew, or their respective heirs. I bequeath my books, except such as my wife shall choose, to be equally divided among my children, and my bookcase with glass doors to Mr. Ewing.

"The twenty-six hundred acres of land in the County of Ohio and State of Virginia, for which I hold a patent, I give and devise to be equally divided among my children above named and my grandson, Abraham Stout, son of my son Samuel, deceased, but if the said tract hereby devised should be worth a thousand six hundred and sixty-six dollars and sixty-seven cents, clear of all expenses, then they must pay to the heirs of William Stout, deceased, two hundred and sixty-six dollars and sixty-seven cents according to my agreement with him." He appointed his sons, Ira and Andrew, executors, and the witnesses to the will were Doctor Benjamin Van Kirk, Isaac Dunn and Rev. James Ewing.

Samuel Stout, Junior, born 1756, died April 22, 1795, married April 24, 1779, Hellena Cruzer, a daughter of his neighbor, Abraham Cruzer, living just over the line in Somerset County. She was born June 1, 1759, and died January 30, 1821. By this marriage they had one child, Abraham C. Stout, who became a man of great prominence in this part of the state. He was born May 26, 1780, and died August 23, 1849. He served for a time in the war of 1812, being stationed at Sandy Hook, and was a member of the Legislature 1817–1819. He married September 24, 1801, Anna, daughter of Ruliff Hagaman, of near Skillman's Station, Somerset County.

Mr. Hagaman was also a revolutionary soldier and served as Sergeant in Cap. Joseph Babcock's Company, Second Battalion, Somerset County, Brig. Gen. Nathaniel Heard's Brigade, State Troops. Ruliff Hagaman died in 1802, aged 62 years. His widow, Catharine Hagaman, applied for a pension, and the papers containing the testimony taken in her behalf are in possession of her great grandson, J. Hervey Stout, of Stoutsburg. We will publish them as interesting items of revolutionary history, giving some of the experience of two of our Hopewell heroes who were with Mr. Hagaman.

The testimony is in part as follows: "Richard Stout says that he was well acquainted with Ruliff Hagaman and he was out on duty a good while in the time of the revolution. He recollects seeing him out and believes that all of the family were good whigs in the time of the war, and further, that he saw him married to Catharine Holmes by the Rev. John Blackwell on the 10th day of September, 1780. The family bible says so also."

Mr. John Swaim (who has been previously mentioned in these articles) testified that he was well acquainted with Ruliff Hagaman and enlisted with him under Capt. Babcock for five months, and marched immediately to New York—this was the next year after the British laid in Boston. "We were at the battle of White Plains, and at the fight at Vannest's Mills, and took nearly all the British baggage wagons loaded with plunder. We were at the battle of Germantown and I was with him all through the war and we acted as minute men. He was a good soldier. We crossed over the river Delaware together and were on duty at the battles of Trenton, Princeton and Monmouth, and also at West Point."

Mr. Hagaman also served for a time as Sergeant in Capt. Simon Duryee's Company, First Battalion, Somerset County Militia. Mrs. Hagaman became the second wife of Capt. Nathan Stout, another old revolutionary veteran, a sketch of whose history has been given in previous articles. Mrs. Catharine Holmes Hagaman Stout died at the home of her son, John R. Hagaman, at Stoutsburg in 1847, aged about 90 years.

For several years after the marriage of Abraham C. Stout and Anna Hagaman, they resided on the farm now occupied by Mr. Peter O. Voorhees of Stoutsburg, and later in life they resided on the farm east of Stoutsburg Station, now owned by Mr. William S. Stryker. They had children as follows: Helen, born December 21, 1804, died July 2, 1889; Samuel Holmes, born February 26, 1808, died January 1, 1887, and Augustus, born January 1, 1825, died in infancy. Helen Stout married January 27, 1825, Doctor James Hervey Baldwin, who was born September 25, 1798, near Burnt Tavern, Millstone Township, Monmouth County, and died at Stoutsburg, May 2, 1869.

Dr. Baldwin was a student of Dr. Gilbert S. Woodhull, attended two courses of lectures at the University of Pennsylvania, and was licensed April 24, 1820. He came to Stoutsburg in 1822, making his home in the family of Judge Peter Voorhees, until his marriage, after which he resided a few years with his father-in-law, Abraham C. Stout. His first purchase of a home was the old Colonial house in Stoutsburg, which from time out of mind had been known as the "Old Doctor House." His next purchase was the small farm of John R. Hagaman, where he spent the last twenty years of his life, taking a great pride in improving it and making it an ideal country home. He also introduced the most improved methods of farming and gained the reputation of being a progressive up-to-date farmer in a community where good farming was the rule. This farm is now owned by his niece, Miss Sarah D. Stout of Stoutsburg.

Dr. Baldwin was a very remarkable man, and besides being a most estimable and useful citizen, was one of the most popular physicians of his time. He was a man of marked ability and had a most successful career, attaining a high reputation as a skillful physician. He was held in the highest regard and esteem by his professional brethren, the neighboring physicians of Pennington, Princeton and Harlingen, all of whom stood high in their profession. He attended rich and poor alike and wore himself out in riding day and night in all weathers, over his very large territory which extended from the Millstone on the east to Woodsville and beyond on the west.

His frank open countenance, pleasing address and very easy courteous manner won the esteem and confidence of all with whom he came in contact. His bright and cheerful disposition was such that many of his disheartened and discouraged patients made the remark that they always felt better as soon as Dr. Baldwin entered the room, he brought so much of hope and cheer and sunshine with him.

Dr. Baldwin was not only a bright and shining light in his profession, but in the church and community as well, being for many years one of the Ruling Elders in the Reformed Church of Blawenburg, and a very faithful and efficient Superintendent of the Sunday School at Stoutsburg. It was the good fortune of Dr. Baldwin to be blessed with a helpmeet who was much above the average in all that is beautiful and lovely in character, and it may be truly said that all the christian graces were exemplified in her to a remarkable degree.

The following account of the exercises at the funeral of Mrs. Baldwin is clipped from the Hopewell Herald of July 11, 1889:

"The funeral services of Mrs. Helen Baldwin were held in the Reformed church of Blawenburg on Friday morning. A large number of friends and relatives were assembled to pay their last tribute of respect and affection to one so long beloved and esteemed among us. A requiem was played by Miss Emma G. Weart as the procession entered the church, followed by reading the scriptures by Rev. W. B. Voorhees. A selection, 'She's gone to the better land,' was sung by a quartette, followed with prayer by Elder Purington.

"A short address was then made by the pastor from the text, 'The memory of the just is blessed,' in which he spoke of the lovely, true and just life of the deceased, her more than ordinary intelligence, kindness of heart endearing her to all, and her devoted piety which was manifested in childlike trust and faith to the last. Her last days were cheered and comforted by the tender ministrations of her niece, Miss Sarah Stout. Mrs. Baldwin will be much missed in the church of which she had been so long a member, and in whose welfare she had always expressed so sincere an interest, giving to it freely of her means and prayers."

1905.

NUMBER XLVII.

Samuel Holmes, son of Abraham C. Stout and Anna Hagamen, born February 26, 1808, spent his whole life of nearly fourscore years in the vicinity of Stoutsburg, his house and mills standing over the line in Somerset, within a few rods of the Mercer County line, and about a half mile south of the village of Stoutsburg. Although not a resident of Old Hopewell, all his interests socially and religiously were identified with Hopewell, and all the married members of his family found their companions in Hopewell Township. Like his distinguished brother-in-law of whom we gave a sketch in our last, he was a model man of the community; and his many sterling qualities and virtues won for him a very large circle of warm friends and admirers.

Honorable and upright in all his dealings, he was held in the highest esteem and regard by those who only knew him in a business way and trusted his integrity. He was one of those who understood the art of growing old gracefully, and in his declining years was a most congenial and agreeable companion for the young as well as those of his own age. He was one of those whose smile and handshake always seemed to carry a benediction with them, and an illustration from the writer's own experience is in point.

When a very young man the writer frequently attended the Old Hopewell church; but as it was not his home church, many of the elderly people were estrangers. Not so, however, with Mr. Stout; everybody young and old knew him, and somehow the writer always had a consciousness when he left the old church, that he was the better and stronger man for having felt the warm and friendly grasp of Holmes Stout. How many who read these lines have had the same experience?

Samuel Holmes Stout married February 14, 1833, Deborah, daughter of Elnathan Drake, and granddaughter of Dr. Benjamin Van Kirk, who one hundred years ago owned the farm and mills which were owned by Mr. Stout during his life, and are now the property of his son, J. Hervey Stout. Samuel H. Stout and Deborah Drake had children as follows: Helen Baldwin, Sarah Drake, Anna Hagaman, Abraham, died in infancy, James Hervey, Samuel Holmes, died in childhood, and Mary Titus.

Helen married David L. Blackwell of Hopewell, and had children: Anna, wife of Joseph H. Moore of Glen Moore; William D., who married Belle Gandy and resides at Cordova, Nebraska; Fanny, married Joseph B. Hill, a lumber and coal dealer in Hopewell; Sarah, married Harvey Boice of Griggstown, and James Hervey who died in childhood.

Anna, daughter of Samuel H. Stout, married Nelson D. Blackwell, who for forty years was engaged in the mercantile business in Hopewell. Their children were Hervey Stout, died in childhood; Elizabeth, died at the age of 15; Samuel H., for many years cashier of the First National Bank of Princeton, now in business in New York, married Bessie Bartine of Princeton; Helen, married Thomas B. Jackson, who is in business in Trenton; Mary, married Dr. George Boice of Princeton; George and David died in infancy.

Mary, daughter of Samuel H. Stout, married Edward Updike, a civil war veteran, of Pennington, and in 1879, they removed to Harvard, Nebraska, where he opened a banking and brokerage business with his brother-in-law, Johnson L. Titus, and was very successful. They had children as follows: Peter Holmes, married Hattie Boyden of Illinois; Nelson B., married Meta Babcock of Broken Bow, Nebraska; Edward, Louisa and Robert B., unmarried.

J. Hervey, son of Samuel H. Stout, and his sister, Miss Sarah, are unmarried and remain on the homestead. Mr. Stout is a civil war veteran, and a very active member of James M. Weart Post of Hopewell. He and Miss Sarah enjoy the enviable distinction of possessing one of the most hospitable homes in the Hopewell valley, thus maintaining the reputation of their ancestors of whom hospitality was one of the distinguishing traits.

At the time of the death of Samuel Holmes Stout, a lengthy obituary was published in "Signs of the Times," a denominational paper of the church of which Mr. Stout was for over half a century one of the leading members and officers. We will publish an abstract of this to show the great esteem in which he was held by his church.

"Our dearly beloved brother, Samuel H. Stout, departed this life January 1, 1887, aged seventy-eight years, ten months and six days. During his illness of nearly two months, he was always cheerful and much pleased to have the members of his church as well as his friends visit him, and not a murmuring word escaped his lips, but he would remark, 'I feel comfortable and this is all right.' Our dear departed brother had certainly been a remarkable man, and we as a church, feel his loss very much, but we would be still and know that our God does all things right however dark and inscrutable His providential dealings with us may appear. Our dear departed brother discharged the duties incumbent upon him as a member of the church long and faithfully, for he was a member of the church fifty-four years, fifty-two of which he was leader and conductor of the singing, forty-nine years clerk of the church, and thirty-five years a member of the board of trustees, and but very few of the church meetings during that long period of time was he prevented from attending, except the two previous to his death.

"His home and the hospitality there shown will be sweetly remembered by the brethren of this church, as well as our Association and the many strangers from distant churches. While reason remains we will not forget the calm and peaceful expression that mantled his brow when we reviewed his remains and bade our last sad farewell, saying in our hearts, 'Well done, good and faithful servant, enter thou into the joy of thy Lord.'

"The funeral was numerously attended at the Brick Meeting House in Hopewell village Wednesday, the 5th inst., and the text used was I Cor. 15: 22-26."

Of the ten children of Samuel Stout, Esq., whose family record is given in number 46, it is quite probable that at least six went to Ohio and settled on the twenty-six hundred acre tract, which by will he divided equally among his children. Ira, who was next to the youngest of the family, married Sarah Burroughs and settled on the homestead in Hopewell now occupied by Mr. Gustav Johnson. Mr. Stout earned the title of "Col. Ira" by which he was known during his long life by several years service in the Hunterdon County militia.

Col. Ira was a man of much prominence in public affairs, and very popular among his friends. To quote a familiar phrase as used by one of his old friends, Col. Ira was the man "who always got there," whether it was an election, a general training or a district school meeting. He was a noted breeder of fine horses about the time of the war of 1812, when good horses were very much in demand, and this fact extended his acquaintance all over the northern part of this state, and in other states. He suffered an irreparable loss at one time from the disease known as glanders, which nearly ruined his well stocked stables.

One of his distinguishing traits of character was his hospitality, which was known and appreciated far and wide. Mere acquaintances riding over the much frequented highway yielded to the impulse to halt at the beautifully shaded spot by the babbling brook and take dinner with Col. Ira, in preference to patronizing the public house which was not far distant. They were always sure of a most cordial welcome and no matter what the time of day the standing invitation was, "Come in boys and have something." Mrs. Stout was a most estimable woman and was called one of the excellent of the earth by her most intimate friends. For many years she was a hopeless but not helpless invalid, and as she could go out but little, she was always glad to see her friends.

The family were among the society leaders of the Township, and their home was frequently crowded for weeks at a time, with visitors from a distance, all invariably receiving a warm welcome from the hospitable host and his amiable spouse. The popular, and in fact about the only mode of conveyance among farmers one hundred years ago was the farm wagon which was frequently covered with white canvas when long trips were made to town. Tradition says that one inmate of that hospitable house, upon whom devolved the labor of providing entertainment for the guests, dreaded to see the old white covered wagon return from the city, as it so frequently brought a lot of new recruits to the already over-crowded house. The suggestion that such generous open handed hospitality was wearing out his family and wasting his resources would have been warmly resented by the chivalrous old colonel, even if at times he had admitted it to himself. However, his sympathetic neighbors whispered among themselves that he began to see it, when in 1821, the new turnpike from New Brunswick to Lambertville was in the course of construction and he and his son, Simpson, fitted up the house in Hopewell now known as the Upper Hotel, and opened a public house.

Margaret, the eldest of Col. Ira's family, married William Poulson and they resided in New York. Their children who lived to maturity were Hannah, who never married; Harriet, married William Boscowen, and Emma, married Reuben Beebe, and had one son, Leslie Stout, all of whom reside in New York.

Phebe, daughter of Col. Ira, married Jacob Drake and removed to Ohio.

Letitia Burroughs, third daughter of Col. Ira, was a lady of much culture and refinement. She resided in New York, but frequently visited Hopewell friends fifty years ago. She died unmarried.

Ann, the fourth daughter of Col. Ira, married Newton Boggs, son of Elder John Boggs of Hopewell. He was a teacher and he and Mrs. Boggs both died in middle life, leaving two children: Joseph, who married Caroline Wade and had no children, and Sarah Francis, who married John B. Voorhees, son of Peter J. of Hopewell. Their children were Charles M., Peter, died in childhood, and Anna.

Charles M. Voorhees, born February 25, 1853, married Sarah J., daughter of John S. Nevius of Raritan, Illinois. They settled near Brooks, Iowa, where they were visited in their pleasant prairie home by the writer in 1877. Their children were Francis, John and Charles. Charles M. Voorhees died at Brooks, April 12, 1879.

Anna, daughter of John B. Voorhees, married Westley, son of Simpson Van Dyke, and had children: Sarah Josephine, Albert and Mary. Sarah Josephine married C. Emmett Voorhees and had children: Adlyn, died in 1905, aged 11; Clara and Hilda. Albert, son of Westley Van Dyke, married Anna, daughter of S. Smith Ege of Hopewell, and had one child, Helen Dane, died in infancy. Mr. and Mrs. Van Dyke reside in New Mexico. Mary, daughter of Westley Van Dyke, married Isaac Woodward.

Burroughs, son of Col. Ira, never married. He died in New York aged 45. Simpson, son of Col. Ira, died unmarried. Mrs. Stout, wife of Col. Ira, died September 14, 1825, aged 55.

One of the inmates in this interesting household of Col. Ira was Mary Praal, who never married, and so far as known, had no relatives. She had a host of friends, however, of all ages and was known to old and young alike as "Aunt Polly Praal." As Mrs. Stout was an invalid, upon Aunt Polly devolved the management and much of the work of providing for this large family, including the ever present visitors. The daughters assisted and they had servants for much of the hard work, but Aunt Polly's energy and competency was very much in evidence in every department. She was a woman of excellent character and highly respected in the community, but she was invariably spoken of as a "character." This may be explained by stating that she possessed a most unique and extraordinary personality, and perhaps her equal in some respects has never existed in this community before nor since.

Her amusing criticisms of some of Col. Ira's aristocratic visitors, and her observations of events generally, as seen from her standpoint, coupled with a vivid imagination and powers of imitation and mimicry were ludicrous to the extreme. She could see the ridiculous side to every passing event, and when she ran in to one of the neighbors for a minute just to relieve her mind, they could always expect something decidedly rich and original. Her quaint maxims and proverbs continued to be quoted for at least half a century after she had passed away, and people who lived after her time were often heard to remark, "Oh, if Aunt Polly Praal could only have lived in my day, life would never become monotonous " Her death occurred about eighty years ago, and the text from which her funeral sermon was preached has probably never been used on a similar occasion. It may be found in the Book of Job, 3d chapter, 17th, 18th, 19th verses.

Col. Ira Stout married second, Elizabeth, daughter of Richard Ketcham of Hopewell, and in his declining years resided with his brother-in-law, William Ketcham, who resided on the farm now owned by Mr. John Kennedy on the hill one mile south of the Borough.

1905.

NUMBER XLVIII.

Capt. David Stout, son of Jonathan the pioneer, who as stated in article number 45 was left in 1722 the half share of the undivided one sixteenth of a whole proprietary, had the farm on the north side of the road opposite his brother Samuel. David's tract extended from the first cross roads east of Hopewell Borough to the Province line at Stoutsburg, and was bounded on the north by the Col. Joseph Stout tract, now occupied by Mr. George E. Weart. It is a fact worthy of note that these two brothers had divided this tract so evenly between them, that in 1753, thirty years after they had inherited it, when an assessment was made to create a fund for the extermination of wolves and panthers, there was a difference of only seven pence in the amount of their assessment.

The residence of David Stout stood on the road between Hopewell and Stoutsburg, a little southeast of the present brick mansion of Peter W. Sheppard. The old house was the home of three generations of the family, until David Stout, Esq., grandson of the first David, built in 1822, the mansion now standing.

David Stout senior was born in 1706, and in 1726, married Elizabeth Larison as we have stated in previous articles. Captain Nathan Stout, the author of the "History of the Stout Family," was very sparing in his compliments, but passes a glowing eulogy on David Stout as an honest man and a Christian. In Dr. Benjamin Van Kirk's Ledgers he is called Captain David, and he was doubtless a Captain with Colonial militia.

The children of David Stout and Elizabeth Larison were: Jonathan, born 1727; Andrew, born September 2, 1728; Hannah, born 1730; James, David, Sarah, Elizabeth, Anna and Mary. David Stout died in 1788, aged 82. He was an invalid for several years before his death, and the arm chair in which he sat is one of the much prized relics in the family of the writer. His will is dated May 28, 1779, which probably marks about the beginning of his disability. The will is proved December 26, 1788, and during this long period he was probably a paralytic, as tradition says that he was unable to walk. We will give a few extracts from his will, as it gives the boundaries of the homestead tract.

He first leaves his wife 225 pounds in money, and she is to have her home in his house during her lifetime. He next gives his oldest son, Jonathan, 5 pounds as his birthright. To his son Andrew, he gives 169 acres, being the part of the homestead on which David then resided. This is described as beginning at the northern corner in the line of his brother Benjamin's land, thence along a road to the four rod road leading from Hopewell to Stoutsburg, thence along said road east to land in possession of John Stout, thence northeasterly to his corner, thence southwesterly (and a parallel line to the four rod road) as many chains as will make the complement of acres herein devised by running a parallel line with the first mentioned line between his land and his brother Benjamin's to the line between "me and Joseph Stout," thence along to the place of beginning, "excepting one acre whereon my daughter Anna Merrill lives with the buildings thereon."

"To my son David Stout I give the remaining part of the plantation I now live on. To my son James Stout a lot of land adjoining the land I have given him by deed 104 acres." He then makes a special bequest to his daughter Hannah Wykoff, and gives the balance of his estate to his five daughters as follows: Elizabeth, Anna, Mary, Sarah and Hannah, all the personal property to be sold and divided. He appoints his sons Andrew and David executors, and the witnesses are Samuel Stout, Nehemiah Stout and Mary Sexton.

Of the above named children of David Stout and Elizabeth Larison, Jonathan, the eldest, married Rachel, daughter of Thomas Burroughs, Junior, and granddaughter of Thomas, Senior, who bought the first tract of land for settlement in the southwestern part of Hopewell Township as now constituted since the organization of Ewing. Thomas Burroughs purchased his tract November 17, 1699. It was located on the path leading from the settlements at Maidenhead to those on the Neshaminy in Bucks County, Pennsylvania, which at that time was only an Indian path.

Jonathan Stout and Rachel Burroughs had at least five children: Moses who went in early life to Dayton, Ohio, where his descendants are still to be found; David and Job who went to Kentucky; Elizabeth, who married a Mr. Updyke of Hopewell, and Charity, who married Elijah Leigh, son of Ichabod Leigh and Anna Stout.

David Stout married first, Amy, daughter of Nehemiah Stout, and after her death married her sister Rachel, and removed to Mays Lick, now Maysville, Kentucky. He had at least two sons, Jonathan and Nathan, but we have no further record of the family. Job, born February 21, 1763, married Rhoda, daughter of Abner and Mary Howell. They were a Quaker family, living in Bucks County, Pennsylvania, near Trenton, New Jersey.

Rhoda Howell was born May 3, 1771, and they were married in 1786, when she was fifteen years of age. Soon after their marriage they removed to Mays Lick, Mason County, Kentucky, where he purchased and improved a fine farm. Mrs. B. B. Clark, wife of the President of the First National Bank of Red Oak, Iowa, and a great grand daughter of Job Stout, informed the writer in 1899, that although Mr. Stout resided in a slave state, he never owned a slave, and was very strongly opposed to the institution. His feelings were so outraged by the almost universal treatment of them by his neighbors, that he sold his fine farm and removed to Franklin County, Indiana, where he again started in the wilderness and cleared another farm, where he died February 28, 1833, aged 70 years.

The children of Job Stout and Rhoda Howell were as follows: Jonathan, born July 10, 1788; Mary, March 3, 1791; Rachel, January 13, 1793; Elizabeth, March 18, 1795; Abner, August 23, 1797; Margaret, December 2, 1799; Joab, January 15, 1802; Rebecca, May 30, 1804; David, August 4, 1806; Sarah, September 18, 1808; Ira, July 16, 1812; Aaron, September 10, 1814; Anna, November 11, 1818. The youngest child of the above family was still living in 1899. She married William Waldorf, and resided at Whitcomb, Franklin County, Ohio. She had in her possession a gold spoon which she prized very highly as a relic of her ancestors. Jonathan and Job Stout, father and son, were both soldiers of the revolution, and Jonathan either removed to Kentucky with his sons David and Job, or followed soon after.

The writer has in his possession an old book published in 1794, in which an account is given of a sensational trial held at Mays Lick, Kentucky, in which Jonathan Stout figured prominently as one of the Justices. A brief notice of the trial is given in number 18 of these articles, but we will publish all the leading features in this connection as Mr. Stout had been a very few years before this occurrence a resident of Hopewell.

Three Justices of the Peace, viz: Jonathan Stout, Joseph Desha and John Young had met at Mays Lick, Mason County, Kentucky, for the purpose of taking depositions and trying about forty civil causes which were set for trial at that time and place. On a short consultation it was agreed that Magistrates Desha and Young should retire to one corner of the large room in which they had met and attend to taking the depositions, whilst Jonathan Stout, the other magistrate, should try the causes. A case came on to be heard in which the sum in dispute was seventy-five cents, neither party having any testimony to produce. Mr. Stout permitted the parties to enter into a conversation on the subject of their dealings. This conversation is too lengthy to be repeated here, but it appeared that not long previous the defendant had called on the plaintiff to make a settlement in reference to taking up an estray. In the presence of Mr. Stout the defendant was asked if he did not remember falling fifty cents short of paying the expense of taking up the estray. He replied that he did, and after a long consultation as to events that had taken place at the hotel where they had met, the plaintiff told the defendant that if he would swear that he had paid the full amount, he would drop it. The defendant said that he would, and asked Mr. Stout to administer the oath.

Mr. Stout had overheard the consultation and was satisfied that the defendant intended to commit wilful perjury, so positively refused to administer the oath, and made a great effort to persuade the man to pay the difference in dispute which was such a trifling sum. The man had become very obstinate, and while Mr. Stout's attention was momentarily called off, he stepped to the other corner of the room, and Mr. Young who knew nothing of the consultation, administered the oath. The man then swore in the most solemn manner to the payment of the money, and immediately informed Mr. Stout that he had found a man willing to take his testimony.

Previous to this the man seemed to be in robust health, but as soon as he turned about to inform Mr. Stout of his successful attempt to commit the horrid crime of perjury, a deathlike paleness was visible in his countenance, and people in the room observed with astonishment the change so instantaneously effected in his appearance. Mr. Stout himself remarked when relating the circumstance that he had the appearance of a man who had been dead two days. Judgment was entered for fifty cents and the guilty man retired from the room and went to his home. He took no refreshment, and for two nights and one day tossed and rolled on his bed in the most intense agony of mind.

The morning of the second day he went to the field where some men were working in harvest, and gave some incoherent directions, and soon after this was seen running through the corn field on all fours, shrieking that the devil and John Johnson were after him (John Johnson was the constable who had attended the trial). He ran through the field giving the most agonizing shrieks and tearing up the hills of corn, and while engaged in this way, fell and immediately expired in horrible agony. His remorse of conscience had produced a nervous condition closely resembling hydrophobia, and the event produced a most profound impression in that community. The occurrence was widely published in the newspapers at that time, and was the subject of much comment. Mr. Stout's conscience was much relieved that he had strongly opposed his being sworn, and had used his influence to obtain a settlement.

Andrew, the second son of Capt. David Stout and Elizabeth Larison, married January 24, 1753, Anna, daughter of his uncle Jonathan Stout, and had children as follows: Elizabeth, born January 11, 1754; Mary, born June 11, 1755, died September 13, 1773; child not named, born February 5, 1758, died aged two weeks; Anna and Sarah, twins, born February 23, 1759, Anna died aged 5 months, Sarah died aged 24 years; child not named, born July 9, 1761, died aged six weeks; Anna, born March 6, 1763; Andrew and Ruth, twins, born December 18, 1766, Andrew died aged two months, Ruth died aged 12 years; Andrew, born September 19, 1768; Joab, born August 24, 1771, died aged 15 months; Ure, born March 6, 1775, died aged 9 months; child not named, born January 22, 1777, died aged three months.

It will be seen that all but three of this large family died in infancy, childhood, or early maturity. Anna, wife of Andrew Stout, died March 31, 1777, aged 43 years. She was survived by an infant two months old who died the following month. Her daughter Ruth died before the close of the summer, and another daughter a few years later.

Andrew Stout married, second, Sarah Morgan, widow of Moses Morgan, and a sister of his first wife. Their children were David, born June 10, 1778; Ruth, born February 16, 1781, and Jonathan, born January 18, 1782. Andrew Stout died March 28, 1807. His will is dated June 10, 1806, and he leaves first, his wife Sarah one room in his house, and all his household and kitchen furniture during her widowhood, and at her decease "to be divided amongst my children, Andrew, David, Jonathan, Elizabeth Leigh, Anna Titus, Ruth Hart, Susannah Hart and Anna Hunt.* My son to maintain my widow on the farm I now live on, and to pay her two pounds ten shillings per year."

He gives the farm he lives on to his sons David and Jonathan, they to pay out legacies as hereafter specified and also his just debts and funeral expenses. His son Andrew to have all the land he holds by deed, and to pay 5 pounds each to his daughters Anna and Betsy. "My son David to pay my daughters Elizabeth Leigh and Anna Titus 30 pounds each, Elizabeth Leigh four years after my decease, and Anna Titus in five years. My son Jonathan to pay my daughter Ruth Hart 30 pounds in 4 years after my decease. My son Jonathan to pay my widow two pounds 10 shillings pr year." He names sons David and Jonathan as executors. The witnesses to the will are David Stout, Senior, Abraham Stout and John Wert, Junior, who were all neighbors of the testator.

---

*It will be seen that there is an error both in the family record and in recording the will which is in the office of the Secretary of State at Trenton. First, Susannah is not named in the family record. This may be accounted for by the fact that the bible in which the record is found was not purchased until several years after the children were born, and after most of them had been deceased many years, and Susannah's name may have been overlooked in copying it from an older Bible.

Second, we find the names of his daughters Anna Titus and Anna Hunt, both of whom were living in 1806. This is doubtless caused by the carelessness of the one who recorded the will. All who have had experience in looking up old wills come in contact with the most inexcusable errors nearly every day, both in names and dates. We shall of course take the will as we find it, with the mental reservation that there were not two in the family of the Christian name of Anna.

1905.

APPENDIX.

The family of the author being in possession of memoranda concerning the Stout family take the liberty of adding to these articles.

The Stouts of New Jersey are descended from John Stout of Nottinghamshire, England, whose son Richard emigrated to Long Island about 1640. A vessel from Holland, numbering among its passengers a man named Van Princes and his wife Penelope, was stranded near Sandy Hook about the same time. The young man having been ill on the voyage was unable to travel further, so they remained on the Jersey coast where he was killed by the Indians, and Penelope, badly wounded, left to die. She crept to a hollow tree where she was discovered by a friendly Indian, who cared for her wounds until her recovery. Afterwards she met and married Richard Stout. This incident is fully described on page 65 of "Smith's History of New Jersey."

Richard Stout was one of the patentees of Gravesend, Long Island, in 1645, and in 1665 he was one of the twelve men to whom the Monmouth patent was granted, and so was one of the original and permanent settlers of East Jersey. Richard and Penelope Stout settled on a farm about three miles west of the village of Middletown, and are buried there.

In Richard Stout's will dated June 9, 1703, on file in the office of the Secretary of State, Trenton, he mentions his sons, John, Richard, James Jonathan, David and Benjamin, his daughters, Mary, Alice and Sarah; his daughter-in-law, Mary Stout, and her son John, and his "kinswoman, Mary Stout, the daughter formerly of Peter Stout."

Jonathan, son of Richard and Penelope Stout, married Anne Bullen and was the pioneer of the family in Hopewell. (Article 45.)

The last article carries the history down to the birth of David Stout, eldest son of Andrew Stout and Sarah Stout Morgan, and great grandson of Jonathan the pioneer. David Stout, known as "Esquire David," was one of the most prominent men in this region. He married December 16, 1802, Margaretta, daughter of John Weart, Sr., and Mary Magdalene Varse. They had seven children, viz: Henrietta, born May 31, 1804; Charles W., born November 19, 1806; Mary, born August 21, 1809; Susan, born July 19, 1812; James Monroe, born April 21, 1816; Jacob Weart, born July 20, 1820; Andrew Gilbert Hunt, born March 17, 1825.

Esquire David Stout, who built and lived in the house now owned by P. W. Sheppard, was a Justice of the Peace, and famous for his liberality and hospitality. When court was in session the lawyers of the county used to travel by wagon road from Trenton to Flemington, and his house was always a stopping place during the journey. He was a staunch supporter of the Baptist Church. When the present edifice was being built, he burned all the brick used for it on his own place, and on the day the church was dedicated gave a dinner at his house to all who had done any work upon it.

David Stout died Sept. 19, 1849, and Margaretta Stout July 23, 1854.

Charles Weart, eldest son of David Stout and Margaretta Weart, married Sarah Merrill, and had eight children: (1) Daniel Webster (see Article 13). (2) Mary Ann, married Abram Manners, and had one son Fred. (3) Furman, died unmarried. (4) Adrianna, married Israel Hunt, and had four children, David Livingston, Alfred, Lizzie, who died at the age of twenty-one, and Wesley, who died in infancy. (5) Wesley, died in childhood. (6) David, married Gertrude Hoagland of Griggstown and had three children, Emma, Fanny and a child who died in infancy. (7) Charles, married Rhoda Holcombe and has five children, Edwin G., Chester, Fred, Bertha and Gladys. (8) Carrie, married Henry Holcombe of Mount Airy.

Mary, daughter of David Stout and Margaretta Weart, married Peter Sutphin Van Zant, and had three children: (1) David, who died in childhood. (2) Peter, married Susan Booker of Clarksville, New Jersey, and had one child. (3) Mary, married Charles Larison, and had one daughter, Ada.

Susan, daughter of David Stout and Margaretta Weart, married October, 1835, Caleb Baker and had two children: (1) David Stout, married Mary Fow and had two children. (2) William Henry, born February 5, 1842, married his first cousin, Mary Stout,

October 8, 1879, and had one son, Frederick Stout, who is the owner of the Stout Bible bearing records back to 1728.

James Monroe, son of David Stout and Margaretta Weart, married Margaret Jane Van Dyke and had eleven children: (1) Sarah E., married Benjamin S. Hill and had three children, Jessie, Edward S. and Jane. (2) Mary, married William Roberts and had one son, Harry S. (3) Cornelius Van Dyke, married Margaret Hill and has five children, Welford, Lillian, Julia, David and Frank. (4) Caleb, died in childhood. (5) James Monroe, Jr., married Rachel Stryker and has three children. (6) Kate Adelaide, died unmarried. (7) Edward L., died in childhood. (8) Archibald. (9) Maggie, married Walter Perrot and had no children. (10) Carrie, married Mahlon C. Daniels and has one son, Claude. (11) Minnie, married Frank B. Jamison and has four children, Frank, Esaias, Joseph Stout and Kate.

Jacob Weart, son of David Stout and Margaretta Weart, married first, Emma Woolmer, who died one month after marriage, and second, Mary English. They had three children, Weart, who was drowned at Atlantic City when about 18 years of age; Howard, and Mary, married Harry Lawmaster.

Andrew Gilbert H., son of David Stout and Margaretta Weart, married Ann Adelaide Van Dyke and had four children: (1) Emma Elizabeth, married Peter VanDerveer Campbell, June 6, 1866, and has eleven children, Edgar, Arthur I., Gilbert S., P. VanDerveer, Walter M., William V., Margaret, Harry B., George W., John and Adelaide. (2) Mary Margaret, born August 14, 1851, married her cousin, William Henry Baker, as previously stated. Mary Margaret Baker died January 10, 1897, and William Henry Baker died April 29, 1897. (3) Edward, married Lucy Jenkins of Jamestown, Ohio, and had one son, Fred Bruce. (4) Elmer Ellsworth, married Mary Hart and had three children, Clarence, Gilbert and Martha.

Henrietta, eldest child of David Stout and Margaretta Weart, married March 1, 1827, Abraham Skillman, born November 27, 1802, and settled on his father's farm which adjoined that of her father (Article 44). They had four children: Charles Augustus, born December 16, 1827; Caroline Matilda, born May 2, 1830; Ida Stryker, born February 12, 1832; Mary Emma, born May 20, 1844.

Abraham Skillman, son of Cornelius Skillman and Ida Stryker, is the sixth generation in the line of Thomas Skillman, who came to this country with the English forces in 1664. He was a musician

in the English Army and was with them when New York was captured from the Dutch.   He was discharged in 1668 and settled on
Long Island.   His great grandson, Thomas, father of Cornelius,
married Mary Beekman, daughter of Gerardus Beekman of Griggstown.

The Beekmans are descendants of Wilhelmus Beekman, who
was sent to this country from Holland in 1647, by the Dutch West
India Company as one of their agents, and was among the earliest
Magistrates of New Amsterdam.   His lands lay principally in the
vicinity of what are now Beekman and William Streets.

Ida Stryker, the mother of Abraham Skillman, was the sixth
generation in the line of Jan Stryker who emigrated to New Amsterdam from Holland in 1652.

When Lafayette made his last visit to the United States in
1825, Abraham Skillman was one of his body guard during the
journey through New Jersey.   The sword which Abraham Skillman carried at that time is one of the most valued possessions of
his son's family.

In 1865, the Skillmans moved to Lambertville, where they
spent the remaining years of their lives.   Abraham Skillman died
July 1, 1881, and his wife Henrietta November 22, 1889.

Charles Augustus Skillman married March 2, 1854, Sarah,
daughter of Stryker Skillman of Ringoes, and settled in Lambertville.   They had four children, viz: (1) Ida, who died in infancy;
(2) Mary, married James Stryker Studdiford of Lambertville, and
has one son, James Ogilvie.   (3) Charles Hervey, who died February 9, 1908.   (4) Carrie Disbrow, married Samuel W. Cochran of
Lambertville, and has one daughter, Margaret Studdiford.   Their
eldest child, Stanley, died at the age of four years.   Charles Augustus Skillman died on September 20, 1906.   He was one of the ablest
lawyers of Hunterdon County, and was very active in the business
and social affairs of his city.

Caroline Matilda, eldest daughter of Abraham Skillman, married February 6, 1856, William Jewell of Hopewell.   The history of
this family is given in Article 39.

Ida Stryker, daughter of Abraham Skillman, married January
22, 1862, Dr. Edward Page Hawke, and has five children, viz.:

1. Caroline, married Peter Voorhees Bergen of Princeton, and
has one daughter, Mary Disbrow.   Their sons, Edward Page and
Martin Voorhees, died in childhood.

2. Dr. William Wetherill of Flemington, married Elizabeth Bartles, and has two children, William Bartles and Elizabeth.

3. Dr. Edward Skillman of Trenton, married Adelaide Knapp, and has two children, Edward Knapp and Isabelle.

4. Henrietta Skillman married Stephen Van Rensselaer Martling of Ridgefield, New Jersey, and has one daughter.

5. Mary Emma, who lives with her mother.

Dr. Edward Page Hawke died December 12, 1898, aged 65. He was a very skillful physician, and his practice was a large one, extending over parts of three counties.

The youngest daughter of Abraham Skillman is Mary Emma, who married Ralph Ege, the author of "Pioneers of Old Hopewell."

M. E. E.

1908.

INDEX

Bechtel, Anna 71
  Charles 71
Beebe, Emma 278
  Reuben 278
Beekman, Gerardus 289
  Mary 289
  Wilhelmus 289
Beihl, Edward 107
Benner, Charlotte A. 79
  Henry 79
Bennett, James 257
Bergen, Caroline 289
  Edward P. 289
  Martin V. 289
  Mary D. 289
  Peter V. 289
Betts, Joana 89
  Richard 89
  Sarah 89
Biddle, William 115
Biles, Alexander Jr. 171
Birch, R. J. 8,22,210
  Rensaler, J. 18
Blachley, Henry W. 175
Black, Dora G. 37
  Elizabeth 37
  Henry H. 37
  John Hardenbrook 37
Blackwell, Actia 134
  Albert 214
  Alice 230
  Amy 134
  Anna 134,275
  Anna D. 163
  Annie 214
Blackwell, Augustus 218
  Belle 215,275
  Benjamin 238
  Bessie 275
  Carrie 217,230
  Catherine 230
  Catherine F. 230
  Charles 136,214,230
  Charles H. 117,134,162
  Clara 230
  Clarissa 136
  Clifton W. 47,56
  Daniel 134,174
  Daniel J. 174
  David 275
  David L. 117,134,163,174,275
  Deborah 134
  Edgar 230
  Edith 214,230
  Elijah 134,135,149
  Elizabeth 134,136,137,148,162,174,
    230,275
  Emily 214
  Fanny 275
  Francis 96,133,134,148,149,152,
    154,159
  Franey 134
  George 275

  Helen 249,275
  Helen M. 104,105
  Henry 136
  Henry C. 230
  Henry J. 174
  Hervey S. 275
  Ira V. 222
  Jacob 134,135,148
  James H. 136,275
  Jemima 134,136
  Jerusha 143
  John 96,105,133,135-138,148,14?
    159,214,270
  John P. 136
  John T. 136
  John V. 174
  Johnson T. 217
  Jonathan 134,135
  Jonathan H. 230,249
  Katherine 218
  Lewis 135-137
  Liscombe B. 215
  Liscombe T. 214
  Lizzie 230
  Margaret 137
  Maria 136
  Martha 134
  Mary 104,134,275
  Mary A. 70
  Morgan D. 87,215,222
  Nathaniel 134
  Nathaniel D. 70
  N. D. 229
  Nelson D. 117,134,174,275
  Oliver H. 136
  Penelope 174
  Rachel 96
  R. M. J. 174
  Robert 134,149,167,214
  Samuel H. 134,275
  Sarah 134,136,275
  Sarah F. 104,105
  Stephen 96,134,135,229,230
  Stephen C. 104,105
  Susan 136,230
  Thomas 134,136,143
  Viola 214
  William B. 171
  William D. 275
  William J. 230
  Willis 230
  Willis B. 230
  Wilson 136
Block, Eleanor L. 235
  William S. 235
Blythe, Elizabeth 163
  Joseph W. 163
Boden, James 266
Bodine, Augustus 247
  Josephine 247
Bogart, Ruth 161
Boggs, Ann 278
  Caroline 278

293

John W. 63
Jonathan 75,81
Joseph 18,33,38-43,45,46,49-56,59,75,
  78,111,154,243
Joseph H. 65
Josephine 37
J. Price 69
Judson 78
Julia 37
Julia A. 37,71
J. Woodhull 71
Katie S. 78
Kesiah 53,56
Leah 56
Lester 65
Letitia 63
Levi 78
Lydia 63
Margaret 69,81
Golden, Margaret A. 80
  Maritje 39
  Martha 62
  Martha A. 69
  Mary 53,54,56,62-65,71,81
  Mary E. 69
  Mary M. 162
  Matilda 77
  Maude 69
  Nancy 65, 79
  Newell H. 77
  Noah R. 69
  Pamelia 75,76
  Peninah 33,56
  Peter Schenck 42
  Phebe 70,82
  Philemon 71
  Rachel 75,78
  Rebecca 63
  Reuben 64,65
  Rhoda 64
  Rhoda S. 64
  Ruth 75
  Sarah 36,37,56,63,69,78,81
  Sarah E. 64
  Sarah M. 69
  Stephen H. 62
  Susan 69,78
  Temperance 35,36
  Theodosia 75
  Theresa 71,78
  Ure 79
  Urie 75,82
  Wildal 71
  William 8,38-42,75-79,81,232
  William E. 77
  William F. 8,13,18,23,46,75,78,227
Golding, William 141
Gooch, General 177
Goodyear, Ida H. 127
Gorcher, Emily 233
Gordon, Kesiah 256
  Lewis 256
  P. 172

Peter 239,250
Gray, Nomer 20
Green, Benjamin 111
  Catherine 163
  Christian 170
  George 113
  Harriet 163
  Helen 163
  Joseph 163
  Mary 163,170
  Maxwell 163
  Miss 227
  Richard 170
  Samuel 163
  William 170
  William A. 163
Griggs, Julia A. 71
Groom, John 63
  Peter 63
  Sarah E. 63
Guild, Benjamin 153
  John 17,95,210
  Ralph 210,267
Gulick, Joachim 42
  Minne (Menne) 45
  Minnie 256

H

Hagaman, Anna 270,271,274
  Catherine 270,271
  John R. 271
  Joseph 246
  Ruliff 270,271
  Samuel 70
  Sarah 246
  Susan S. 70
Hale, Dr. 173
  Mary L. 148
Hallock, Sarah 241
Halsey, Jemima 225
  Josephine 37
Hamilton, James 177
  John 176,177
Hanley, Emma 127
Harding, Ellen 234
Harlin, Rudolph 109
Harrison, John 116
Hart, Abigail 121
  Abner 65
  Alanson 256
  Alfred 256
  Alvin 217
  Amanda 127
  Andrew 65
  Anna M. 104
  Anna S. 127
  Arinda 127
  Benjamin 63
  Betsy 255
  Caroline 23,127
  Caroline H. 127
  Catherine 82,127,152

298

303

Suydam, William 18,22,249
Swager, Maria 213
Swaim, John 204,206,271
Swallow, Peter 248
  Phebe A. 248
Sykes, Thomas 187

T

Talbert, Elizabeth 258
Tavener, Charles 83
  Kate 83
Taylor, Catherine 230
  George M. 229
  John 144
  Lavinia 229
Temple, Abraham 168
  Benjamin 169
  Joanna 169
  Sarah 169
  Timothy 111
Tenbrook, Elizabeth 221
Tennent, Gilbert 99,210
Terry, Franklin 217
  Mary 217
Thomas, David 136
  Elizabeth 245
  John 136,257
  Nancy 256
  Sarah 135,136
Thompson, Mary 62
Throckmorton, Elizabeth 143,144
Tidd, Dr. James 92
Tilton, John Jr. 41
Timbrook, Mrs. 263
Tindal, Isaac 52
Tindall, John 16
  Joseph 52
  Robert 13,16,18,52,107,108
  Thomas 13,14,16,38,50,51,52,55,
    91,111,115
Titus, Abbie 216
  Abiel 72
  Abigail W. 65
  Adelia 217
  Albert 218
  Alfred 218
  Ambrose 65
  Ann 174
  Anna 4,71,72,217,218,285
  Anna M. 217
  Asa 110,213
  Belle 214
  C. A. 72
  Catherine 216
  Catherine E. 214
  Charles J. 215
  Constantia 131
  Content 72,73,131,165
  Cornelius L. 217
  David 218
  David L. 138
  E. S. 8,44,50,107,235,241,243,250

Edgar 217
Edmund 72
Edna 218
Edwin S. 104,215,218
Elizabeth 125,127,131,167,213
Emily 65,214,217
Emma K. 70
Enoch 159
Enoch A. 22,70,110
Enos 215,217
Era 217
Etta 217
Mrs. Eure 214
Fannie 217
Frances 70
Francina 217
George 217
George G. 70
George W. 214
Gertrude 65
Gladys 218
Hannah 72,130
Harold 218
Henry B. 215
Howard 216
James 217
James S. 70
James T. 217
Jane M. 213
J. Elwood 65
Titus, Joab 70-72
  John 71-74,104,134,167,239
  John Jr. 4,71,72,73
  John M. 67
  John P. 213
  Johnson 72
  Johnson L. 275
  Jonathan 83
  Joseph 74,130
  Josephine 217
  Julia E. 70
  Katherine 218
  Laura 218
  Maria 213
  Mary 104,217,218
  Mary A. 70,217
  Mary Emma 218
  Maud 218
  Nathaniel R. 174
  Oliver 216
  Pamelia 213,217
  Patience 131
  Peter 9,231
  Phebe 70,130,138
  Rachel 214,217
  Rachel R. 215
  Rebecca 71,83,213
  Reuben 65,70,72
  Reuben C. 71
  Robert 71,72,131
  Ruth A. 214
  Samuel 72,213
  Samuel B 214

312